INQUEST ON AN ALLY

INQUEST ON AN ALLY

BY

PAUL WINTERTON

LONDON
THE CRESSET PRESS
MCMXLVIII

To
MOSCOW RADIO
without whose help this book could not have been written

Printed in Great Britain by
THE SHENVAL PRESS
LONDON AND HERTFORD

CONTENTS

FOREWORD

IN THIS book I have quoted many Soviet press and radio commentators without identifying them other than by name. To do more would serve no useful purpose, for they have no individuality in their public work. Collectively, they make up the voice of the Kremlin. They are the loudspeakers through which the party line is relayed to the Russian people and the world. The characteristics of each loudspeaker are of no interest.

In the western countries, quotations from press and radio would have little value as evidence of the outlook and intentions of those countries, since every expression of view would be cancelled out by a conflicting view. In totalitarian Russia, however, statements in newspapers and on the radio can safely be taken as a reflection of Soviet policy. The censorship sees to that. The rare exceptions are usually marked by public reprimands.

London
May 1948   P. W.

CHAPTER I

THE RUSSIAN ATTITUDE

It is a remarkable fact that while no one would attempt to understand a book without first learning the alphabet of letters, many people seek to understand the post-war behaviour of Soviet Russia without first studying the alphabet of communism. Often they come to the conclusion that Russian policy is an insoluble political crossword without taking even a glance at the available clues.

There is no puzzle about Russia's basic aims. No political intentions in the history of the world have ever been so widely and vociferously trumpeted or so consistently adhered to.

Soviet Russia believes, and always has believed, in a religion of universal revolution. The human race can achieve freedom, equality, prosperity and peace only through 'true socialism'—by which, of course, the Russians mean *their* sort of socialism, sometimes called bolshevism. Capitalism, very broadly interpreted, is the enemy. Social democrats like Mr Attlee and Mr Bevin, who, according to the Russians, believe in the wrong sort of socialism, are just the 'lackeys' of capitalism and will be destroyed with it. Capitalism, which is aggressive and self-destructive, will *inevitably* be superseded everywhere by true socialism. True socialism will not be secure until the remnants of capitalism have been made powerless. The transition period will *inevitably* be one of violent and bloody struggle. Russia, the only true socialist country, together with the communist parties of the world, will lead the struggle. Russia's mission is to liberate mankind by her help and example. This is the law—laid down in Marxist-Leninist-Stalinist tablets of stone. It is the lucid and coherent dogma to which all communists everywhere subscribe; it is the chief inspiration of all Soviet action. If Soviet Russia abandoned the dogma, she would cease to be Soviet Russia. There is not the least sign of any such retreat.

The communists formally declared war on non-communism in the Communist Manifesto of 1848, which bluntly stated:

9

'The Communists openly declare that their aims can only be achieved by the violent overthrow of the whole contemporary social order.' That pronouncement has often been re-stated by communist leaders but it has mellowed little with age. The assumption of unavoidable violent struggle has never been repudiated. On the contrary, it has been emphasized decade after decade until the present time.

Lenin put the position starkly. 'We are living,' he wrote,* 'not merely in a state but in a system of states; and it is inconceivable that the Soviet republic should continue for a long period side by side with imperialist states. Ultimately one or the other must conquer. Meanwhile a number of terrible clashes between the Soviet republic and the *bourgeois* states is inevitable.'

The Sixth Congress of the Communist International held at Moscow in 1928 adopted a resolution saying, 'The overthrow of capitalism is impossible without violence—i.e. without armed uprisings and wars against the *bourgeoisie*. In our era of imperialist wars and world revolution, revolutionary civil wars of the proletarian dictatorship against the *bourgeoisie,* wars of the proletariat against the *bourgeois* states and world capitalism as well as national revolutionary wars of oppressed peoples against imperialism, are unavoidable.'

As recently as 1945 there was published in Moscow an English translation of Stalin's earlier book, *Problems of Leninism.* It is one of the fundamental textbooks for the political training of Soviet youth today; an authentic guide to contemporary Soviet thinking. It says, among other things, 'The overthrow of the power of the *bourgeoisie* and establishment of the power of the proletariat in one country does not mean that the complete victory of socialism has been ensured. . . . The victory of the revolution *in at least several countries* is needed.' Elsewhere in the book the italicized words become *in all countries.*

This book has been called 'Stalin's *Mein Kampf',* and with good reason. It shares with Hitler's famous work what the Nuremberg judgment called 'an unmistakable attitude of aggression' and an uninhibited frankness about the tasks ahead. 'The development and support of the revolution in other countries,' says Stalin, 'is an essential task of the victorious revolution. Thus the revolution victorious in one country must not

* *Collected Works,* Vol. XXIV, p. 122, Russian edition.

consider itself a self-contained entity, but a support, a means of speeding the victory of the proletariat in other countries.' Note carefully that word 'support'. It hardly squares with the re-assuring picture sometimes drawn of a non-intervening Russia watching with purely academic interest the spontaneous working out of events in other countries.

Stalin outlines the tactics suitable for the period of struggle which was inaugurated by the success of the revolution in Russia. The terminology is significantly military.

'Aim—consolidation of the dictatorship of the proletariat in one country, using it as a point of support for the overthrow of imperialism in all countries. The revolution extends beyond the borders of one country, and the epoch of world revolution has begun. Main force of the revolution: dictatorship of the proletariat in one country and revolutionary movement of the proletariat in all others. Main reserves: the semi-proletarian and petty-peasant masses in the advanced countries and the movements for the liberation of colonies and dependent areas. Direction of the main blow: the isolation of the petty-*bourgeois* democrats and of the parties of the Second International that form the main support of the policy of *compromise* with imperialism. Plan of disposition for our forces: an alliance of the proletarian revolution with the liberation movement in the colonies and dependent areas.'

The official communist dogma, as presented by Marx, Engels, Lenin and Stalin, had by 1937 been circulated in Russia in 360 million copies of their works, published in 85 Soviet languages, and since the war the stream has grown. It is odd that we should underrate a creed on which so much emphasis is placed.

Another work which gives us all the clues to Russia's wide open secret is called *A History of the Communist Party (Bolshevik), Short Course.* This book is one of the world's best-sellers. It was edited and authorized by the Central Committee of the Communist party of the Soviet Union in 1938 and was first published in Moscow in 1939. Stalin had a good deal to do with its preparation. It is the Bible of the orthodox communist in all countries. In October 1946 the army newspaper *Red Star* called it 'the great book of our epoch' and 'an essential reference book for all Soviet people'. Indeed, it was more than that. 'Communists and progressive workers abroad,' said *Red Star,* 'in studying Stalin's work are learning to fight imperialism and reaction in the workers' interest.' *Pravda* in 1945 stressed the importance of the *Short Course* for training new cadres and giving basic political knowledge to recruits. Its practical significance was emphasized. 'To a Bolshevik, theory is a guide to action.' By 1946 the total issue of the *Short Course* had reached 31,317,000 copies, and it had been published in sixteen foreign languages as well as in sixty-one national languages of the Soviet Union.

Now what does the book say? It says precisely what all the other communist books say, what all the communist spokesmen say everywhere except when they are deliberately trying to mislead; it consistently repeats what so many people have refused to believe. There is no suggestion that Russia will be satisfied with communism in one country. 'The study of the history of the Communist Party of the Soviet Union,' says the Introduction, 'strengthens our certainty of the ultimate victory of the great cause of Lenin-Stalin, the victory of Communism throughout the world.' Page nine recalls the teaching of Marx and Engels that it is 'impossible to get rid of the power of capital and convert capitalist property into public property by peaceful means', and that 'the working-class could achieve this only by revolutionary violence against the *bourgeoisie*'. A quotation from Lenin on page seventy-two stresses Russia's role of encouraging others. 'Nothing will raise the revolutionary energy of the world proletariat so much, nothing will shorten the path leading to its complete victory to such an extent, as this decisive victory of the revolution that has now started in Russia.' Page 273 refers significantly to the *delay* of the revolution in the West. On page 275 we read, 'The victory of the proletarian revolution in the capitalist countries was a matter of vital concern to the working people of the USSR.'

Dogmas so widely circulated and intentions so often re-stated are evidently of the very stuff of contemporary Soviet political life. These classical doctrines are not dead, as the Latin language is dead. They are not presented in Soviet schools as a healthy mental exercise or a beautiful heritage, but as a guide to action. Every Soviet child today believes in world revolution under Russian leadership. A set of Notes on the programme for secondary schools, issued a year or two ago by the People's Commissariat for Education of the RSFSR, said that reading must be devoted, among other things, to inculcating 'a selfless love and devo-

12

tion . . . to the leader of the workers of the whole world, Comrade Stalin' and that 'a feeling of solidarity with the workers of the whole world who are fighting to free themselves from the yoke of capitalism must be awakened in the pupils'.

The dogma has never been pressed upon the Soviet people with greater zeal than in the post-war years. If the Russian Communist party lost something of its hold in the war years, when new ideological themes had to be introduced and when so many Russians were seeing the outside world for themselves, every effort has been made to recapture lost ground. Demobilized communists—'young untempered communists'—have been shepherded into a special fold and given a course in first principles. In the autumn of 1946 a higher party school was founded to train workers for local party duties. *Pravda* emphasized that more than half the members of the party consisted of persons admitted during the war who had not had time to receive the necessary Marxist-Leninist training. This gap was to be filled. In November 1946 a new journal appeared called *Party Life,* with the task of injecting fresh vigour into the stream of propaganda activity. The war—to the orthodox communist a passing incident in a continuous epochal struggle—had brought its special problems for the agitator, but the balance of advantage was considered favourable. 'If as a result of the first World War,' wrote *Pravda* in October 1947, 'there occurred the first serious break in the imperialist chain and the mighty Soviet Union emerged in one-sixth of the world, the second World War inflicted a new serious defeat on the capitalist world.'

Authoritative speeches, broadcasts and writings in the post-war years show with what vigour the whole body of the dogma flourishes. In March 1946 Dimitrov, former Comintern chief and more recently Prime Minister of Bulgaria, declared, 'When the time is ripe for action, only one party will remain on the historical stage; the Communist Party, the party of Lenin and Stalin. . . . Our party has to last and will last up to the historical moment when Communism, when the ideal communist society, becomes a reality . . . then all the political parties will be superfluous.' In July 1946 Academician Varga, writing in a Soviet publication, *World Economy and World Politics,* said the inclusion of Russia on the allied side during the war had had the effect of abating or halting the struggle between the 'two sys-

13

tems' but 'of course, it did not indicate the end of that struggle'. In July 1946, the newspaper *Bolshevik* spoke with the authentic timeless voice of revolutionary Russia. 'Reaction, militarism, imperialist aggression and war are inseparable features of capitalism in its present imperialist stage. . . . The fight is spreading to all the corners of the world; liberated Europe, the vast expanses of the colonial empires, the United States and England.' In September 1946 a special youth transmission was broadcast in the Moscow home service reminding young communists that one of the important tasks ahead was to use the power of the proletariat in Russia to form lasting ties with the proletariats of other countries 'for the development and victory of the revolution in all countries'. In August 1947 *Pravda* took pride in the fact that, contrary to an old Russian saying, the 'rays of socialism' were coming not from the West but from the East. On May Day 1947 a slogan called on 'workers of all countries' to join in the common struggle. In November 1947, in his speech on the anniversary of the Revolution, Molotov said, 'People in whom knowledge has brought awakening see in the successes of the Soviet Union the approach of their own liberation from the yoke of enslavement.' *Pravda* next day put one passage from the speech in a special panel. 'The revolution has opened the eyes of the people to the fact that the age of capitalism is coming to an end. . . . The feverish attempts of the imperialists, under whose feet the soil is trembling, will not save capitalists from the approaching peril. We are living in an age when all roads lead to communism.' This last sentence, it was stated, had 'a particularly enthusiastic reception' among the workers.

One of the basic convictions of the Soviet dogmatists is that capitalism, particularly American capitalism, stands on the edge of a crisis which will destroy it. This crisis is none the less to be assisted and encouraged because it is inevitable. Even destiny is none the worse for a helping hand. From Stalin downwards, therefore, the Russians have watched the economic indices of the capitalist West as a water diviner watches his twig. The coming slump is a theme with which Moscow radio often heartens its vast provincial audience. In June 1946, a broadcast by Lapitsky gloated over the fact that there were already four to five million unemployed in the United States. In such broadcasts, Russia's happy lot was usually contrasted. 'The Soviet people,' said Zhdanov, in November 1946, 'are marching ahead confidently, unafraid of economic crises and unemployment. . . . We know, of course, that such a situation is by no means true of other countries.' A little later, Professor Varga became more prophetic than an academician ought to be. 'In the not distant future,' he wrote in *Pravda*, 'probably not later than 1948 or even earlier, a fresh economic crisis may be expected in the USA, which will inevitably exert an enormous influence on the position in other capitalist countries as well.' Poslanski, broadcasting in the home service in April 1947, held out even brighter hopes of American calamity. 'Irrefutable indications' testified to the approach of a fresh slump. If, as was predicted, United States production dropped to the level of 1940, there would be an army of unemployed totalling nineteen millions. Stalin himself, when interviewed by Mr Stassen in Moscow in April 1947, displayed what can only be described as a ghoulish interest in the forthcoming cataclysm. When Mr Stassen said he thought there was just a possibility that it might not happen, Stalin patently disbelieved him.

One of the things which differentiate the communist from the rest of humanity is his conviction of infallibility. This unshakable certainty, which alone is sufficient to make co-operation between communists and erring mortals virtually impossible, has never been more precisely expressed than on page 355 of the *Short Course,* where we find these remarkable words. 'The power of the Marxist-Leninist theory lies in the fact that it enables the party to find the right orientation in any situation, to understand the inner connection of current events, to foresee their course and to perceive not only how and in what direction they are developing in the present but how and in what direction they are bound to develop in the future.'

This monstrous claim, which is responsible for so many of our contemporary ills, has, of course, been roughly handled by events. Had the Russians foreseen the staggering triumphs of Hitler in the early stages of the war, they would hardly have been so ready to help him with their propaganda, their raw materials, and their offers of advanced bases for his naval operations. The Soviet leaders and the communist parties, notwithstanding their boasted prescience, have indeed made many grave miscalculations. There have even been subsequent con-

15

fessions of error. But the communists are resilient—however wrong they may have been in the past, they are always right now. Like Aleksandrov, the head of the Propaganda Department of the Russian Communist Party, they 'look with pity on those people whose capacity to understand the real significance of the political phenomena of our times is very relative'. But they do not learn any other lesson from Aleksandrov, who in 1947 was publicly reprimanded and humiliated by Zhdanov for a philosophical heresy.

*   *   *   *   *

Russia's fanatical devotion to the cause of world communism, her implacable hostility to all forms of non-communism, is the main factor in her post-war attitude to the rest of the world. But there is another factor, too. The quite peculiar difficulty which we have experienced in our relations with Russia arises not only from her uncompromising dogma, but also from her being Russia. When a country's leaders embrace a new religion, they do not automatically shed the heritage, prejudices and ambitions of that country or purge their blood of ancestral characteristics. Every intelligent visitor to Russia since the 15th century has remarked on the suspiciousness of the official mind. That is a quality which has nothing whatever to do with ideology. There are others, equally persistent. There is pride of race, strongly developed among the Slavs and far from subdued in spite of Marx and the brotherhood of man. There is pride in Russian national power. There are the old expansionist dreams. The product of the Frunze Military Academy can also read a map and knows where Constantinople used to be. The young Red sailor, watching a new destroyer being launched, does not congratulate himself that another blow has been struck for the workers of the world. He draws himself up a little higher and thinks how good it is to be a Russian. He is a patriot at least as much as he is a communist. Moreover, because Russia has only recently come to full World Power status, because in many material and cultural respects she is so backward, the Russian is inclined to be even more crudely boastful than patriots usually are. One hardly needs a deep knowledge of psychology to understand that.

We can no more ignore these purely Russian elements in

16

seeking an explanation of the Soviet Union's attitude than we can ignore her ideology. Dogmatic communism and naïve chauvinism are strange bedfellows, but there they lie. The amalgam has, in Russia, been officially recognized and given the name of 'Soviet patriotism'. We are seriously told by learned professors that in the Soviet Union a new type of human being is emerging —'the new Soviet man'; a type far in advance of 'western man' or 'capitalist man'. In the post-war world, therefore, it is with the psychology of the 'Soviet patriot' that we have to deal; the psychology of the Marxist Russian who hates not merely the ideology of the West but the West itself.

To popularize 'Soviet patriotism', a new organization was set up in Russia in 1947 under the name of the All-Union Society for the Propagation of Political and Scientific Knowledge. It was intended that this society should have a wider appeal than the Communist party, and that its propaganda should cover not merely the old dogma but the new Soviet self-esteem. Its aims were clearly set out in a special home broadcast in April 1947.

'The successful realization of the great task of building a communist society demands systematic and extensive work to develop the culture of the workers, improve the communist education of the Soviet people, and eradicate completely the remnants of capitalism from the minds of the people. . . . We propose to create a new society. . . . Its task . . . must be to organize the widespread propagation of scientific and political knowledge by means of public lectures on international politics and Soviet economy, science, culture, literature, and the arts. . . . In public lectures the members of this society will undertake to explain the foreign policy of the Soviet state, to expose the provokers of a new war and of aggression, to indicate the falsehood and limitations of *bourgeois* democracy and to reveal the reactionary substance of the ideology of the contemporary imperialist *bourgeoisie* and its servants. These lectures will reveal the advantage of the Soviet public and state system over capitalism and will indicate our successes. . . . We must show the greatness of our socialist fatherland and we must encourage among the people the feeling of pride in their Soviet country by waging a decisive struggle against the kowtowing of individual citizens of the USSR before contemporary *bourgeois* culture . . . .'

This was a sort of keynote speech, which Soviet publicists at once proceeded to amplify and expound, bringing out much

17

more plainly the theme of the 'new Soviet man'. Fadeev, writing in *Pravda* in June 1947 on 'The Upward Surge of Soviet Literature', said, 'The central and main theme of the moment, in which we are united, which encompasses all other themes, is that of Soviet patriotism. We must show to our people and to the whole of humanity what our Soviet society is; what we, the Soviet people are, as compared with capitalist society and with men reared by capitalism and imperialism. We, the authors, can and must more than everyone else say what our Soviet regime actually is, demonstrate its advantages and the greatness of Soviet men and women. Such is our basic theme for a long time to come.'

Sometimes the patriotic note took the form of a broad generalization of superiority. 'Today,' said Kovalev in a home broadcast, 'the Soviet Union has become the most advanced and progressive country in the world.' Sometimes it was old-fashioned jingoism. 'The Russian navy was created before the British navy made its appearance,' said Vishnevsky in a home broadcast. 'Russia, the Soviet Union, is a sea power. She was it, she is it now, and she is going to remain it.' *Pravda,* about the same time, declared that the peoples of the Soviet Union wanted to see their navy stronger and mightier still and would do everything they could to have ships of all classes and types superior to the best ships of foreign navies.

Sometimes the patriotism of the 'new Soviet man' assumed a less healthy tone. In 1947, *Bolshevik* printed a long article, the gist of which was as follows: 'Before the Revolution the exploiting classes of the western European states sought to subjugate Russia spiritually. They implanted the idea of the superiority of western over Russian culture. We were to be the pupils, fawning on the foreigner. Foreigners sought to undermine our faith in our creative forces. But the Revolution dealt a powerful blow at the idea that Russia must always be an imitator. It paved the way for the achievement of mental superiority of the Soviet people over the people of *bourgeois* western culture. We have refuted the slander that we are an inferior nation. The thirty-year history of the Soviet State has once and for all destroyed the legend of Russia as a country guided by the West. By being the first country in the world to build a socialist society we have outstripped western Europe by an entire historical epoch. Yet there

18

are still writers and scientists who fawn before reactionary culture.'

Any Soviet intellectual who 'fawned on the West' was now certain of professional extinction. Sycophantic publicists rushed into battle on behalf of the 'new Soviet man'. Mental autarchy became the order of the day. There must be no imitation, no admiration, no acknowledgment, no association with the decadent West—barely even common civility where western knowledge and culture were concerned. The one aim of authors, artists, poets, scientists, actors, historians, film producers, composers, even clowns, must be to turn themselves into good non-kow-towing patriotic Soviet prigs. All their work must be related to orthodox Soviet purposes. Many fell by the wayside, if only temporarily. There were 'ideological impurities' even in a Shostakovich symphony. The famed Professor Varga was unanimously condemned by a gathering of prominent economists for praising Britain's war-time rationing system. The biologist Zhebrak was disgraced because, in his political ignorance, he had imagined that genetics was a pure science. 'How unsightly,' said *Pravda,* 'is the role of Zhebrak, the detestable fawner on *bourgeois* science!' Men were hounded for dabbling in 'capitalist art', which had 'poisoned its consciousness by praising low instincts, and represented the human being as a beast, as a monster from the physical and moral point of view'. Notable literary figures like Akhmatova and Zoschenko were scourged for practising 'art for art's sake'—a conception, declared a broadcast from Moscow in English in September 1946, 'entirely alien to the very essence and spirit of Soviet life'. Zoschenko has since been working his passage home by devoting his considerable talents to the compilation of a book about the prowess of the Leningrad guerillas. 'If the book is a good one he will regain the trust of the people and re-enter the family of Soviet writers,' said a fellow-writer, Boris Gorbatov, at a press conference. Aleksandrov, one of the party's leading theoreticians and a man whose claim to infallibility has already been noticed, was castigated for his subservience to foreign philosophers and for 'seeing in every philosopher first of all a professional ally and only afterwards an adversary'. He forgot that the only safe rule where the West was concerned was to 'Speak no good, see no good, hear no good'.

Scientists were particularly badly mauled in this battle for

'Soviet patriotism'. *Pravda* was hot on the trail of the unenlightened when it wrote in September 1947, 'It is not by chance that certain elements are full of admiration for foreigners, as is evident from their theses and lectures which are full of quotations from foreign publications, the scientific value and authoritativeness of which is nil. Some local scientific workers, in quest of a dubious popularity, endeavour to print their works in these insignificant magazines, forgetting their dignity and pride as Soviet citizens and Soviet savants.' This point was taken up again in a decree of the Presidium of the Soviet Trade Union Central Committee in October 1947, which, after condemning certain of the intelligentsia for unworthy adulation and servility towards 'the putrefying reactionary culture of the *bourgeois* West' denounced some inventors for 'making haste to publish abroad articles on their work, which is really the property of the Soviet state'.

The view that the *bourgeois* world has consistently stolen Russian inventions and taken the credit for them was developed to the point of paranoia. The patient listener to Moscow radio in the post-war period would have learned that the lightning conductor was invented by Lomonosov in 1752, though for many years the results of his researches were attributed to Franklin. Petrov anticipated the Davy lamp by ten years. Ladygin's incandescent lamp of 1873 was subsequently perfected by Edison. Three Russians had successfully originated the electric motor. The Russian physicist Schilling had developed the electric telegraph system, 'five years before the inventor Morse'. Everyone knew that Russian technicians had endowed the world with radio. The 'father of radio' was A. S. Popov. Russians had also invented electric welding. Four Russians were responsible for the work 'forming the basis of the use of atomic energy and radio location'. In September 1947, Moscow radio, after the usual fraternal criticisms of the tanks which Britain sent to Russia during the war, said that 'the honour of inventing the tank belonged to the Russians'. A certain Tsalkovsky was the inventor whose brain child, 'jet propulsion as applied to aircraft', was 'taken up by the West'. As for penicillin, it was not, as is commonly supposed, first discovered by Professors Fleming and Florey, but by two Russians, Manasein and Polopevnov, fifty years ago. The unearthing of this fact was modestly described in an English broadcast from Moscow as 'among the best pieces of research work this year'.

The evidence of a peculiarly unpleasant national psychosis was even stronger during a visit to Oxford in 1947 of Professor Palladin, president of the Ukrainian Academy of Science. The Professor, at least, was taking no chances of being accused of 'toadying to the West'. He was unfavourably impressed by the poor hospitality, the lack of publicity given to the international conference he was attending, the lack of running water in the rooms, having to eat with the students, the darkness of our streets at night, our 'pitiful' prefabs and indeed practically everything else about our country. Of the conference he said subsequently, 'I cannot think of any foreign scientist who at this congress produced a single new question or new basic principle. Mostly they dealt with details of problems which in the main had already been thrashed out before the war. Quite naturally, on the other hand, our papers produced a great impression, for we established in them some radically new facts and acquainted our audience with phenomena until then unexplored by scientists.' Comment, though tempting, appears superfluous.

It is in the context of 'Soviet patriotism' that we must seek an explanation of the Soviet Government's post-war views on the marriage of Soviet women to foreigners. No explanation covers its obstinate refusal to release the Russian wives of former allied Servicemen except that it believes the 'new Soviet woman' should be content, indeed proud, to marry the 'new Soviet man' and no one else. Its refusal of visas was not confined to the wives of Britons, and had little if anything to do with Anglo-Soviet relations. The universality of the ban was shown by the decree of March 1947 which forbade any Soviet citizen to marry an alien.

'Soviet patriotism', in its xenophobic aspect, is closely linked with fear of espionage. The anxiety of the Soviet authorities to keep their scientific inventions to themselves has already been noted. In June 1947 a new decree was promulgated greatly increasing the penalties for revealing, by design or accident, a very wide range of 'State secrets'. Shepilov, broadcasting in July 1947 on the theme of Anglo-Saxon espionage, referred to 'the inordinate talkativeness of certain organs of our Press'. Internal propaganda ceaselessly stressed the need for constant vigilance 'so as to prevent any tricks of the foe'. Judge Ulrich, in a lecture in August 1947, discussed the dangers of careless talk and said, 'Citizens should remember that it makes no difference whether a particular capitalist country is at war or peace with the Soviet Union'.

'Soviet patriotism' has many distressing features. Let us therefore end this section on a note of comic relief. 'The Soviet chess team,' said a home broadcast in October 1947, 'is undoubtedly the strongest in the world. . . . It is not a matter of favourable climatic conditions. The explanation is that we live in the freest country in the world, in the great Soviet Union, where in the last thirty years culture has been the property of the whole people and where consequently conditions for the development of creative possibilities are particularly favourable.'

*　　*　　*　　*　　*

Russia's frame of mind throughout the post-war period was aggressive. The frame of mind of the West was largely defensive. This difference will be discussed in more detail later. For the moment, it is sufficient to bear in mind that in the ideological struggle between communism and non-communism, it was communism which first took the world offensive. Chronology does matter. No magistrate hearing charges against two participants in a brawl could properly fail to ask who struck the first blow. It can be argued that capitalism was always at war with the idea of socialism in every country, but there is nothing in *bourgeois* ideology which declares inevitable a world-wide struggle to the death with communism. We in the West have never taken the view that it is impossible for non-communism, in its various phases, to co-exist peacefully with non-aggressive communist states. It is communist dogma which drives the world forward to the fatal clash. Yet the communists, by a hypnotic propaganda, have succeeded in saddling the West with much of the blame for the present struggle. How often has it not been said that Russia's suspicion of the West is fully justified by the abominable way in which she was first attacked and then isolated by the capitalist powers after the Revolution? Yet how did the Russian communists expect to be treated? They had declared unprovoked global warfare on the whole of organized society.

Did they expect bouquets? In so far as their activities were mis-represented in the capitalist press—and no doubt they were—that was wrong, as well as unnecessary. But tolerance, let alone support, for communism between the wars would have been sensible only if the West had approved the aims of communism.

In the years following World War II, the communists again tried to put the onus for the world's divisions on the non-communist states, while maintaining their own offensive initiative unabated. 'It is the influential reactionary groups,' said the Soviet periodical *New Times,* in October 1946, 'who . . . at every step sow the venomous seed of distrust and suspicion and hope to reap a rich harvest of hate and jingoism.' Melnikov, in an English broadcast in the same month said, 'The world reactionaries' number one aim today is precisely to create a permanent quarrel among the freedom-loving nations, and among the Great Powers first and foremost.' It seems a cool charge from a party which avowedly set out to achieve 'the violent overthrow of the whole contemporary social order'. In the chapters which follow, Russia will be found repeatedly accusing the West of working for the headlong collision the inevitability of which is the very keystone of communist theory. The reader will judge for himself where responsibility lies.

*　　*　　*　　*　　*

Anyone studying the dogma and its many manifestations must be impressed by the consistency of the pattern. There is, however, one discordant voice which must be noticed—discordant, at least, if words mean what they appear to mean. It is the voice of Stalin, some of whose post-war pronouncements on the subject of Russia's relations with the West seemed to contradict what was written on the tablets of stone, and to offer new hope to westerners hungry for Russian co-operation and eager to magnify a crumb into a meal.

Careful examination of Stalin's statements shows that the crumb was, in fact, very small. He told Mr Stassen in April 1947 that 'of course' the United States and the Soviet economies could collaborate. There is, of course, nothing in the dogma to rule out mutually beneficial economic collaboration between communism and capitalism up to the moment when the latter collapses—though such collaboration is hardly in accordance with the spirit of the dogma and in practice never amounts to much. In February 1947, replying to a query from a Russian, Stalin said that Marxist theory laid down only general guiding principles, the particular adaptation of which must be different in different countries. In August 1946 he had touched on the same point when he told a British Labour Party delegation that he thought Britain had the opportunity of a more peaceful approach to socialism than Russia had had. That might seem like a crumb, but the dogma has always allowed the possibility of capitalism 'going quietly' in a few exceptional places which prove the rule of general violent change. In January 1946, Stalin, in conversation with Elliott Roosevelt, pooh-poohed the idea of a new war for the time being. That was an even smaller crumb. Russia would clearly not risk a war in a period of relative weakness.

Some statements by Stalin, however, were superficially startling and undoubtedly contradicted the dogma. In September 1946 he told the British journalist Alexander Werth in a written reply that he had an absolute belief in friendly co-operation with the West and in friendly competition between the two systems, capitalism and communism. This theme was taken up by *New Times* which said in November 1946, 'International co-operation under present conditions implies the collaboration of nations with differing social systems and differing ideologies. It has been repeatedly declared in Soviet quarters that differences of social system and ideology constitute no obstacle to effective co-operation between the Soviet Union and other countries.' Commentator Lemin, in an English broadcast in February 1947, said, 'The basis of our relations with capitalist countries consists in allowing for the co-existence of two opposite systems.' In April 1947 Stalin told Mr Stassen that 'each people stood by the system it desired and could stand by it. One should respect,' he said, 'the systems approved of by the people.'

It would be improper, in an examination of the Soviet post-war attitude and intention, to ignore such utterances. Stalin, presenting himself to the world as a benevolent uncle or a great liberal statesman, deserves at least a passing glance. The value to be attached to his words is a different matter. This writer attaches no importance to them whatsoever. He believes that, like Hitler's disavowal of further territorial ambitions, they were flung in the path of pursuing realists with the sole object of diverting attention and gaining time. They were the sweet syrup to soothe 'men of goodwill'. They were written or spoken with intent to deceive. Against the general propaganda background, they make no sense otherwise.

*   *   *   *   *

Let us now briefly summarize the Soviet attitude and intention in the post-war world, as it emerges from classic communist dogma and contemporary re-statement.

We see Russia with a fanatical sense of mission. Her task is to save the world. 'Past experience has demonstrated,' said Yermashov in December 1946, 'that the fate of socialism in the Soviet Union and the fate of civilization and culture are inseparable, and that victories achieved by the Soviet are victories of light over darkness, of progress over deadly stagnation.' Nothing could be clearer.

We see Russia implacably hostile to non-communism. We see an arrogant Soviet patriotism superimposed upon and reinforcing the embedded dogma. There is no gleam of toleration, no break whatever in the solid wall of hatred, no chink admitting the possibility of error. We are talking, of course, of those who lead Russia. What the Russian people may think is interesting, but in practice largely irrelevant.

Now what is to be concluded about Russia's attitude in the light of the evidence so far available? Are we to decide there is no hope whatever of co-operation? A verdict in accordance with the evidence may seem to some people to involve a death sentence on humanity, but no other verdict is permissible. If the Russians had declared themselves to be the sworn enemies of the non-communist West, and yet in their actions had been friendly, we should be right to hold that actions speak louder than words, and to be hopeful. If the Russians, though invariably hostile to the West in their day-to-day actions, had been theoretically loyal to the idea of good-neighbourliness, we should be right to hope that the deadlock was due to temporary circumstances and would pass. But when theory and practice coincide (and later we shall see how they do), when both words and deeds are the words and deeds of warfare, then we are not entitled to disregard their clear meaning.

To many people it may seem that the evidence produced so far in this chapter has been tediously familiar and unnecessary —that the writer has been 'kicking at an open door', since the facts are only too well known. The justification for an admittedly wearisome re-statement is that so many other people, finding the facts distasteful, have refused to believe them. Repetition will continue to be necessary as long as a great body of opinion still thinks of Russia as just another country—a difficult one, admittedly, and therefore needing limitless patience in negotiation —instead of a dynamic revolutionary force uninterested in good relations with the non-communist world and hell-bent for mischief everywhere.

*   *   *   *   *

The ultimate purpose of Soviet Russia has never varied, but the means by which it was to be accomplished have always been elastic. Lenin was a master in the use of adjustable tactics, and his advice on the subject has been enshrined in the *Short Course*. Writing about the events of the 1905 revolution, he said, 'All this showed that one had to know not only how to advance resolutely, to advance in the front ranks, when the revolution was in the ascendant, but also how to retreat properly . . . when the revolution was no longer in the ascendant, changing one's tactics as the situation changed; to retreat not in disorder but in an organized way, calmly and without panic, utilizing every minute opportunity to withdraw the cadres from under enemy fire, to re-form one's ranks, to muster one's forces, and to prepare for a new offensive against the enemy.' Writing in his pamphlet *Left-wing Communism: An Infantile Disorder,* he used the following much-quoted but much-forgotten sentence, 'It is necessary . . . to use any ruse, cunning, unlawful method, evasion, concealment of truth.' Stalin could certainly justify his 'soothing syrup' under this rule.

Lenin's precepts have been faithfully observed by Russia and by communists in all countries. Seeking to take full advantage of every opportunity, they have never worried about *tactical* consistency. In the past thirty years we have seen them in every

26

tactical phase. Sometimes they have appeared in full revolution- ary cry; sometimes they have gone to ground. Sometimes they have flattered and fraternized with social democracy; sometimes they have made it the object of venomous attack. Sometimes they have presented themselves in the guise of a respectable, constitutional and co-operative political party, quietly sharing the duties of government; sometimes they have behaved like irre- sponsible political hooligans. At no time has there necessarily been any correlation between what they said and what they thought. They have been tortuous and self-contradictory; unre- liable and opportunist. That is why it has been impossible for any non-communist to co-operate with them for long. Though they are undeviating in their goal, they are without scruple over the means of reaching it. Success is the only test of morality.

Of the many instruments which Russia and the communists have brought into their service, the communist party in the vari- ous countries of the world is, of course, the most important. The party is selfless, reliable and compact—a tempered weapon. Its members are politically informed, devotees of the dogma, and unlikely to lose sight of the end however confusing the means. Their task, in every country, is to prepare for 'the day' and lead the local struggle.

No question has been more keenly argued in non-communist circles than the extent to which the communist parties are units independent of Moscow. Gouzenko, the cipher clerk who dis- closed the facts of Soviet espionage in Canada, declared that the parties were simply an instrument of Russia, a Soviet 'fifth column'. Stalin, in September 1946, said that the accusation that the policy of the western communist parties was dictated from Moscow was 'an absurdity borrowed from the bankrupt arsenal of Hitler and Goebbels'. He was perhaps not unaware that noth- ing has so hampered the growth of communism in a nation-con- scious world as the belief that it was an unpatriotic movement.

It is almost certainly a mistaken approach to think of Moscow dictating instructions, in the Soviet interest, to every satellite party. That, as Stalin has said, would not be realistic. It is diffi- cult to conceive, for instance, of an American Communist party —once it had reached the parapet of power—taking its orders from the Kremlin. The truth is that all communists are priests of one church. While the foundations of the church stand it is

27

virtually impossible that Soviet policy and local communist policy should clash. The identity of approach is automatic and basic. What is good for Moscow is good for communism; what is good for communism is good for Moscow. Most of the leadership comes from Moscow at the moment because most of the power is in Moscow. It is not necessary for Moscow to make a habit of issuing instructions to Mr Pollitt or M Thorez or Signor Togliatti, since these gentlemen religiously take their cue. The fact that no communist party has ever for long pursued a line out of step with Moscow is due to the accident of history which set the 'Ark of the Covenant' in the Russian capital. For the communists, it may prove to have been an unfortunate accident since it gives to their activities an unpatriotic and treasonable flavour which would have been less apparent if the initial Revolution had succeeded in two or three big countries simultaneously.

Though communism, in its present phase, cannot dispense with the support of Russian State power and cannot, therefore, avoid being seen as its instrument, the communist movement is, of course, a *horizontal* conspiracy where nations are concerned. It was because the West was unduly conscious of Russia's direction of the Communist International that it gave such a sigh of relief when the dissolution of the organization was announced from Moscow in 1943. But the men and women who signed the statement of dissolution did not go into retirement. On the contrary, they were soon to enter upon their most active and fruitful period. Of the signatories, Togliatti was shortly to play a leading part in Italy; Dimitrov was to become virtual dictator of Bulgaria; Gottwald was to be Prime Minister of Czechoslovakia; Thorez and Marty were to lead a revolutionary bid in France; Pieck was to become the potential communist leader in the Soviet zone of Germany; Anna Pauker was to be foreign minister of Rumania; Rakosi was to be the dominant figure in Hungarian politics. When the Cominform was set up, seven signatories of the old Comintern deed of dissolution turned out to be foundation members of the new organization. Nothing but plain ignorance of communism and an infinite gullibility could ever have led the peoples of the democracies to believe that the horizontal conspiracy was over.

*   *   *   *   *

Not all communists openly avow their creed. Some pretend allegiance to other organizations, hoping thereby to increase their effectiveness. It is an old tactic. The *Short Course*, page 57, tells how in 1905 there was a plan to present a workers' petition to the Tsar. 'The petition was discussed at workers' meetings where amendments were made. Bolsheviks spoke at these meetings without openly announcing themselves.' They have been doing the same thing ever since.

Then there are the 'sympathizers'—the genuine idealists, the liberal intellectuals, the occasional misguided cleric—who do not go all the way with the communists but seem to. Theirs is a heavy responsibility, for they give to communist propaganda an appearance of respectability and integrity to which it has no title.

Openly and secretly, the communists seek to gain control or influence in every kind of organization by persistent infiltration. This, too, is a time-honoured technique. The *Short Course* tells on page 138 of the great influence which the Bolsheviks exercised, at a time when their own organization was illegal in Russia, 'on the workers' groups at four legally-held congresses . . . a congress of people's universities, a women's congress, a congress of factory physicians and a temperance congress'. There is no end to the diversity of their interests. They are most energetic in the trade unions, control of which can, at the right moment, be turned to decisive revolutionary purpose, but they are busy, too, in co-operative movements and civic institutes and indeed wherever two or three are gathered together.

They are adept at creating new organizations which may serve their purpose. Before the war they had never made much headway in the international trade union movement, but in 1945, when goodwill towards Russia was still high, the communists were able to take the lead in forming a World Federation of Trade Unions, to which the adherence of the British TUC gave an appearance of moderation. The declared aims of the Federation were laudable enough. 'We must create,' said the Soviet trade union leader Kuznetzov, 'a trade union organization capable of uniting and organizing the working class of the world and directing all its efforts towards the struggle to achieve lasting peace, freedom and democracy.' But soon the organization was becoming a world-wide instrument of agitation and propaganda

29

for many of the causes which the Soviet Union and the communists had sponsored. Federation delegates were found reporting adversely on the British zone of Germany, backing up Russian charges about conditions in the Anglo-Persian oilfield, deploring 'fascism' in Greece, and stirring up trouble in Japan.

Another apparently respectable organization which the communists had a big hand in creating was the World Federation of Democratic Youth. It had its origins in the World Youth Congress movement started in Geneva in 1936 on the initiative of young British communists. Soon it had the support of many young people who were not communists and were unaware of the movement's communist leadership. By 1946 a World Youth Conference was able to muster 437 delegates from 62 countries, and the Federation was beginning to send its own busybody delegations round the world, including one to report adversely on Anglo-Dutch imperialism in Indonesia.

One of the most active of the communist instruments in the post-war period was the network of societies for 'cultural relations' with Russia and 'friendship societies' in a host of countries. The effect of such organizations was to attract the support of amiable and idealistic people interested in Russia or in the development of good relations with Russia, and to use them as a cloak for communist propaganda. The British-Soviet Society did precisely this; so did the Society for Cultural Relations. The nature of the British-Soviet Society was excellently described by an unhappy delegate in a letter to *The Times* on September 27th, 1947:

'The Society . . . the self-appointed mouthpiece of the Soviet Government . . . consistently disparages and criticizes our Foreign Office. The Society is permeated with an ideological sympathy which creates an unhealthy bias. The Soviet point of view is well-presented to us and quite uncritically into the bargain. I have no evidence that the British case is put to the Russian people. If and when attempts are made to establish contacts at popular levels, they are always on a 'one-way-traffic' basis. British and foreign supporters of the Society are free to move about this country and comment as they please. Similar facilities are not allowed in the Soviet Union. The Society is not dignified. Its demeanour is not that of free, proud and independent men and women offering friendship on an esteemed reciprocal basis. There is a distasteful atmosphere of subservience. The Soviet contribution to the desired concord is an officially-sponsored stream of mis-statements, rebuffs and snubs calculated to hurt and wound us in our personal and national feelings. Any expression of our admiration for Russian efforts or appreciation of her difficulties is accepted with condescending patronage.'

Another instrument which the communists used with vigour and effect in the post-war years was the theme of Slav solidarity. It was used, of course, solely as a means to an end. The dogma frowns on racial emphasis and of the many races in Russia, most are not Slav. But Slav propaganda could serve the double purpose of consolidating the strategically important Slav area of eastern Europe, and of exploiting a ready-made emotional support elsewhere in the world. Hitler, with his *Bunds,* had shown the way. Much could be said and done under the banner of Slav solidarity which would have been impossible under the hammer and sickle. In September 1946, for instance, the third national convention of the American-Slav Congress was held in Madison Square Garden, New York. Fifteen thousand Americans of Slav descent heard speeches by the Polish and Yugoslav ambassadors, the Soviet Consul-General and the Polish Vice-Minister of Defence. The congress was severely critical of American foreign policy and adopted some denunciatory resolutions.

The manner in which the Slav theme was used in Czechoslovakia illustrates once again how no weapon comes amiss to the communist. Speaking on the deportations from the Sudetenland after the war, the communist Minister of Propaganda, Kopecky, declared, 'We shall expel all the Germans, we shall confiscate all their property, we shall denationalize . . . the whole area . . . so that the victorious spirit of Slavdom shall permeate the country from the frontier to the interior.'

* * * * *

One of the important tasks which Russia and the communists set themselves in the post-war period was to divide Britain and America. To communism, all capitalism is the enemy but by its nature it is not a homogeneous thing. Existing strains and stresses between rival imperialisms can be usefully aggravated. At post-war conferences of the Powers, particularly the early conferences, attempts were made to play off Britain and America against each other, and they had a limited and temporary measure of success. Radio talks from Moscow repeatedly stressed the conflict of interests and the points of maximum irritation. Much salt was rubbed into the wound of Britain's postwar financial dependence. *New Times* ranged the world for fruitful squabbles. It declared 'the United States policy of establishing undivided US rule has clashed with the more modest plans of Britain and her Dominions' in the Far East. In March 1947, Hassanov, broadcasting in Arabic, said the Americans were chasing the British from Iran and that this was typical of the overall situation, for the British had lost their position in the Near East and were retreating before the Americans. In April 1947 a broadcast in German on the congenial theme of 'Anti-American Tendencies in British Public Opinion' spoke of the alarm of the British people at the fact that their country was becoming a junior partner of the United States. In October 1947, Professor Varga wrote, 'The United States is systematically working for the realization of its plan of world supremacy and the liquidation of Britain as a World Power.' The sustained Russian effort to set Britain and America at loggerheads was given some support by Mr Wallace, who declared that British imperialism was dragging America into war, and by Mr Zilliacus, who declared that American imperialism was dragging Britain into war. A number of Labour MPs with concealed affiliations or suicidal instincts lent themselves to the task of underscoring Anglo-American differences and problems. Happily, they had little success. Transatlantic discords are sometimes harsh, but the ties are strong, and Russia could safely be relied upon to prevent any loosening of them.

Another aspect of Russia's policy was the sowing of division in all the countries not under her control. It cannot be too strongly emphasized that the military and economic power of the Soviet Union is only a part, and perhaps only a minor part, of the danger which threatens the non-communist world. By far the strongest weapon in the hands of Moscow and the communists is the power to create a horizontal split in the enemy camp. It would be foolish to take too much comfort from the power predominance of the western countries; that power balance can shift very quickly. Much communist propaganda may have fallen on hard ground in Britain and America, but the seeds lie dormant and in suitable conditions may germinate. Several allied countries outside the Russian sphere of influence have already been effectively neutralized by spoiling tactics. Others could go the same way. In October 1947, *Tass* from Bucharest quoted a statement alleged to have been made by an itinerant Labour MP to the effect that he 'would like to tell provocateurs who were trying to scare the world with the spectre of a new war that British workers would not fight against the Soviet Union— that British dockers would refuse to load munitions and British miners would not dig a single ounce of coal'. If that kind of prediction came true—and it might in favourable circumstances— communist propaganda would have achieved a victory greater than any bloody triumph on a battlefield. A Soviet Union, isolated from the disturbing stream of world doubt and solidly united in its conditioned ignorance, could face confidently the last struggle with a non-communist world torn by internal strife.

The other main tasks which Russia set herself in the post-war world were, first, to seize the opportunities afforded by victory to extend her territorial, political and economic power as far afield as possible; secondly, to hasten the disintegration of the British Empire; and thirdly, to undermine and discredit Britain and America in the eyes of the world. These and associated topics form the subject matter of the rest of this book.

CHAPTER II

THE WESTERN INITIATIVE

It was stated in the last chapter that in any proper assessment of responsibility for a quarrel, an answer to the question 'Who began it?' is fundamental. An uninformed third party, instructed to give a verdict on the relative culpability of the chief belligerents at the end of World War II without considering the war's origins, might have found it very hard to pronounce on the respective demerits of unrestricted sea warfare, Nazi death camps, British saturation bombing and American atomizing. Similarly, a dispassionate observer of the present division of the world, ignoring its causes, would find it very difficult to decide which party was the worse offender. He would see both sides interfering in other people's affairs, both seeking new footholds and bases, both arming fast, both supporting undemocratic governments for strategic purposes, both abusive and intolerant. He would be able to make a case at will that either Russia or America aimed at world domination. To every charge he would find a counter-charge; rights and wrongs would be buried in the inextricable confusion of events, and he would probably conclude that it was just another case of 'six of one and half a dozen of the other'.

Yet such a judgment would be untrue and it is necessary to go back to the beginning to see why. It is almost always difficult to say where the beginning of a quarrel starts. Where relations between Russia and the West are concerned, however, there is an obvious and proper starting point. It is the period when the hatchet was declared by both sides to be buried; when, for four years and a few days, Russia and the West were technically allies. If we can show that one side never really regarded it as buried at all, or hastened to dig it up again at the first safe opportunity, we shall be able to answer the question 'Who began it?' to the satisfaction of most people.

*   *   *   *   *

34

Britain and America, having no dogma of hate, were whole-hearted during the war in their desire that bygones should be bygones. The few who cherished old grievances were isolated, silent and morally disarmed. The Anglo-Saxon peoples were exuberant in their admiration and friendship for Russia, and they were sincere. Their press and radio gave the Soviet Union support and praise without limit. The West sought ceaselessly to widen the area of co-operation. No assistance that could be given to the Russians was ever refused. On British and American soil, Russians were treated as comrades; on Russian soil the most conscientious efforts were made to avoid offending Russian susceptibilities or arousing Russian suspicions. Undue curiosity about Soviet military tactics, plans and equipment was studiously avoided on instructions from above. Constant rebuffs were accepted with patience and in the hope that things would improve. Conciliation was the order of the day, even though it involved humiliation. On the material side, the United States gave top priority to shipments to Russia at a time when British and American forces were themselves in acute need of supplies. Between October 1st, 1941, and May 31st, 1945, America sent to Russia 16½ million tons of material, including nearly 4½ million tons of foodstuffs—enough to give an army of ten million men a square meal every day throughout the greater part of the war. No 'strings' were attached to any of these supplies, even when it became increasingly apparent that Russian demands were not wholly related to the prosecution of the war.

Now what was Russia's war-time attitude? The fact is that the dogma prevailed. The struggle with the West was in abeyance while Germans were killed—that was all. The officially correct Russian approach—broadening into friendship only at banquets—barely concealed the underlying hostility and distrust. Only on the rarest occasions was there any co-operation. There was not even effective military co-operation. The more the war could be kept in two separate compartments, the better the Russians were pleased. Adequate liaison was made difficult by their obstruction and procrastination. Allied military missions were given almost no information and allowed almost no facilities. The Russian air was virtually banned to allied aircraft; the Americans were not allowed to set up their own communications system in Moscow; even meteorological co-operation was for long avoided. Allied parties going into Russia to help the common war effort frequently had as much difficulty in getting visas as though they had been suspected enemy agents. In a northern port, hospital units sent from England to save the lives of British sailors wounded or frostbitten in the dangerous convoy run were refused admission. In the latter stages of the war, Anglo-American efforts to reach war prisoners liberated by the advancing Red Army were systematically obstructed. Throughout, every initiative for co-operation came from the West. In the words of General Deane, former head of the United States military mission in Moscow, 'Not once during the war did Stalin or his subordinates seek a meeting with British or American authorities in order to present proposals for improving our co-operative effort.'

Virtually no information was given to the Russian people about allied aid. Very little appeared in the Soviet press about allied military successes. No attempt was ever made by the Russians to create a feeling of allied solidarity in any but the most transient form. If such a feeling appeared to be taking root, it was eradicated by the sort of report which in 1944 ascribed to Britain the intention to make a separate peace. Anglo-American nationals in Russia—military, diplomatic and press—were virtually segregated from the ordinary Russian people. All press messages from Moscow were subjected to a deliberately misleading political censorship.

To mention facts like these during the war was, of course, impossible; in Britain, as late as 1946, to do so was unpopular, as this writer has reason to remember; now such things are taken for granted. But that is no reason why they should be forgotten. They are vital evidence. They show that the Soviet Government never buried the hatchet; that the hand outstretched to them in friendship was never grasped; that to the Kremlin, Britain and America never ceased to look like potential enemies of Russia. And if the Russians could not bring themselves to co-operate during war, there was never a chance that they would co-operate after the war.

* * * * *

Because the dogma said so, the Russians always believed

that Britain and America would prove unreliable allies. They thought and still think that the western allies deliberately 'pulled their punches' and that the 'second front' was purposely delayed until the very last minute. That it was delayed is indisputable; that it could have succeeded earlier is the dubious thesis of a minority of military strategists; that it was consciously withheld in order to weaken the Russians is not likely to be the view of history. But it will be the view of Russian history. The belief was incorporated in the script of the post-war Russian film *The Battle of Stalingrad*. 'Everything is perfectly plain,' soliloquizes Stalin. 'They want us to bleed white so as to dictate to us later on. . . . They want to achieve their aims with other people's arms. . . . They hope that we shall surrender Stalingrad and lose our base for the offensive.'

The view that the Normandy landing took place only when it could no longer be safely postponed has been put on record in the *Short Biography of J. V. Stalin*, published in Moscow in 1947. Describing events in 1944, this book says, 'The military situation created meant that the Soviet Union was in a position, without the assistance of its allies and relying on its own forces, to occupy the whole of Germany and to bring about the liberation of France. This circumstance compelled the former Prime Minister of England, Churchill, who until this time had opposed the opening of a second front in Europe, to undertake the invasion of western Europe.' This is what every Russian schoolboy is now learning. Nobody will tell him that General Eisenhower was ordered to England in June 1942 to prepare for a cross-Channel attack and that plans went ahead from that time until the assault was actually launched.

While the war was on, the Russians usually contrived to present with some caution and qualification the view that the Soviet Union was fighting virtually single-handed and that the western allies were not really trying. After the war, it was asserted more crisply. 'The Anglo-American reactionaries,' wrote Zaslavsky in November 1946, 'did not wish to destroy German fascism. They only wanted to weaken it in order to rise to the top themselves.' In May 1947 he said that the war could have been ended with complete victory a year earlier except that a speedy and complete victory was 'not in the interests of certain politicians'. Mikhailov, in a VE-day broadcast in German in 1947, attacked

37

Churchill for 'in every way sabotaging the second front' until the moment of the Red Army's decisive victories 'which had not been included in Churchill's plans'. Moran, writing in *Izvestia*, did not trouble to qualify the myth when he starkly referred to 'the war fronts, where we fought single-handed'. But it was left to the embittered Ehrenburg to declare of the western allies, 'They did not hurry to arm themselves during the struggle against the enemy'. At least, one could retort, they did not hurry to supply the enemy with oil and grain.

Russian suspicions of the intentions of the West were intensified when Churchill argued at Teheran in 1943 in favour of a Balkan front rather than a Channel crossing. That political as well as military considerations were in his mind is hardly open to doubt. Such an invasion, if it could have been agreed upon, would have prevented Russia's unilateral control of south-eastern Europe. Precisely for that reason, it could never have been agreed upon. Stalin did not want it and he had his way, backed up by Roosevelt and General Marshall. In short, what the Russians have insisted on regarding as proof of Anglo-Saxon hostility in fact turned out to be yet another indication that in the interests of co-operation the West was at this period always prepared to give way.

Russia's belief that her allies would 'double-cross' her never wavered, and as the war drew to a close she repeatedly declared that they were doing so. The Soviet war correspondent Kraminov accused the British in October 1947 of having planned to seize Berlin with mobile forces before the Russians could reach it when they discovered 'not long before the end of the war' that there was no German front ahead. In fact, the project of advancing on Berlin from the west had been considered and rejected, in part to allay Soviet fears. Kraminov also accused the western allies of crossing the agreed demarcation line; as fighting was still going on they would no doubt have been accused of breaking off the battle had they stood pat on the line. Finally, 'reactionary circles in Britain violated their obligations as allies and rescued fragments of fascist armies. The Germans were only too grateful to accept this help. They felt that the spirit of Munich was coming to life again'. Actually, as *The Times* military correspondent pointed out, these 'rescued' Germans were sealed off in the Baltic peninsulas where they spent a winter of acute discomfort. Short of shooting them all, no more effective means of liquidating them could have been found.

In the final days of Germany's dissolution, the western allies exercised the greatest care to keep the Russians informed of all events, fully maintaining their initiative in seeking military co-operation. Their thoughtfulness was in vain. When Kesselring made the first tentative approaches to Alexander on the Italian front, Stalin decided that the western allies were bribing the enemy to open the front to them with a promise of easier peace terms. He insisted on the correctness of his view even after it had been denied by Roosevelt, and compelled the usually restrained President to nail it as a 'vile misrepresentation'.

The Russians, with their preconceived view of the way in which capitalist powers must necessarily act, preferred the doc-trine to the facts. The blood jointly shed, the dangers jointly survived, the four years of common struggle towards one goal meant nothing to the Russians. To them, peace was the resump-tion of war by other means.

*　　*　　*　　*　　*

The chief architect of Anglo-American war-time policy to-wards Russia was President Roosevelt. To call his policy one of sustained concession would be to do less than justice to a noble if fleeting vision. Roosevelt saw American-Soviet collaboration as the indispensable basis of post-war peace. He hoped that in time the Russians might be weaned away from their rigid dogma; that the Kremlin might abandon its creed of world revo-lution, and that American democracy and Soviet communism, avoiding conflict, might move nearer to each other over the years. He believed this would be all the more likely if Russia could be persuaded to enter an international organization to maintain post-war security and co-operation. His 'great design' was for a law-abiding and peaceful world with the Soviet Union as a willing partner, and he believed that Russia could be per-suaded that her own interests would be best served by such an association. He felt that if he could meet Stalin face to face, it would be possible to convince and reassure him, and he tried repeatedly to bring about such a meeting. The Teheran confer-ence was for Roosevelt a hopeful adventure to which he looked eagerly forward as an opportunity for a 'meeting of the minds'. We are told that at Teheran he 'conducted a seminar in the good-neighbour policy'.* As an earnest of that policy, and to disarm Russian suspicions, he was prepared to make very great material concessions to the Soviet Union. It is inconceivable that any man could have shown greater sincerity or determination in seeking to enrol Russia as an equal and permanent partner. But the attempt failed.

Of the British attitude over the same period, it need only be said that Britain fully shared the President's hopes and that her policy, under Churchill and Eden, followed the same broad aims—at a similar, or greater, cost.

The records show unmistakably that before he died Roosevelt was disillusioned about the possibility of achieving his aim. Before we glance at the many concessions which the western allies made to Russia in pursuance of the Roosevelt purpose, it is useful to follow one of the main threads of disillusionment to its end.

The test case for Roosevelt was the attitude which Russia would adopt towards the liberated and satellite countries near her borders. He accepted the often-repeated Soviet claim that the border governments must be 'friendly'. That in itself was a big concession from principle to realism. Friendship is a prize which normally has to be earned. No country which is compelled to be friendly with a neighbour, irrespective of what the characteristics of that neighbour may happen to be, can be fully independent or democratic. Would Hitler have been justified in demanding a change in the government of Czechoslovakia before Munich because Dr Benes was unfriendly to Nazism—as he undoubtedly was? And if the right to friendly border governments is conceded, does not a logical extension of the principle require friendly governments still farther afield? A friendly Poland could never save Russia from the impact of a strong and hostile Germany.

Roosevelt no doubt had these considerations fully in mind, but in the interests of collaboration he agreed that Russia could not be expected to tolerate hostile governments on her frontiers. Within the framework of 'friendliness', however, he required

* James F. Byrnes, *Speaking Frankly*. Harper & Bros (New York), Heinemann (London).

that the liberated and satellite countries should be given a real opportunity to rule themselves on democratic lines and should not be treated as an annexe of the Soviet Union. He knew that at their first meeting in Moscow, Stalin and Churchill had reached a verbal understanding that Russia should have a predominant interest in east and south-east Europe and that Britain should have a predominant interest in Greece. But this understanding was set in a military context, and was never intended to mean the mutual recognition of exclusive control.

At the Yalta conference in February 1945, the President succeeded in gaining the approval of Stalin to a Big Three Declaration of principle on the subject of liberated Europe. The three governments pledged themselves to 'concert' their policies in assisting the liberated and satellite countries to solve their political and economic problems by democratic means. They also declared that they would 'jointly assist' these peoples 'to form interim governmental authorities broadly representative of all democratic elements in the population and pledged to the earliest possible establishment, through free elections, of governments responsive to the will of the people'.

One of the countries coming within the scope of this Declaration was Poland. There were, at this period, two governments of Poland—the London government, which had directed the 'underground' in Poland throughout the war and was recognized by the West, and the Lublin government, which had been set up under Russia's aegis in the rear of the Red Army. At Teheran, Roosevelt had refused to take sides in the bitter dispute which developed between Churchill and Stalin. At Yalta, he put forward proposals for an amicable settlement in line with the principles of the Declaration. As a result, it was agreed that the Lublin government should be 'reorganized on a broader democratic basis with the inclusion of democratic leaders from Poland itself and from Poles abroad'.

Like many agreements of the period, the text was so loosely framed as to open the way for endless disputes over interpretation. But the discussions at Yalta seemed to leave no doubt about the spirit of the understanding between the Big Three. Roosevelt made his intentions quite plain. Molotov envisaged elections in Poland 'within a month's time', though actually they did not take place for twenty-three months. Roosevelt stressed

41

that the 'free elections' must be 'like Caesar's wife' and Stalin took the point.

The Yalta meeting was hardly over, however, before it became apparent that the Kremlin's idea of reorganizing a government on a broader democratic basis differed sharply from Roosevelt's. The British and Americans were thinking in terms of a new government embracing all elements not hostile to Russia; the Russians were thinking in terms of a slightly expanded Lublin government which would remain subservient to them.

Very shortly before his death, Roosevelt submitted to Churchill a draft message to Stalin. In it he said that he could not conceal 'the concern with which I view the development of events'. He could not, he declared, reconcile the Soviet view that the new government should be little more than a continuation of the old, with the tenor of the agreement reached at Yalta. 'Any such solution which would result in a thinly-disguised continuation of the present government would be entirely unacceptable, and would cause our people to regard the Yalta agreement as a failure.' Stalin's reply held out no hope of satisfactory compromise.

An even more flagrant breach of the spirit of Yalta occurred almost simultaneously in Rumania, where the Red Army was in control. Hardly a fortnight after the close of the conference at which 'concerted policies' and 'joint assistance' for the ex-satellites had been pledged, the Russians brushed aside an American request for consultations over the Rumanian situation, where communist-led strikes were threatening order. Vishinsky rushed to Bucharest at the end of February 1945, compelled the resignation of the Government which was declared to be 'unfriendly', refused to accept a Government which, though 'friendly', would not have been servile, and installed a puppet Government under threat of force. Throughout the *coup* the western allies were treated with the utmost contempt. This plain indication that Russia proposed to do exactly as she pleased in south-eastern Europe and had no desire to co-operate with her allies was given, let it be remembered, at a time when Anglo-American appeasement was at its height and when the joint war was still being fought. The atom bomb had not fallen, the Truman doctrine was not even an embryo. No Anglo-American action had provoked the Russian step.

For Roosevelt, these events in Rumania and Poland appear to have been a turning point. To Mr Byrnes he expressed his 'grave misgivings' about the future. As far as he was concerned, the Yalta agreements had been reached in good faith and he had always intended that they should be scrupulously carried out. Had he lived, there is little doubt that he would soon have shared Churchill's prominent place in Soviet demonology, for his high hopes were incompatible with Soviet plans.

When he could no longer speak for himself, the Russians built a myth around him. Roosevelt had been their friend; he had understood them; he had been a sincere believer in co-operation. It was the departure from Roosevelt's policy, said Orlov, in an English broadcast in June 1946, which had caused the differences between America and Russia.

We have only to follow the story of Poland and Rumania through to the end to see how baseless is that claim. Far from stiffening in its attitude over the non-observance of the Yalta Declaration, as Roosevelt would almost certainly have done, American foreign policy took a headlong plunge into appeasement at all costs, with Britain in close if unenthusiastic attendance. Following a visit by Harry Hopkins to Stalin immediately after Roosevelt's death, agreement was reached on the formation of a provisional government in Poland on terms which left every vestige of real power in the hands of Russia's nominees and paved the way for the communist domination of the country. Superficially, the agreement just managed to 'save the face' of the West; in fact, it was an unconditional surrender.

As for the establishment of democratic government in Rumania (now linked with the associated problem of Bulgaria), principles were cast away in Moscow in December 1945 after Mr Byrnes and Mr Bevin had made a brief stand in London in September. This time, not even face was saved. At the instigation of Mr Byrnes, the West agreed to recognize the Soviet-installed governments of Rumania and Bulgaria provided these governments took in representatives of 'democratic parties not hitherto participating in them'. The subsequent developments arising out of this formula were farcical. Bulgaria's government could not be 'reorganized' since that country had just held elections, but Russia undertook to 'advise' the Bulgarian government to take in two opposition members. This undertaking failed to bear any fruit and the whole subject was discreetly dropped. As regards Rumania, it was agreed to send the British and American ambassadors in Moscow and Mr Vishinsky to Bucharest to secure the necessary changes. After the customary difficulties, the West finally 'settled' for the inclusion of two opposition gentlemen whose brief tenure of unimportant office hardly cast a ripple on the communist-controlled surface of Rumanian political life.

* * * * *

It is now necessary to return to Roosevelt. As has been seen, he believed that the key to the whole future lay in Russia's collaboration in a world organization. It is significant that all the initiative and drive in this essentially peaceful, co-operative and good-neighbourly enterprise came from the United States and Britain. Russia, with her eyes on the dogma, did not at first see how valuable it would be to her and had to be cajoled and prodded into joining it.

The Dumbarton Oaks Conference in the autumn of 1944 on proposals for setting up such an organization had left the question of voting unsettled. The Russians had wanted a much wider veto right for the Great Powers than either America or Britain had thought desirable. Roosevelt was determined to get a settlement of the unagreed clauses at Yalta, and two months before the Yalta meeting he had sent off compromise proposals by air to Moscow so that Stalin should have plenty of opportunity to study them. But when the Big Three met, Stalin had not even read them, so slight was his interest. Nevertheless, Russia accepted the American proposals since, in the matter of the veto, they conceded virtually all that Russia had required.

Another big concession was the agreement that Russia should have three votes in the new organization, Byelorussia and the Ukraine being given separate representation. This enabled the Soviet Union not merely to vote three times but to talk three times on every issue which subsequently arose in UNO—an opportunity of which she never failed to take advantage and which added greatly to the value of UNO as a Russian soap-box on the international street corner.

* * * * *

The conciliatory attitude of Britain and America was shown with unmistakable clarity in the matter of Russia's territorial acquisitions during the war and post-war period. The most striking transfers were those made under the secret clauses of the Yalta agreement relating to the Far East. They were in a military, rather than a politically-appeasing category, for the *quid pro quo* was a Russian declaration of war on Japan after Germany was defeated. In return for this undertaking, Russia was to get back everything in the Far East which she had lost as a result of her defeat by Japan in 1904—southern Sakhalin, the Kuriles, a naval base at Port Arthur, pre-eminence in the commercial port of Dairen and such a measure of control of the Manchurian railways as would give her economic predominance in that country.

In return for the quiet acceptance of Russia's other territorial acquisitions, no *quid pro quo* was expected by the West except a more co-operative relationship. There was a little private criticism, of course, both in Britain and America, but officially there was not even a whisper about the Atlantic Charter which had pledged the powers to 'seek no aggrandisement, territorial or other'. Both the British and American Governments were ready to accept the thesis that after all Russia could hardly be blamed for taking back what had belonged to her before the Revolution, and to overlook the fact that in some places she had actually taken a great deal more. Her annexations included the very valuable Petsamo nickel area, a naval base near Helsinki and a slice of the Karelian Isthmus from Finland; Königsberg and its hinterland from East Prussia; nearly half of Poland; Bessarabia and Northern Bukovina from Rumania, and Ruthenia from Czechoslovakia. These were in addition to the three Baltic states annexed in 1940. Altogether, more than a quarter of a million square miles of territory and some twenty-four million largely unwilling people were added to the Soviet sixth of the world. These territorial changes, many effected by force and without prior consultation with anyone, were all tacitly accepted by the West in the name of friendship. It should be noted in passing that Britain acquired no new territory as a result of the war, while American 'expansion' was confined to the administration of about 1,000 square miles of sparsely populated islands.

One of Russia's annexations—the eastern half of pre-war Poland—started a new chain of problems which called for western concessions all along the line. Russia's title to territory east of the Curzon Line had been widely accepted. At Yalta Stalin insisted on an approximation to the Curzon Line as the new Russo-Polish frontier and proposed that Poland should be given 'compensation in the west'. He favoured the Oder-Neisse line as the new Polish-German frontier, giving Poland an area of indisputably German land formerly peopled by nine million Germans.

The western Powers did not agree to this at Yalta, and they have never agreed to it, but they came so perilously near agreeing that they have been hopelessly compromised ever since. Against their better judgment, and in the context of Stalin's plain intentions, they recognized that Poland must receive 'substantial accessions of territory in the North and West' and that the final delimitation of the frontier should await the peace conference. Before long, Russia had handed over the debated areas of Germany to Polish administration, making them a *de facto* part of the new Polish State, and at Potsdam the western Powers were persuaded to give their blessing to the transfer. Great firmness by the West at Yalta might have prevented this abuse of power; nothing short of war is likely to undo it. The new frontier will never be acceptable to Germany, which is now—in the words of Mr R. R. Stokes, MP—'a country of thirteen million irredentists with fifty-three million supporters'.

One thoroughly bad decision, acquiesced in for the sake of Big Three harmony, inevitably led to another, more patently wicked. If Poland was to have a 'substantial accession' of German territory, hundreds of thousands of Germans would have to be deported westwards from their former homes. Stalin, characteristically casual about inconvenient figures, said at Potsdam that 'no single German remained in the area to be given to Poland', though later it turned out that there were more than a million and a half. The deportations would mean not only increased hardship for the population of the overcrowded and underfed western zones, and greater subsidies from America and Britain, but would inevitably involve the deportees in fearful sufferings. Though the whole idea was repugnant to Britain and America, they agreed, salving their consciences with a phrase at Potsdam requiring that the deportations should be carried out in 'a humane and orderly manner'. Yet they knew that once the principle was accepted they would have little or no control over the manner of its execution.

That proved to be the case. Before the eyes of the alarmed but committed West, the fruits of 'co-operation at all costs' were soon displayed. Thousands upon thousands of eastern Germans, men, women and children, were turned out of their homes at a moment's notice and packed into slow trains for the western zones without adequate food or water. Newspaper correspondents and outside observers were unanimous in recording the cruelty and horror of this traffic in human wreckage which was to continue on and off for eighteen months. It is sufficient to quote just one statement out of scores—an eye-witness report sent in August 1945 by Norman Clark, the able and conscientious correspondent of the *News Chronicle*.

'Under the bomb-wrecked roof of the Stettiner railway station—the Euston or King's Cross of Berlin—I looked this afternoon inside a cattle-truck shunted beside the buffers of No. 2 platform. On one side, four forms lay dead under blankets on cane and raffia stretchers; in another corner four more, all women, were dying. One, in a voice we could hardly hear, was crying out for water. Sitting on a stretcher, so weakened by starvation that he could not move his head or his mouth, his eyes open in a deranged uncomprehending stare, was the wasted frame of a man. He was dying, too. As I walked about the station a score of others came up to me, all ravenous and starved, for whom also, like those in the cattle-truck mortuary, nothing could be done—until death. Two women sanitary helpers did what they could in ministering to the small wants of the dying.

'The train from Danzig had come in. It had taken seven days on the journey.'

* * * * *

Finally, it is necessary to consider the arrangements which were made towards the end of the war for dealing with a defeated Germany. The pattern of events was largely dictated by Russia. The contribution of Britain and America was to speak up boldly against proposals which they later reluctantly agreed to; to insist on safeguards and qualifications which were not subsequently respected; and to continue to implement the full agreements as though the safeguards had not been brushed aside.

At Yalta, Mr Maisky proposed that the allies should confiscate eighty per cent of all German industry. Russia wanted £2,500 millions in reparations for herself. Churchill and Roosevelt both doubted the practicability of anything approaching that figure, and said so. Nevertheless, they later accepted the figure 'as a basis of discussion' by the Allied Reparations Commission —thus conceding irrecoverable ground. For a brief moment, the West was even manoeuvred into approving the use of German slave labour as a form of reparations. At Potsdam, the western allies were induced to give their consent to three indefensible projects—the large-scale annexation of German territory, the indiscriminate looting of German industry and the mass deportation of German populations. Britain and America, who had fought doggedly and successfully for freedom over half a decade, squandered the moral fruits of victory almost overnight at the demand of a totalitarian ally, and at Potsdam put their signatures to a document which, in its subsequent interpretation if not in its text, has rarely been exceeded for savagery, shortsightedness and sheer impracticality.

* * * * *

It was, of course, proper that the western allies should seek to meet Russian wishes where no vital principle was at stake. They invariably did so. Both at Teheran and at Yalta, Roosevelt made it clear that he accepted Russia's right to a fair share of the oil resources of Persia. Bulgaria's title to an Aegean outlet, championed by Russia, was provisionally conceded in 1945 and proposals put forward by America to that effect. The necessity of revising the Montreux Convention in Russia's favour was accepted, and it was actually the United States which initiated discussions on revision. All these were legitimate attempts to consolidate good relations with an ally.

But concession went far beyond what was legitimate. It had no apparent limits. It is difficult to think of a single disputed matter of importance in this period on which the West was not prepared to surrender for the sake of agreement. For Britain and America it was a period of moral debacle. Because of their desire to maintain the war-time alliance and disperse Russian distrust, they threw away the negotiating power which their combined military strength undoubtedly gave them, they connived at territorial settlements which they knew were wrong and dangerous, they acquiesced in monstrous cruelties, they approved unbridled spoliation of the beaten enemy, they abandoned allied as well as enemy countries to exclusive alien control, and they allowed a wrecking veto to be bolted into the machinery of the new international organization which was to be the hope of the world. They can fairly be accused of having been unprincipled, vacillating, naïve, cowardly and blind.

But this chapter has not been written to condemn Anglo-American policy. It has been written to show that the one thing Britain and America cannot be fairly accused of is a dictatorial and non-co-operative attitude at the close of the war. *They* did not launch the world struggle with the Soviet Union; *they* did not 'begin it'.

In defence of their attitude, this must be said. It was well-meaning. A high ideal lay behind the succession of retreats—the ideal of a lasting working arrangement with their former ally which alone could ensure world peace. That aim was not realized but no one can say, looking back, that the attempt bore no fruit at all.

It was Neville Chamberlain's unsuccessful efforts to appease Hitler which finally convinced the British people that the Nazis wanted war. The equally unsuccessful efforts of Britain and America to appease Soviet Russia undoubtedly helped to convince the democracies that the Kremlin still clung to its dogma and wanted not co-operation but victorious struggle.

CHAPTER III

THE BORDER STATES

There is not the slightest reason to suppose that the Russians ever intended to have free and independent countries on their borders after the war, or to allow the western allies any say whatever in the working out of events in eastern Europe if they could help it. What they did intend was to exploit to the limit the opportunities for communist expansion resulting from military victory. To have let such a unique chance slip would indeed have been a disloyalty to the cause. They planned to impose communist minority rule on largely hostile populations by a combination of force and fraud; to turn six considerable countries—Yugoslavia, Czechoslovakia, Poland, Hungary, Rumania and Bulgaria—into a communist *bloc* from which western influence would be as far as possible excluded. Conditions varied greatly from country to country, and therefore there would have to be some difference in tempo and approach. But there were no differences about the ultimate aim.

Many western apologists made the mistake in the post-war years of considering events in these eastern European countries as though they were unrelated to each other, as though they were the spontaneous outcome of purely local conditions in each country. These observers concentrated on the detail and declined to see the pattern. It was as though a Health Department, faced with a sudden epidemic of typhoid cases, were to send inspectors to examine hundreds of individual drains instead of testing the common water supply. What the apologists failed to see, in their eagerness to find extenuating circumstances in each country, was the overall plan of wholesale political aggression. They did not realize that basically there was only one plan and only one event.

Yet the pointers were plain enough. The Moscow-trained revolutionaries were lined up in advance for their co-ordinated assault on the freedom and independence of their respective nations. There was Joseph Broz (Tito) for Yugoslavia, Dimitrov

for Bulgaria, Anna Pauker for Rumania, Berut and Gomulka
for Poland, Rakosi for Hungary, Gottwald for Czechoslovakia.
They were all old Comintern figures or trusted agents, and each
was the centre of a powerful nucleus. When the moment seemed
ripe, these zealots were sent 'over the top' with the rank and file
of the party in close support. Drawing on a common armoury of
tactics, they fought their battles on broadly similar lines. They
set to work to gain control of the security police and militia, to
dominate the trade unions, to muzzle the press and capture the
radio. They spread the view that the only fight was against fascism, and hustled all parties into National Fronts in which they
secured the chief positions. They used the Centre to destroy the
Right; then they used the socialists to destroy the Centre; finally
they insisted that the socialists should merge with them, and
declared open war on all socialists who stood out against them.
They intrigued and manoeuvred; uncovered and magnified con-
spiracies; organized purges and trials; terrorized, imprisoned
and tortured; all in the belief that finally they would be left in
triumphant possession of the stricken field and would be able
to weld a huge block of territory and a vast population into one
great communist unit, almost another communist Great Power,
economically and politically integrated, largely closed to the
West, and indissolubly bound to Russia.

It is true, as the apologists never tired of repeating, that in many
of these border countries there was little freedom before the war.
It is true that since the war they have effected some important
and long-overdue economic and social reforms. But the new
eastern Europe is not something we can afford to embrace and
applaud simply because it has shed its feudal past and made
some progress with its two- and three-year plans. In the context
of a world struggle between communism and non-communism,
these things are as dangerously irrelevant as was the fact, in the
struggle between liberal democracy and Fascism, that the Duce
made his trains run punctually and drained the Pontine
marshes.

It is true that in all these border countries some 'reactionary'
and 'near-fascist' elements were still in existence in the post-war
period. What is not true is that they were ever a menace justify-
ing the subsequent course of events. With Russian troops standing by, and the communists controlling police and militia and

51

armed forces everywhere, there was no possibility in any eastern European country of a successful post-war *coup* to restore an old regime or bring back any kind of fascism. The proved war criminals, the genuine collaborators, were easily rounded up with the support of all parties. So, in a short time, were most of the patriotic, anti-communist insurgent bands. They were not the real issue. It will be seen in this chapter that the main communist offensive was directed not against these elements but against good democrats, peasants and socialists, men with fine resistance records, men who had always fought for the people. They had to bear the brunt because it was precisely their honest and courageous liberalism—and not the plots of fascists—which constituted the chief obstacle to a ruthless minority bent on imposing its will.

Finally, it has often been stated that Russia's sole purpose in eastern Europe was defensive—that all she wanted was to set up a screen of friendly states between herself and a possible aggressor. The theory was attractive to men of goodwill outside Russia who wished to make every possible excuse for her. But her other activities showed that her ambitions extended much farther west than the satellite fringe. At one time she had high hopes of capturing Germany, France and Italy, and made great efforts to do so. In any case, the claim of a nation to total domination of its neighbours in the supposed interests of its own security must be rejected—as it was rightly rejected when Hitler swallowed Czechoslovakia because it was 'a pistol pointed at the heart of Germany'. The logical end of such a claim is domination of the world, which offers the best security of all.

In the following examination of post-war events in six eastern European countries, it will be seen that the communist aim was not uniformly accomplished. By the end of 1947, one or two socialist parties still retained a measure of independence and were even showing signs of revolt against their communist masters. The apologists were quick to draw public attention to this fact, but they can take no credit for it. In so far as Russia and the communists failed locally in the full execution of their plans, the failure was due solely to a belated political counter-offensive by the West, which the apologists opposed, and to the encouragement which Continental socialists derived from it. Even so, as these words are written, the chances that an independent socialism will survive in any eastern European country are slight indeed.

* * * * *

We need not spend very long on Yugoslavia, which was swept into the post-war Russian orbit with streamlined efficiency. Tito, the chief instrument of the change, had everything on his side. As a long-standing member of the communist party and a pupil of the Moscow school, he had naturally enjoyed full Russian support in the struggle against his only dangerous rival, the Serb patriot, General Mihailovitch. When the western allies were persuaded to transfer their support from Mihailovitch to Tito—thereby giving the clearest proof that they attached much more importance to quick military victory than to the post-war balance of power—his position became unchallengeable. As the war ended, he commanded a well-armed and communist-led partisan army of considerable size. To many of his countrymen he was a romantic and heroic figure. Russia, mother of the Slavs, had never been more popular. The masses, as in the Russia of 1917, were largely illiterate and politically passive—ideal material for an imposed revolution.

Almost all the opposition leaders were abroad, either in lonely exile or working for the Royal Yugoslav Government in London. To consolidate his position before the world, Tito came to an agreement with the London Prime Minister, Subasitch, in the summer of 1944 for a union of forces. But the new government formed in March 1945 was still under communist control. Subasitch himself, who for a short time was Foreign Minister in the new government, had a communist in charge of his political department and another in charge of his personnel. The Serb leader Milan Grol, who was given a minor post, was soon being accused of 'strengthening the anti-democratic and reactionary forces' and was forced to resign about the middle of 1945.

By the time elections were held in November 1945, there was no organized opposition outside Tito's 'People's Front', and little effective criticism inside it. Though the Front incorporated many elements, the communists directed it. No candidates were allowed to stand for election who had not been approved by the communist-controlled National Council of Liberation; no one could vote who was not a loyal supporter of the Front. At election register conferences, anyone could be struck off by popular acclamation. The communist paper *Borba* wrote in September, 'The people will decide who is to vote and who not.' No opposition newspapers were permitted. Press, printing and radio were under State control. The whole campaign was carried out under the watchful eyes of OZNA, Tito's security police. There were no ballot papers on polling day; the voting process consisted of dropping a ball from the clenched fist into one of several boxes, in the presence of Tito's men. In these circumstances, it was not perhaps surprising that Tito was able to declare afterwards that no election had ever been conducted with such order, tranquillity and peace.

The Times thought that 'very great moral pressure' had been used!

The communists now proceeded to complete the building of a 'People's Republic' more or less on the Russian pattern. The Stalin Constitution provided a framework; the nationalities policy was similar to that of Russia; Tito's army, like the Red Army, had its political commissars; the trade unions were government instruments; People's Courts dispensed justice. Yugoslav propaganda methods were modelled on the Russian. One cartoon in a Yugoslav newspaper showed British soldiers whipping colonial slaves in Trieste.

The remaining opposition elements were soon liquidated. Mihailovitch was tried and executed and the bulk of his supporters were rounded up. Archbishop Stepinac, voicing the conscience of the Catholic Church, was sentenced to a long term of imprisonment, and many more priests were subsequently arrested and confined.

Of the few independent voices inside the 'People's Front', the outstanding personality was Dr Dragoljub Yovanovitch. Before the war he had been the leader of the left wing of the Peasant Party, an advocate of far-reaching reforms, and an ardent friend of Russia. Imprisoned under the dictatorship of King Alexander, he had joined Tito's Front at its inception. In earlier disputes between Tito and the Royal Yugoslav Government, Yovanovitch had been usefully cited as evidence of the broad character of Tito's movement. Now he had served his purpose. In the middle of 1946, the communists began to close down local branches of his party. When he protested, he was denounced for attacking the Communist party, for alleging Soviet interference in the internal life of the country, for being a political intriguer in the international field, and for assembling 'fascist elements' around himself. In August 1946 his expulsion from the Peasant party was engineered and he was deprived of his seat in Parliament. In the autumn of 1947 he was arrested with many other Peasant party politicians and in October he was sentenced to nine years' hard labour after a farcical trial.

Other opponents of communist dictatorship were disposed of with equal efficiency. Among a considerable group of Slovene intellectuals arrested in 1947 was Professor Furlan, a distinguished legal scholar who escaped from Yugoslavia during the war in time to evade the execution of an Italian death sentence. For a year he broadcast in the partisan cause and in 1944 he returned secretly to his country to help Tito's forces. In August 1947 he was tried on a charge of 'spying' and sentenced to death —a punishment subsequently commuted to imprisonment for life.

Long before the end of 1947, Tito and his communists were in supreme control of a single-party police state and a regimented people, and Yugoslavia was geared in all important respects to the Soviet Union.

* * * * *

Post-war Czechoslovakia presented a unique and complex problem for the Russians. It was a Slav country. It was aware, in more ways than one, that it had been liberated by the Red Army. The prestige of the communists was high, and it is possible that at the end of the war they could have seized power by a *coup*. But there were risks. Czechoslovakia was the farthest outpost of Russian western penetration, it had a special place in the regard of the western allies and its politically-conscious population had tried western democracy and liked it. The Russians, and their instrument—the Czech communist leader Klement Gottwald—decided to move cautiously.

Post-war government was in the hands of a Provisional National Assembly, elected indirectly by local National Committees which were dominated by the ever-active communists.

Nominally, the government was a four-party coalition. In Bohemia, the four participating parties were the Communists, the closely-associated Social Democrats, Dr Benes's National Socialist party and a Catholic People's party. In Slovakia, there were Communists, a Labour party, a Democratic party and a Catholic Freedom party.

In May 1946, the first post-war elections were held. No parties opposing the coalition were permitted. All parties subscribed to a common programme called the 'Kosice programme' which included land reform, nationalization of industry, and the ejection of Hungarian and German minorities. The powers of the Ministry of the Interior were used by the communists with caution. There was more liberty than in most other countries in the Russian sphere of influence, but it was still qualified liberty. A Catholic newspaper declared during the election campaign, 'There certainly is freedom of speech in this country but it takes a brave man to exercise it.' The press was 'free', in the sense that any organization which supported the broad policy of the government was entitled to a share in it. There was no censorship, because there was no need for it. The election campaign was conducted, on the whole, in a gentlemanly fashion. The Soviet authorities, dissuaded at the last minute from marching 100,000 troops through the country while the campaign was in progress, did not intervene. Voting was compulsory, but electors could return a blank white paper if they wanted to register their disapproval of the coalition. Though it was most unlikely that any of these blanks would be put in by communist voters, it was agreed that subsequently they should be divided equally among the parties. One of the posters of the Right showed a ballot paper going into the box white and coming out red. But the little device was of no practical consequence. As a result of fair elections, the communists emerged as the largest party in Bohemia. In Slovakia, however, the conservative Democratic party won a clear majority. In the country as a whole, the communists and socialists together had won just sufficient mandates to control the coalition, and the communist leader Gottwald became Prime Minister.

The Slovak Democratic party—a perfectly legal and constitutional party with a great following—at once found itself the target of angry abuse and threats from the Left. The communist-controlled Printers' Union refused to print the Democratic party newspaper. The communist Minister of the Interior set up a special commission to report on the Slovak elections. Fierlinger, the near-communist leader of the Social Democrats in Bohemia, joined in the chorus of denunciations, declaring Slovakia to be 'far behind'. The communists were particularly worried by the results because constitutionally no law passed by the National Assembly of Czechoslovakia had validity in Slovakia unless it had also been approved by a majority of the Slovak deputies. There was a real danger that Slovakia might remain an independent island in a communist sea. In an atmosphere of crisis, a conspiracy against the Czechoslovak republic was discovered. The Slovak Democrats re-affirmed their loyalty to the unified Czechoslovak state, a temporary agreement was patched up with the communists, and the Democrat newspaper—a little chastened in tone—was allowed by the printers to reappear. The first round was over, with a win on points for the communists.

The second round began almost before the Democrats had recovered their breath. The communists were in a good position to take the offensive. They had a firm grip on the central government, where they controlled the portfolios of the Interior, Justice and Defence. They had paramount influence in the trade unions and in the local National Committees. In the army they had instituted something very similar to the Russian system of political commissars. Prague radio was a communist pocket borough. Moreover, their hands were strengthened by the fact that the other parties in the Czech coalition, though genuinely concerned to preserve democratic liberties, were uneasy about Slovak separatist tendencies.

In September 1947 the communists unearthed a Slovak plot. There were scores of arrests in Slovakia and a purge of the Democratic party was begun. The immunity of two Slovak deputies was suspended to permit their arrest. In November, Slovakia's regional government, the Board of Trustees, was forced into dissolution by the resignation of the communist members, who demanded that the departments of Internal Affairs and Justice should be placed in the hands of 'non-party members of the resistance movement'—in other words, of disguised communists. Bodies claiming the right to nominate representatives included the Slovak Trade Union Council, the Partisan Union, the Union of Political Prisoners and the War Veterans' Association, all *aliases* of the communist Pooh Bah. The trade unions were persuaded to threaten a general strike if the demands were not met. The Democrats would not give way, since the whole attack was highly unconstitutional. Presently the National Assembly dispatched Gottwald to Bratislava with the task of forming a new Board of Trustees. His powers of persuasion were increased by the fact that two of the three secretaries of the Slovak Democratic party were under arrest. Gottwald finally succeeded in forcing a new Board of Trustees upon the Slovak Democrats, depriving them of their majority. The results of the election in Slovakia were thus reversed, and the Democratic party was on its way to extinction.

In the meantime, however, the communists were having trouble in Bohemia. The National Front had been badly shaken by the reversal of the government's decision to adhere to the Marshall Plan. It was common knowledge that Gottwald had received his orders in Moscow, and that the *volte face* had taken place in a climate of threats. The autumn session of the National Assembly met in an atmosphere of crisis. The communists picked a quarrel with their colleagues on the subject of a new capital levy to aid farmers hit by the drought. Social Democrats and Communists, who had recently agreed to form a Marxist *bloc,* found themselves on opposite sides. For the first time, vigorous attacks on the communists appeared in the Social Democratic paper *Pravo Lidu.* The communists appeared to be isolated. They were particularly concerned about the growing independence of the socialists because elections were due the following spring and socialist collaboration was essential.

Suddenly the Social Democratic leader Fierlinger almost destroyed his party by concluding a provisional electoral pact with the communists, without the party's knowledge or permission. The socialists were thrown into confusion. For a time it seemed that they might submit to the communist will but they recovered. Strengthened by the vigorous international socialist reaction to the Cominform and by the increasing firmness of the West in relation to Russia, they dismissed Fierlinger from the chairmanship of the party at a conference in November 1947. By the end of 1947, the communists had still to win their battle for Czechoslovakia, and no one could prophesy with certainty whether they would do so or not.

* * * * *

Of all the countries lying near Russia's borders, Poland was the one which the Soviet leaders were most determined to bring to heel. Their whole Polish policy, both during the war and after, was directed to this end. Most of the long and shameful story—the partition of the country by agreement with Hitler, the mass deportation and callous ill-treatment of Polish civilians, the sabotage of the Warsaw rising, the organization of the Lublin puppet government, the persecution of the 'underground' and the treacherous arrest of its leaders—these things are outside the scope of this book. Our interest begins when British and American recognition of a re-organized Government in 1946 officially brought the Polish 'problem' to an end. This Government, which was to have included all elements on a broad and representative basis, in fact included no independent Pole of authority except the Peasant leader and Prime Minister of the London Government, Stanislav Mikolajczyk, who became Minister of Agriculture and second Vice-Premier in the new communist-controlled coalition Cabinet.

The process of fixing totalitarian shackles on Poland was already far advanced. A Russian army, in inconspicuous but none the less effective occupation, stood by in case of need. Many Russian officers in Polish uniform were incorporated in the new Polish forces. There were representatives of the Russian security police in every district. The Polish security police was firmly in communist hands. The concentration camps were filling up again, the press was heavily censored, the radio was under communist direction. The President of the Republic was a communist. So were many of the leading ministers. Support for the communists in the country was negligible; the Russians were hated and feared.

First the communists tried to disrupt Mikolajczyk's Peasant party, which was by far the strongest and most popular political organization in the country, but their efforts to establish a competing Peasant party under their own control met with little success. Then they decided to woo the Peasant leader. He was invited to join an electoral *bloc* formed by the communists and socialists, but on a minority basis. In view of his strength in the country, he declined. His refusal was the signal for a concerted attack on himself and his colleagues in the controlled press. He was a 'British agent', a 'crypto-fascist'. The first of a series of raids took place on his party headquarters in Warsaw and some of his officials were arrested. Local branches of the party were dissolved. His daily paper—the only opposition daily in all Poland—was heavily censored. He was accused, without any foundation, of complicity in 'underground' terrorism.

In June 1946 a national referendum was held on the questions of the new western frontiers, the economic reforms which were taking place, and the suppression of the Senate. To test his strength, Mikolajczyk asked his supporters to vote against the suppression of the Senate. For the communists, the referendum was a rehearsal in the technique of electoral manipulation. By this time, 1,200 members of the Peasant party were in jail. The party was not allowed adequate propaganda facilities. Its representatives were not allowed to be present at the count. The results, which showed overwhelming 'Yes' majorities in all questions, were faked.

But the communists made one bad blunder. Through some failure in organization, the voting in the city of Cracow was not properly 'fixed'. By very large majorities, the city voted down all the government's proposals. What happened afterwards perfectly illustrated the prevailing political conditions. The communist-controlled city council passed a special resolution condemning those who 'blotted the good name of the city' and announced that reactionary elements not usefully employed in Cracow would be deported elsewhere. Cracow garrison, 'amidst the unparalleled enthusiasm of officers and men', demanded that the 'good-for-nothings' who in their scores of thousands had exercised their franchise so shamefully should be turned out of their homes and put to work on national reconstruction. 'Down with the Hitlerite stooges!' the resolution ended. The press and radio dwelt on 'the Cracow infamy'. A leading member of the government wrote an article entitled 'Cracow—the Sick City'. Warsaw radio reported a protest by the 'Cracow world of labour' against the results. This was 'eastern democracy' in full flower.

Particularly significant was the attitude of Cyrankievicz,

later to be 'socialist' Prime Minister. 'The Cracow working class,' he wrote, 'rightly demand the expulsion from the city of the people whose behaviour constitutes a provocation and challenge to Polish democracy. The people who voted three times "No" are those who expect a third world war and wait for the atom bomb.'

The elections which were to set the seal on the fate of Poland took place in January 1947. The socialists, through their left-wing officials, were closely tied to communist leadership. Mikolajczyk's party constituted the only opposition element and it was now to be destroyed. By election day, twelve thousand members of his party were under arrest. Others were beaten and murdered. In many districts his representatives were prevented from scrutinizing the poll or being present at the counting of the votes. In ten districts he was not allowed to put up any candidates at all. In a village ten miles outside Warsaw, members of the electoral commission distributed blocks of voting tickets. Opposition voters were intimidated and there was compulsory collective voting by employees at some government factories. With complex ingenuity, the unity of the Polish people was being forged.

Apart from the communists, foreign correspondents and outside observers were unanimous about the nature of the elections. Sefton Delmer, for the *Daily Express,* summed up the contest as 'an efficient combination of intimidation and fraud'. William Forrest, in a dispatch to the *News Chronicle,* said 'All my allotted space would not be enough to catalogue the admitted facts which make the election results a mockery of the people's will'. That was the unanimous view. The 'free and unfettered elections' promised at Yalta had been an impudent travesty under the eyes of the world.

However, the apologists were not silenced. On the day before the poll, *The Times* had thought fit to headline its Warsaw story, 'Eve of Polish elections. Thirteen Communists killed by terrorists'. Its correspondent wrote that the greater activity of the terrorists might 'to a certain extent justify the official Polish measures, however unacceptable these measures are to western ideas'. The *New Statesman and Nation* explained, 'No elections east of the Elbe have ever been fair by British standards'.

The campaign and its results had shattered the Polish Peasant party. In many cities, its leading members were being tried and sentenced to imprisonment and death. The personal attacks on Mikolajczyk were intensified—among other things he was accused of complicity in the tragic accident which had killed his former chief, Sikorsky, during the war. The communist leader, Gomulka, had put the 'black spot' on him. In November 1947 he succeeded in fleeing abroad. Czechoslovakia demonstrated its well-known desire to be a 'bridge' between East and West by capturing some of his companions and handing them over to the Polish security police for trial and sentence.

With the Peasant party disintegrated, the communists could now turn their attention to the socialists. In June 1947, it was announced that the secret police had arrested leading members of the socialist party who opposed fusion with the communists. They were charged with 'terrorist subversive activity and propaganda'. The official socialist organ sycophantically approved the arrests. Those held for trial included not only the secretary and other close associates of the 'Lublin' socialist Premier, Morawski, but also Puzak, a man who had spent years in chains in a Tsarist prison after 1905, and had been general secretary of his party for twenty years and chairman of the council which directed the operations of the Polish 'underground' during the war. In Warsaw a complaisant party meeting passed a resolution affirming that 'the path of the Polish socialist party leads only to the Left. Only the foe is on the Right. A partner with whom it is possible to collaborate is only to be found on the left side of the barricades'. It was not safe to take any other view. By the end of 1947, the advocates of socialist independence were effectively silenced, and the communist grip on Poland appeared to be complete.

*   *   *   *   *

In her drive to turn the border states into obedient communist satellites, Russia found Hungary one of the toughest post-war problems. It had been an enemy country, not an ally; there was no racial affinity to exploit; the behaviour of the Red Army in the first flush of victory had revolted the population, which in any case had no predilection for communism. As in Czechoslovakia, the Russians decided to move carefully, entrusting the working out of the Hungarian revolution to their able lieutenant, the communist leader Matthias Rakosi.

When the Germans were in process of being driven out of Hungary in 1945, a National Front Government was formed at Debrecen by General Miklos, under Russian supervision. It included representatives of four parties—the Communists, Social Democrats, Smallholders and National Peasants. Before the elections of November 1945, it was agreed that whatever the outcome the National Front coalition would continue. On this understanding, the elections were fair and free. They gave an overwhelming majority to the Smallholder Party, whose leader Ferenc Nagy became Prime Minister. The Communists, however, obtained many more offices than their revealed voting strength warranted and the communist Rajk was made Minister of the Interior.

The communists held many strategic positions throughout the country. Locally, they controlled most of the Liberation Committees which had been set up after the expulsion of the Germans. They were strongly entrenched in the trade unions and held more than half the police posts. Communists and socialists together, though they had polled only 45 per cent of the votes, controlled nearly 80 per cent of the posts in the administration and 70 per cent in the police. Soon, the communists succeeded in having the Frontier Guards transferred from the control of the Ministry of War to the Ministry of the Interior. With the Russian occupation forces at their back, they lacked nothing but popular support.

Immediately the elections were over, Rakosi set to work to reverse the results by the skilful erosion of the Smallholder party. The tactic was to accuse the Smallholders of harbouring 'reactionary' elements, and on this pretext to compel the shedding of members who were not reactionaries. The first big fission was achieved in March 1946, when the moderate democrat Dezso Sulyok and nineteen other prominent members were expelled from the party. Throughout 1946 there was a succession of political crises, and on each occasion the communists threatened to leave the coalition unless their demands were met. Usually they were met. A purge of the civil service was agreed to and all 'reactionary' organizations were dissolved. Nagy, a sincere but nervous liberal, saw with some indignation his party taking a back seat in the administration which it was entitled to control. The Soviet representatives were watchful. The Red Army newspaper wrote, 'Soviet Russia would be sorry to see Hungary . . . lose her independence'.

In October 1946 the communists renewed the offensive. 'The reactionary right wing of the Smallholder party,' said a manifesto, 'has put itself at the service of the enemies of democracy; it is breaking the unity of the government and . . . poisoning public life.'

Nagy replied, 'The Smallholder party is proceeding along the road of radicalism; it is not fighting for a bygone world but it cannot allow its lawful position to be undermined by subterfuges about the fight against reaction.' This, in fact, was precisely what it could not prevent. In November the communists, with their Social Democrat allies in tow, put forward a wide range of political demands backed by workers' demonstrations. Menace was in the air. The Social Democrat vice-premier, Szakasits, declared, 'We see democracy in danger. However much we love tranquillity, we are compelled to talk of resistance, street fighting and clenched fists'. It was the authentic voice of the barricades and Nagy was no hero. Once more he made big concessions.

In December 1946, a 'plot against the republic' was uncovered by the Minister of the Interior, Rajk. There was, indeed, a conspiracy of sorts, though it was wildly exaggerated for party purposes. Its extreme element was a small clique of unpractical hotheads who apparently dreamed of restoring the Horthy regime; there was also a much larger group which was planning —with no great secrecy and as it had every constitutional right to do—to evict the communists from office as soon as the Russians left.

This plot was all that Rakosi needed to destroy the Smallholders. 'We must ask the Smallholder party,' he cried, 'how it could have permitted such a black counter-revolutionary reaction to shelter under its roof. . . .' Eight Smallholder deputies were arrested, and the party was induced to expel or encourage the resignation of many more. In a short time, its strength in the Assembly had been reduced by fifty. Momentarily the party stood firm when it was required to vote away the immunity and life of its popular secretary-general, and the architect of the land reform, Bela Kovacs. Seeing its hesitancy, the Russians stepped in and themselves arrested the unfortunate Kovacs, thumbing their noses at their Western colleagues on the Control Commission who protested. The Soviet security police soon succeeded in extorting a 'confession' from Kovacs. When the Russians left the country nine months later, his friends were distressed but not surprised to learn that he had died in prison.

The communists were now ready for new elections. The badly compromised Smallholder party was increasingly appeasing. It called for 'the complete and final liquidation of the conspiracy' and declared Kovacs no longer a party member. Nagy said, 'It is my endeavour to make the viewpoint of the Smallholder party harmonize with that of the left *bloc*. Thus I wish to iron out all controversies between the political parties. The Smallholder party intends to inaugurate such changes in the organizational and personal spheres as will reassure left-wing opinion.'

In March the crisis intensified. As Russian troops began to move menacingly from eastern Austria into Hungary, four Smallholder ministers were dismissed and the emasculated party was left with only a slender and intimidated majority in the Chamber. A few weeks later Nagy, on holiday in Switzerland, learned that Kovacs had allegedly implicated him in the plot, and resigned the Premiership without returning home. His Foreign Minister Gyongyossy, and Speaker of the Assembly Varga, also fled abroad. Many of Hungary's diplomatic representatives, realizing that a *coup* had taken place, withdrew their allegiance to the Government and resigned. Dinnyes, a colourless and tractable member of the Smallholder party, was made Premier. The party ranks voluntarily purged themselves yet again. Nominally, the coalition continued. But Rakosi was publicly jubilant over the major shift of power, and gloated over the success of his 'iron-fisted party'. 'Before the United States could rub its eyes,' he told a meeting of workers in Budapest, 'everything was perfectly put over.'

The next step was to hold new elections. Under the unexceptionable slogan of 'Order, prosperity, independence', the communists under Rakosi proceeded to plot a spectacular electoral swindle. On the pretext of preventing people from voting who had been in any way associated with the old regime, something like one-fifth of the electorate was disfranchised by communist-controlled registration committees. At the same time, large numbers of blue cards were printed permitting electors to vote away from their homes. These two measures were intended to dovetail.

Other preliminary steps were taken. The 'Right' was disposed of by a coalition decision forbidding anyone to stand as a candidate who had been a deputy in a pre-war government party. Sulyok, who after his dismissal from the Smallholders had been permitted by the Control Commission to form a Freedom party, came under this category. The fact that he was a liberal and a patriot, that he had been the first man in Hungary to denounce the Arrow Cross leader Szalasy as a German agent, and that for three years during the war he had been hunted by the Gestapo, was conveniently forgotten. Pursued by a creeping barrage of abuse and threats, he was compelled to dissolve his party and leave the country.

Among the coalition parties, all candidates suspected of an anti-communist attitude had been successfully eliminated. The Smallholder list, in particular, had been purged of every person who had previously played any major role in the party. Only just over one-third of the Smallholder deputies in the last Chamber were standing again; in Budapest only five out of thirty-three. The Social Democratic party had been split, part working closely with the communists, but some social democrats were following the courageous lead of Charles Peyer who, because of his denunciation of communist methods, had been expelled from the party which he had led for twenty-five years. The Opposition had been sliced up into seven different groups; for tactical reasons, licences had been granted to a Catholic People's Democratic party under Barankovitch, to an Independent Democratic party under a former Smallholder, Father Balogh, and to a Hungarian Independence party under Zoltan Pfeiffer.

The stage was set. Just before polling day, Rakosi made a speech saying that he awaited the results with confidence, 'convinced of having accomplished good work'.

Unofficial estimates of the disfranchised shortly before polling day put the figure at about a million, or one-fifth of the electorate. Prime Minister Dinnyes himself admitted rather uncomfortably to press correspondents that the number was nearly half a million, and hastened to explain that the cases of 300,000 would be reviewed. But time was now short. The whole process had been incredibly crude. In the first wave of disfranchisements, Jews had been listed as Arrow Cross Nazis, managers of great public concerns as 'mentally deficient' and respectable old ladies as 'prostitutes'. Deletions were wholesale and blatant. On election day, one foreign correspondent reported that in a mining town he had visited, 1,200 voters out of 4,070 had been struck off. Some large apartment blocks could not muster a single voter. In Budapest alone, ten thousand names vanished from the lists at the last moment.

The Times, its blind eye cosily applied to its editorial telescope, commented complacently, 'Universal suffrage in a country striving to rise from the ruins of past failures and oppression and so lately torn by civil war is much to expect'.

There was now plenty of elbow room for fraudulent voters. Minister of the Interior Rajk had thoughtfully printed 500,000 blue voting cards which could be used at any polling station by itinerant electors. Why he should imagine that one out of every ten voters would be on the road on polling day was never explained, for the Minister was subsequently coy about holding a press conference at which the point might have been elucidated. On election day, 'flying squads' of multiple voters toured the country. The Social Democrat secretary in one town told the *Manchester Guardian* correspondent that three hundred people wearing communist badges had arrived in State factory lorries, voted, and gone on to vote elsewhere. The same correspondent recorded that a man in Budapest who had succeeded in getting his vote back at the last minute was told at the polling station that someone else had already voted in his place. In Czegled, a 'hiker' was apprehended with twenty-four blue voting cards on his person. Minister of the Interior Rajk had taken the precaution of ordering that anyone arrested for electoral frauds was not to be searched or detained in police stations, but handed over to his own security police. In so far as these instructions were carried out, the full extent of the fraud was hidden. Rajk himself maintained afterwards that no more than 20,000 blue cards had been used illegally.

The Times was in the Munich mood—the mood to concede 'territorial fringes' of principle. 'In spite of this fraud and distortion,' it wrote, 'the general conduct of the election did not compare unfavourably with the election of 1945.' *The Times* correspondent, in a classic dispatch from Hungary, wrote, 'The election, otherwise correct, was marred by plural voting and unjust disfranchisements.'

So little real support had the communists in Hungary that Rakosi, in spite of all his stage-managing, discovered that he had cut things very fine. His own party polled little more than a fifth of the votes cast. The Smallholders, deserted by the electorate now that they had visibly lost their independence, were reduced to second place. Their former votes went to two new opposition parties—Barankovitch's Progressive Catholics and Pfeiffer's Independent Democrats—who between them polled a third of the total number cast. The government *bloc*, with the help of a narrowly-gained 'bonus', had only a bare majority in the Chamber.

The elections ended, moreover, in what the *Manchester Guardian* correspondent described as 'a hangover of the first order'. The day after the election, the socialist Minister of Justice, Riess, tendered his resignation on the ground that Minister of the Interior Rajk had obstructed his investigators sent to examine the 'flying squads'. The Social Democrat leaders seriously debated whether they should denounce the results, and at one time all five of their Ministers had decided to resign. In the factories, socialist workers were seething with indignation.

Gradually, the chaos was sorted out. The Minister of Justice and the Minister of the Interior settled their quarrel, declaring that it had 'arisen out of a mutual misinterpretation of the law'. The Social Democrat Ministers had second thoughts about resigning after a heart-to-heart session with the Russian military authorities. The Smallholders, who in a last wriggle of independence had selected a right-wing committee, were obliged to rescind their choice after the intervention of the puppet President Tildy.

Meanwhile, Rakosi was busy re-arranging the popular verdict. Pfeiffer, whose electoral success had somehow survived the unexplained loss of 50,000 of his votes in a second count, was soon disposed of. Despite the fact that he had worked with Rajk and Szakasits in the Hungarian 'underground', he was denounced as a 'fascist'. Scores of his provincial organizers were arrested and shortly afterwards all of his fifty-or-so deputies were deprived of their mandates, six being cast into prison. Pfeiffer himself succeeded in escaping abroad as he was about to be arrested on a fantastic charge of supplying forged documents to a member of the Hungarian SS. The independent socialist, Charles Peyer, whose small party had succeeded in winning a few seats, also managed to leave the country just in time to avoid arrest.

With the Smallholders broken, the socialists docile, and the main opposition dispersed, the communists by the end of 1947 were far advanced along the road to supreme and exclusive power. The only thing they had to smash now was the spirit of the people.

* * * * *

Rumania's transition to complete Soviet puppetdom began shortly after the anti-Nazi rising in Bucharest in August 1944. The Liberal, Peasant, Socialist and Communist parties had all had a hand in the *coup,* which was largely organized by the famous Peasant leader Julius Maniu in close consultation with the young King Michael.

In January 1945, the government of Rumania was in the charge of Prime Minister General Radescu, who had been approved in office by all three members of the Allied Control Commission. Towards the end of January the Democratic Union— a largely bogus left-wing *bloc* under active communist leadership—published a revolutionary programme and demanded the removal of Radescu. Printers' strikes and censorship succeeded in closing down many of the non-communist newspapers. 'Spontaneous' demonstrations began to take place in the streets and there were disorders. The blame was put on Radescu. Everything was now ready for the intervention of Mr Vishinsky who —as was noted in the last chapter—hurried to Bucharest to impose Russia's unilateral will. Vishinsky demanded Radescu's instant dismissal, rejected an alternative government suggested by the King, and finally declared that if his own nominee, Peter Groza, was not immediately appointed Prime Minister, Russia would be unable to guarantee the continued independence of Rumania.

Groza accordingly took office at the head of a Democratic Union Government, with the old Comintern leader Anna Pauker as the power behind the administration. Early in 1946 two members of the Opposition—Hatieganu of the Peasant party and Romniceanu of the Liberals—were allowed to join the Government as a sop to the western allies, but they had no authority whatsoever and learned about State affairs only from the newspapers. The historic Peasant and Liberal parties had a great following in the country, and the communists set to work to break them.

Groza had promised 'free and fair' elections for 1946. Disregarding a flurry of protests from the West, the communists proceeded to put their plans into action against a background of support from the Soviet press and radio. The Democratic Union, with its collection of splinter parties and peculiar *ad hoc* bodies like the 'Federation of Rumanian Democratic Women', was given every electoral facility, including the robust assistance of the communist militia. The opposition parties were persecuted. In the course of a few weeks in the spring of 1946, more than a hundred spokesmen of the opposition parties were shot, imprisoned or abducted. The two opposition Ministers were physically assaulted. Maniu, the Peasant leader, was described by *New Times* as an agent of the Gestapo. Opposition newspapers were starved of newsprint and all attacks on the Government were suppressed by the censorship. Opposition demonstrations were broken up. Civil servants in the provinces who did not adhere to the Democratic Union were dismissed. Mr Vishinsky's forecast that the government *bloc* would receive ninety per cent of the votes seemed a safe bet.

Communist tactics matured as election day approached. In many districts members of opposition parties were not registered. The Printers' Union was forbidden to print the forms necessary for voters' claims. As usual, the opposition parties were not allowed proper representation on the electoral commissions, or at the count. Many opposition candidates were arrested before the poll; in some cases voting papers were marked in advance.

One of the most lively accounts of this remarkable election was subsequently given by G. E. R. Gedye, the correspondent of *Tribune*. 'That the whole State machinery,' he wrote from

70

Bucharest, 'was used to ensure the triumph of the "Block of Democratic Parties" and that factory workers and State employees had to vote at their places of employment under the supervision of the Communist trade unions was only the beginning. . . . At the polling booth in the "Unirea" works, I found the long queue of voters held up for over half an hour in an anteroom plastered with Communist propaganda. Outside the town hall, crowds were demonstrating against the refusal of voting papers. I saw dozens of instances of as many as four voting papers having been given to supposed Government supporters. Inside the polling booths, the voter could not himself drop his completed ballot into the urn, but had to hand it, folded over but with no envelope, to the presiding officer—usually a Government appointee. . . . In the villages I met duly authorized scrutineers for the Opposition Parties who had been turned out of polling booths where the Communist presiding officer quite openly examined every ballot and tore up those of the Opposition. Other Opposition scrutineers were kept outside until the urns had been sealed, thus enabling the presiding officer to start off with as many forged ballots as he chose to insert. In less accessible areas Opposition scrutineers, unless they went into hiding, were rounded up by the police one or two nights before the elections and only released when they were over. In village after village I met crowds of furious peasants who had been chased away from voting stations by local Communists. . . . Despite these and many other abuses, so little real support had the Government that there had to be a three-day delay in announcing the results to enable them to be "corrected".' Gedye went on to say that at a cocktail party immediately afterwards government supporters openly admitted that voting had had to be 'controlled' and 'corrected' to avoid an opposition victory.

The elections gave the government *bloc* eighty-four per cent of the votes. Immediately afterwards, widespread arrests were instituted, aimed at breaking the Opposition for all time. The climax of a campaign of terror was reached in July 1947 when the aged Maniu was himself arrested with many of his leading Peasant colleagues and soon afterwards sentenced to solitary confinement for life. A dubious 'liberal' element in the government *bloc* led by the Foreign Minister and old-time politician Tatarescu was expelled for indiscipline and the government was reconstituted with Anna Pauker emerging from the shadows to become the new Foreign Minister. By the end of 1947 the communists were in undisputed control of a tame left-wing coalition.

* * * * *

The Bulgarian story starts in 1944. During the spring and summer of that year, Bulgarian partisans had been fighting bravely and effectively against the Germans under the political leadership of the Fatherland Front, an 'underground' organization formed during the war by Communists, Peasants, Social Democrats and the middle-class Zveno or Republican party. By September 1944, when the Red Army was marching on Sofia, the Fatherland Front had become the rallying point for the whole nation. A *coup d'état* was successfully staged and a communist, Yugov, was given the post of Minister of the Interior in the new Government. For a time, the victorious partisans were the law. Communists took over the civil administration everywhere. More than a hundred Ministers, deputies and members of the late King Boris's household were hustled through People's Courts to the gallows, and soon the number of the purged could be counted in thousands. War and defeat had brought the inevitable revolution and the inevitable retribution.

With the ending of the German menace, however, cracks soon appeared in the structure of the Fatherland Front. The Peasant party was the first to secede. Its leader, Dr G. M. Dimitrov, who had been sentenced to death during the war for his pro-ally activities, returned home from the Middle East in September. He discovered that the communists were using the Fatherland Front for their own purposes under the slogan of 'national solidarity'. In view of the fact that his own party was the most widely supported, he felt that it was entitled to a policy of its own. His independence at once got him into trouble. Despite his record, he was accused of having sabotaged the war effort and acted as a foreign agent. He resigned the leadership of his party in January 1945, escaped abroad, and was subsequently tried *in absentia* and sentenced to twenty years' imprisonment for 'spreading defeatist propaganda'.

His place at the head of the Peasants was taken by Nikola

Petkov. Petkov was a man of the people and came from a family of proletarian fighters. His father and his brother had both lost their lives in the cause to which he himself was devoted—the single-minded and resolute service of the Bulgarian peasantry. Petkov, hunted by reactionary pre-war governments, had spent many years in exile in Paris campaigning against the oppressive rule of the Tsankov and other administrations. On his election to the Bulgarian parliament in 1938 he had returned home, but his advocacy of close co-operation between the Peasants and the communists had soon led to his removal from Parliament. During the war he had attacked the pro-German Filov Government and its police-selected deputies whenever he was not in prison. He was one of the founder-members of the Fatherland Front executive committee, and after the successful *coup* he was for a short time Vice-Premier of the Fatherland Front Government.

This was the man who now took Dr Dimitrov's place at the head of an opposition Peasant party. He was soon ousted. A party meeting packed by the communists displaced him in favour of a certain Obbov. Petkov resigned from the Government and went deeper into opposition, taking the loyal Peasant majority with him. The fiction of Peasant participation in the Fatherland Front was preserved by the followers of Obbov.

The Social Democratic party was similarly split. The pro-communist wing led by Neikov forcibly took possession of the party offices and newspaper with the help of the police and remained in the Fatherland Front, a nucleus without a following. The independent socialists continued in opposition under Pastuchev and Lulchev.

In November 1945 elections were held for the National Assembly. The opposition parties, dissatisfied with the prevailing conditions, refused to take part and the Fatherland Front was returned with a large majority. It was early in 1946 that attempts were made to persuade Petkov and Lulchev to rejoin the government and thus fulfil the decision of the Big Three, which has already been noted, that the administration should be broadened. But the conditions offered would have meant the inclusion of the opposition leaders only as prisoners, and the attempt came to nothing.

The Fatherland Front Government, under the nominal Premiership of the tame Zveno leader Kimon Giorgiev, now instituted a campaign against the opposition which was to end only with its complete extinction. In April 1946, laws were passed to strengthen 'the people's authority'. Newspapers showing 'tendencies damaging to the general interests of the State' could be suppressed. The judiciary under communist control became a 'combat organization' for the furtherance of party interests. Political trials were ordered. In April a district court passed five sentences of death and 38 of imprisonment on supporters of the absent Dr Dimitrov. Members of the Peasant party were arrested all over the country. The two or three opposition newspapers, already restricted in circulation, were subjected to ruthless censorship and frequent suspensions. Socialist meetings were broken up by the communist militia and known anti-communists were deprived of subsidiary food and clothing coupons. By August 1946, through the zeal of the communist Minister of the Interior, three out of fifteen members of the Socialist executive committee and seven out of twenty-two members of the Peasant party presidium were in prison or concentration camp. The 72-year-old veteran socialist Pastuchev had already received a five-year sentence for criticizing a speech made by the communist leader Georgi Dimitrov—not to be confused with the former Peasant leader. It was Georgi Dimitrov who had been narrowly saved from Goering's clutches at the Reichstag Fire trial through the efforts of western liberals. It was Georgi Dimitrov who was to send Petkov to his death.

In July 1946 the communists turned their attention to the army. A Bill was rushed through all its stages in a single day to secure the purging of 'harmful elements' and the establishment of political commissars. General Velchev, the Minister of War, tried to resist the communist encroachment and was relieved of his duties. The new War Minister was General Damianov, a distinguished Soviet officer who had served in the Red Army for twenty-six years.

The communist grip was tightened still farther in the elections of October 1946. Philips Price, MP, reporting on the campaign for the *Manchester Guardian,* wrote, 'The campaign of the last fortnight has been carried on in such a way that the election results cannot reflect the state of feelings in the country. . . . The crux of the matter is the control of army and police by the communist party, which means in effect by Soviet Russia. If Russia was using her undoubted right to have strong influence here no one could object. But when she uses her privileged position to vilify and to terrorize any Bulgarian citizen who deviates one iota from the line she lays down, then it is clear that she is aiming at eliminating all elements from public life that show any independence.'

Two days before the elections, Georgi Dimitrov declared that the opposition leaders had 'a common platform in treachery to the nation'. 'To support such an Opposition,' he said, 'is to commit treason against the people; to vote for this Opposition is to plunge a knife in the back of the People's Republic.' He reminded opposition leaders of the fate of Mihailovitch, who had been executed in Yugoslavia. Such inflammatory language created an atmosphere conducive to unrestrained violence. On October 24th the opposition leaders complained to the Premier, 'For ten days the country has been overrun by organized terrorist groups which break up both public and closed opposition gatherings with sticks, stones, knives and bombs'. Many opposition candidates were jailed before polling day. Many opposition leaders were severely hurt. People distributing election literature for the Opposition were arrested. It was the old story—sickening, heaven knows, in repetition, but necessary for the record. Once more, on polling day, communists were practically the only members of commissions for supervising and counting votes. Once more there was plural voting. In the outcome, two-thirds of the recorded votes were declared to have been given to the communists and their satellites.

All that now remained between Dimitrov and the absolute power of his party were the voices of a few brave men—and these were soon to be silenced. Nikola Petkov, with the shadow of the rope already over him, denounced the communists with passion in the new Chamber. 'Despite the solemn promises made before September 1944 that the form of government would be democratic, with equality of rights and obligations, the Fatherland Front became a screen for the one-party rule of the communist party. . . . Look at the present Government!—there is nothing in it but the communist party. Who represents in it the political organizations of the Fatherland Front?' With deep emotion he read out to the Assembly a letter from his friend and party colleague and fellow deputy Petr Koyev, who had been tortured in prison by Dimitrov's men. 'Shall we speak,' he cried, 'of the sixteen fresh graves of people who belonged to the Peasant party? . . . Or shall we speak of the falsifications, of our torn and burned news-sheets, of the distribution of uncompleted voters' papers, of our authorized representatives being driven away and ill-treated, threatened after the elections, and today still wandering homeless about the streets of Sofia?' He held up a piece of paper. 'Manol Zagrafov, candidate in Kharmanli, was beaten up before the election and while still ill in bed received from the Kharmanli Council a burial certificate sealed with the seal of the communist party. Here is that burial certificate.'

It was proud defiance—as great as anything in the history of freedom. It could have only one end. The new communist Government proceeded to thin out the opposition benches by systematic removals and arrests. For three sessions, the entire Opposition was prevented from entering the Assembly. In June 1947, Petkov was arrested in the Sobranje building and shortly afterwards twenty-three opposition deputies were deprived of their seats. The charge against Petkov was of plotting a *coup d'état*—against the communists entrenched in every position of power and backed by all the might of the occupying Red Army!

Petkov was not the only brave man, nor the only one who should be remembered. Six days later Petr Koyev, whose sufferings had already been described to the Assembly, was brought to trial. Speaking in the Assembly on the motion to withdraw his immunity as a deputy, he told the serried ranks of communists, 'I know that I am seeing you for the last time. . . . Confessions incriminating me were made by Colonel Abramov when he was in such a state that when they brought him to confront me he was unable to stand upright. . . . If any new confessions appear from me, I tell you here and now, that you all may know, that I have made them under absolutely unbearable conditions'.

There were no opposition newspapers to report Petkov's trial to the people whom he had served. Three weeks before the trial began, the Bulgarian Ministry of Information published a pamphlet expatiating on his guilt! The two State prosecutors and the three judges were all communists. So were the defence counsel. Of the few witnesses for the defence, one was arrested immediately after the trial 'for giving false evidence'.

Britain and America asked the Soviet Government to intervene. 'The Soviet Government,' came the reply, 'has complete faith in and respect for the Bulgarian court.'

On September 23rd, 1947, Nikola Petkov was hanged. 'To a dog, a dog's death!' said Sofia radio. Moscow radio applauded. So, to their everlasting dishonour, did some of the 'fellow-travellers' in the British House of Commons. Mr Gromyko in the Security Council said the Bulgarian Government had 'dealt effectively' with an enemy not only of Bulgaria but of all 'peace-loving' States.

But *The Times* headed its leader 'Murder in Bulgaria', and the *Manchester Guardian* wrote of 'a judicial murder, after a trial which was a farce, of an inconvenient opponent who was as good a patriot and as brave a fighter against fascism as his accusers'. Even the *New Statesman,* which had been able to stomach so much, this time had qualms over Petkov. The case was 'very thin', the verdict had 'probably' been decided beforehand, the evidence that Petkov had 'actively' engaged in a murder conspiracy was 'slight and suspect' and the execution was 'an evil and dishonest affair'. Besides, it would inevitably lead to the assumption that political trials in all other eastern European countries were 'frame-ups'. On that account, of course, it was to be deprecated.

With the death of Petkov and the liquidation of the Opposition, Bulgaria became a totalitarian state, indissolubly linked with Russia and completely under her control.

CHAPTER IV

THE SATELLITE PEACE TREATIES

The main collective enterprise of the four Great Powers in the year 1946 was the writing of peace treaties with Germany's former allies—Finland, Hungary, Rumania, Bulgaria and Italy. The peace-making fell into three distinct phases. The first covered preparatory talks and drafting by the Foreign Ministers in London in September 1945, Moscow in December 1945 and Paris in the spring and early summer of 1946. The second was the Peace Conference of twenty-one nations held in Paris in the summer of 1946. The third was the meeting of Foreign Ministers in New York in November 1946 when the final texts of the treaties were agreed upon.

All the five ex-enemy countries were under military control. Finland, Hungary, Rumania and Bulgaria were all in the Russian sphere of influence and the governing factor was the presence or proximity of the Red Army. The West had a voice through formal participation in the respective Allied Control Commissions, but in practice the Russians enjoyed unchallenged authority. Russia was in physical possession, and could, therefore, do as she liked. In Italy, the position was reversed. Western forces were in occupation, and it was Britain and America who had exclusive control. Both Russia and the western allies were in a position to dictate the terms of the treaties in their own sphere, if they wished to do so. Neither side could impose its wishes in the territory controlled by the other.

Russia's broad aims at the peace talks were, first, to preserve intact her exclusive political and economic influence over Finland, Hungary, Rumania and Bulgaria, denying to the West any possibility of infiltration; secondly, to collect from these ex-enemy countries the highest possible total of reparations for herself and her satellites, while whittling down the claims of the West; thirdly, to obtain the greatest possible concessions for herself and her satellites where Italy was concerned. The broad aims of the West were to prevent the eastern states becoming a closed

78

Soviet economic preserve; to prevent them being so mulcted in reparations that their economic life would be ruined; and to defend Italy against unreasonable claims by Russia and her satellites. All these aims emerged clearly during the discussions.

If both sides had shown the same strength of will and stubbornness in safeguarding their interests, we should have expected to find both standing firm on their home ground, with no significant concessions on either side. As a study, the peace negotiations would then have been of comparatively little interest. They are fascinating precisely because they did not work out in that way. As we shall see, Russia stood pat and conceded virtually nothing; the West gave way and conceded a great deal. The treaties as a whole were a Russian triumph.

Chief among the factors which brought this about was the difference in the approach of Russia and the West to the whole question of peace-making. The western allies wanted treaties badly, and wanted them quickly. It was already a year since the European war had ended, and every day without a final settlement worsened the economic plight and political unrest of the defeated nations and consequently increased the danger of collapse throughout Europe. Britain, in particular, rightly foresaw how seriously her own economic problems would be aggravated if Europe were not set quickly on the road to recovery. America, on whom the main burden of relief fell, fully shared that interest. To the West, almost any treaties seemed better than no treaties.

Russia, on the other hand, was in no hurry at all. She had no interest in the recovery of Europe as a whole. Indeed, the dogma required just the opposite. The greater the unsettlement outside her own sphere the better. In the territories which she controlled, delay did not matter. The outcome of the discussions would not affect the situation east of the Stettin-Trieste line; throughout the months of talk, Russia would be completing the subjugation and integration of the eastern States. Every delay was a gain for her, a loss for the ideological enemy.

There was another important difference in approach. The western allies would not contemplate, at this period, the possibility of a final breakdown in their relations with Russia. It was an axiom of the time that world peace was dependent on the maintenance of Big Three unity. Mr Byrnes and Mr Bevin knew that the people at home expected this unity to continue and would not understand the reasons if the wartime allies fell apart. To prevent that happening was the overriding task. Delay and concession were preferable to impatience and deadlock.

Mr Byrnes disclosed the western frame of mind very frankly in some comments he made on the failure of the first meeting of the Foreign Ministers in London—a failure soon to be followed by an appeasing mission to Moscow. 'We were reluctant,' he wrote in *Speaking Frankly*, 'to let the first test of the peacemaking machinery result in complete breakdown. The people were anxious for peace. The public at home did not have the clear view of Soviet ambitions which the President and I got at Potsdam and which was revealed even more clearly here in London. We had refrained, after Potsdam, from publicly expressing our concern because of our desire to maintain friendly relations with our Russian allies. . . . The Soviet leaders knew of our people's strong desire for peace and they thought we would not dare to let the conference fail.' Mr Bevin, representing a political party which had been helped to power by its confident guarantee of a close understanding with Russia, was no less determined that the talks should not collapse. These two men were the prisoners of their own good intentions. Their attitude was reflected in all their public statements. They were often dispirited, bewildered, resentful and exasperated but they did not do or say anything which might lessen the chances of ultimate agreement. Never in history was there more devoted and patient work for peace.

Contrast, now, the Russian attitude. The Soviet Government did not believe, never had believed, in co-operation with the West. The dogma ruled that out. For the Russians, the peace conference was a battlefield. The fighting propaganda speeches of Mr Molotov and Mr Vishinsky, crackling with rancour and abuse, were almost as important to them as the results of the conference itself. The will to be friendly was clearly lacking. Russian reporting of the conference was a succession of snarls. *Tass,* reporting on the conference in August 1946, wrote 'The British Foreign Minister Bevin, who arrived in Paris a few days ago, has only now appeared at the conference. If Bevin's health prevented him from participating in the work of the conference, it did not prevent him from having long talks with the Greek delegate Tsaldaris, with the Italian Premier de Gasperi, with the ambassador of Franco in Paris, with the Turkish ambassador, and from keeping in close contact with the British military authorities in Palestine.' That was characteristic. The motives and the actions of the western allies were distorted and obscured by the tedious jargon of Soviet political warfare. 'Circles' were always creating 'situations' for 'narrowly selfish ends'. 'The enemies of peace,' wrote Zhukov in *Pravda*, 'are now forced to have recourse to outflanking movements and combinations behind the stage.' 'It looks very much,' declared Kudriavtsev, 'as though many of the delegations are not pursuing the aim of establishing a stable and enduring peace but rather their own narrow selfish interests treating the conference as a place where the way can be paved to peace-endangering movements in the future.' The West, as usual, was wholly black. Russia was snow-white. 'The Soviet delegation at the Paris conference,' said Moscow radio, 'is defending the foundation of true peace, based on the co-operation of the nations and on the principles of the defence of democracy, but of course such a peace is not favoured by the magnates of capital and their representatives.' Mr Molotov was the knight in armour, battling brilliantly against the dark dragons of imperialism. Always brilliantly, always successfully! 'Mr Vishinsky again took the floor and exposed the manoeuvre of the Australian delegate.' 'The speech of the Soviet delegate was listened to with rapt attention.' There was never a cool assessment of the facts; there was always a frenzy of hate and an ecstasy of self-congratulation.

* * * *

In one notable respect, this peace-making differed from all others. The western allies enjoyed an undoubted preponderance of world power and a no less striking preponderance of votes, yet it was they who finally emerged defeated and discomforted from the council chamber. The process by which the Russians brought about this remarkable result deserves careful study.

First, they charged the West with wanting to 'impose its will' and dictate the peace. The very magnitude of the falsehood made it difficult to answer, and it touched the West in a most sensitive spot, as Mr Molotov well knew. No accusation at this period

produced such an instinctive recoil as that of 'ganging up' against
Russia. Britain and America had a complex about it. That had
been their great error, so they were told, in the disastrous years
'between the wars'. It must not be repeated. It would not be repeated. They must do anything to avoid it. A watchful public
opinion at home would not permit it. Earnestly they implored
the Russians to believe that there was no such intention.

Very well, said the Russians, the western allies must show by
their actions that the charge was untrue. They must voluntarily
divest themselves of their negotiating advantages. They must accept the Principle of Unanimity. Nothing must be done unless
there was full agreement among the Great Powers, and discussions must continue until there *was* agreement. On the supposi-
tion that both sides would move to meet each other in a spirit of
goodwill, it was an unexceptionable principle and in Britain
won the weighty approval of *The Times*. In practice, it meant
that the western allies must agree with Russia, since unanimity
was otherwise impossible. Whenever they were faced with indiscipline, the Russians reached for the unanimity principle as a
Squeers might reach for his cane. Hardly ever did it fail to bring
the West to order.

Unanimity, the Russians decided, would be much more easily
achieved at a small gathering of Foreign Ministers than in a large
conference. It must, therefore, be agreed that the treaties should
be drafted by the Big Four, and presented to the full peace conference only when they had been completed. The western allies
did not like this procedure, since it was obviously Russia's intention to present the smaller nations with an accomplished fact.
But if they refused, Mr Molotov would say they wanted to 'impose their will' by the use of client votes. Very reluctantly, they
agreed.

The Foreign Ministers prepared their drafts in two main sessions in the early summer of 1946. Great differences developed
at an early stage. The inexhaustible Russians sat tight and waited
for the West to move. They never hesitated to repeat an argument for the tenth or twentieth time, and no topic was ever
closed until it was closed in their favour. One has the impression
that Mr Molotov and his colleagues thoroughly enjoyed these
sessions; all they lacked was a bright light to shine in the eyes
of their victims. Their strongest weapon was a blank refusal to

let the drafts go forward to a full peace conference until agreement was reached. Mr Byrnes and Mr Bevin repeatedly urged that invitations should now be sent out, that a date should now be fixed, and that it should be left to the twenty-one nations to fill in the gaps where the Foreign Ministers could not agree. Mr Molotov was adamant. It had been agreed to convoke the conference, he said, 'when the preparation of all drafts was completed'. He did not insist on 'the last comma', but he intended to see all his main objectives agreed in writing before he exposed himself to the blasts of the full conference. Even the rules of procedure for the coming conference must be more or less cut-and-dried before a date could be named. Patiently he waited, his strength that of the single obstinate juryman facing eleven colleagues who want to go home. In the end, he got agreed drafts which were satisfactory to him. 'As a result of prolonged discussions,' *Tass* cabled jubilantly from Paris, 'in the course of which the Soviet side consistently defended its lawful demands, an agreement has been reached which is built in all its basic points on the proposals made by the Soviet delegation.' On procedural matters, also, Mr Molotov had had his way. 'As to rules of procedure,' said *Tass*, 'agreement was reached on all disputable issues on the basis of the proposals on the Soviet side.' Unanimity had triumphed. 'The principle championed by the Soviet delegation, namely that agreement be reached on all main points by the four Powers before the opening of the peace conference, did finally win out.'

Mr Molotov's main procedural victory was a provision that voting at the peace conference should be by two-thirds majority rather than by simple majority. He knew that if the western allies really tried, they could muster a majority of more than two-thirds among the twenty-one nations. He also knew that however the voting went he had no intention of accepting any peace conference recommendations which he did not like. But he realized that it would be less easy for him to have his own way at the final session of the Foreign Ministers—the session which would follow the main conference and where the definitive treaties would be written—if the full peace conference had passed on a large number of recommendations which he could not accept. The task of breaking down his colleagues would be that much harder. The two-thirds majority would ease his path.

He calculated that he could continue to bludgeon his fellow Foreign Ministers with the Principle of Unanimity, and that against the combined vote of the Foreign Ministers and their supporters a two-thirds majority would rarely be achieved.

From the start, the peace conference was rebellious over the voting procedure. The two-thirds majority came under sharp attack from most of the smaller countries. The Australian Dr Evatt, in particular, worried Mr Molotov. He was a fresh batsman facing a tired bowler. Tempers rose rapidly on both sides. Russia started a propaganda offensive both inside and outside the conference. Talk of small nations' rights was due to 'a deliberate desire to break up the conference'. Evatt's 'clumsy manoeuvre' was an attempt to carry out the tasks set by his Anglo-American masters. Britain was accused of 'prompting' Dr Evatt and of 'trying to hide behind small nations'. The West was 'playing on the votes', was trying to organize a mechanical voting majority, was 'forsaking unanimity' and trying to 'dominate' and 'impose'. Mr Byrnes, because of his 'stubborn silence', was charged with 'duplicity' and disloyalty to the Foreign Ministers. 'If,' said Mr Molotov, 'the British and American delegations in the Council of Foreign Ministers voted for a certain proposal and are voting for an opposite here, they thus destroy and annul the preparatory work carried out by the Council of Foreign Ministers.' Russia was not so dishonourable. 'If the Soviet delegation voted for and advocated a given procedure to the Council of Foreign Ministers, it regarded it as a point of honour to vote for the same proposal in the conference.' In vain did Mr Byrnes repeat that he had never given any pledge of continued support to purely procedural decisions. To Mr Molotov, this was a boulder that might start an avalanche. His great Principle of Unanimity had given an ominous rumble, and his command of the conference was threatened.

When it seemed that the decision would go against Russia, the battle waxed hotter. *Tass* called it 'a tense struggle'. Mr Molotov insisted that an 'egregious error' was being made. This was 'a highly important question which determines the entire further work of the conference'. Where appeals to loyalty had failed, appeals to emotion might succeed. The wartime sacrifices and losses of Russia were recalled. Mr Molotov flatly refused to accept an adverse vote of fifteen to six. Mr Manuilsky, by a process of logic peculiarly Russian, argued that the vote was 'not in accordance with the wishes of the majority of those present'. Yugoslavia announced that as a sovereign State she could not consider herself bound by decisions of less than a two-thirds majority.

The struggle had now been going on for a week. Since the Russians declined to accept the verdict of the conference and seemed ready to walk out, a 'compromise' had to be reached. Decisions passed by a two-thirds majority would go forward to the Foreign Ministers as 'recommendations'; simple majority decisions would merely go forward! 'This mistake,' said Yermashov, 'will undoubtedly undermine the authority of the decisions which will be adopted by the conference.'

Mr Molotov's stubborn fight on this issue, and the unpleasantness which it caused, actually strengthened the Principle of Unanimity. The West had had its lesson; on no other matter of importance did Britain or America go back on the Foreign Ministers' decisions. It had beeen made plain to them that to do so would involve a breakdown. New machinery was actually set up while the conference was in session to help the four Ministers keep in step. Mr Molotov watched, hawk-eyed, for any deviation. At the first sign of hesitancy, he chivvied, cajoled and reprimanded. Mr Byrnes and Mr Bevin, unhappy 'split personalities', would speak up for resolutions in which they strongly believed before joining with Mr Molotov in voting them down. More often they sat in silence, leaving the struggle to others and knowing that the others must lose. Even their silence was considered culpable. 'Formally,' said *Tass*, 'they do not speak against the agreed decisions but actually they are calmly viewing the tricks of the delegations . . . and never lift a finger to support actively those decisions agreed upon by the Council of Foreign Ministers which they do not like.' They were, said *Tass*, 'preserving innocence while acquiring capital'.

In fact, they acquired no capital. One after another, every amendment of consequence proposed by the smaller countries was swept into oblivion at the crack of Mr Molotov's whip. 'Demining the road', *Tass* called it. As *New Times* agreed after the conference was over, 'the clauses of the treaties which were jointly agreed upon in the Council of Foreign Ministers were, with very few exceptions, approved by the conference'.

Mr Molotov's campaign had been masterly from beginning to end. He had taken over the 'voting machine' of his opponents and used it with their concurrence for his own purposes. He had persuaded them to enter the negotiations with one hand tied behind their backs in proof of friendship, and had then savaged them with all his armament. The various treaties must now be examined in more detail to see how complete was his victory.

* * * * *

Russia's feeling about the treaties with Finland, Hungary, Rumania and Bulgaria was that they were really her exclusive business. She had done most of the fighting; she had suffered most of the losses; she had virtually dictated the armistice terms; she had had the decisive voice in the Allied Control Commissions; she was going to write the treaties. The views of the western allies and of the smaller nations were heard with ill-concealed impatience and automatically rejected. The treaties, as finally approved, were almost identical with the original Russian drafts. As *New Times* said in July 1946, these treaties 'presented no special difficulties'.

Russia's intention was to maintain the stranglehold over the economic life of the four defeated nations which she had acquired as the result of victory. By fixing a reparations figure well in excess of the individual country's capacity to pay, she had an excuse for repeated interventions in their economic arrangements. Reparations fixed at £75 millions for Finland, for instance, were far more than this small and exhausted country could pay without foreign credits. In addition to the fixed reparations figure, Finland had to pay to Russia all the commercial and military debts which she had formerly owed to Germany and to transfer to Russia all German property in the country. She had lost an important slice of territory in Karelia and another near Helsinki, and had been compelled to hand over her Petsamo nickel mines. Everything went to Russia. Almost all her post-war exports went to Russia. For many years, she would be closely bound to Russia by the terms of peace.

Hungary and Rumania had even less economic freedom. During the first months of occupation, both countries had been mercilessly looted. Hungary in particular had been stripped of vast quantities of grain and meat and the Russians had also helped themselves freely to manufactured goods. The provision enabling them to remove 'German property' was liberally interpreted. None of these transfers was at any time accounted for to the western allies, who were expected to approve a reparations figure without knowing how much had been taken already. Moreover, the war was hardly over before Russia had forced Rumania to sign economic agreements giving the Soviet Union a half-interest in mixed companies which would have monopoly rights over the oil, iron and steel and transport industries. A large Soviet share was also secured in the textile industry. These mixed companies were not formed, as the Rumanians hoped, to assist the fruitful exploitation of the country's resources in the joint interest. Russia was not planning any long-term investment. The agreements were little more than a means of extracting the maximum of reparations quickly from the Rumanian economy —a sort of mechanical milker. The textile industry, for instance, was kept busy processing Soviet raw cotton, almost the whole of the product being sent to Russia. A similar procedure was followed in Hungary, where mixed companies were set up to control shipping and air transport, oil and bauxite. In reply to western protests that Russia ought not to be making exclusive economic agreements with former enemy countries when peace treaties were still unsigned, Russia replied that she had made the agreements out of a sincere wish to improve the economic position of the defeated people.

The result of these measures was to make Rumania and Hungary a Soviet economic domain, virtually closed to western trespassers. This was the economic equivalent of the political domination which was studied in the last chapter. The special relationship which was forced upon the defeated nations was achieved with the *allied* border countries by political means. The complete picture showed an eastern Europe with its economic as well as its political face turned to Russia.

The western allies began the peace negotiations hoping that they would be able to loosen Russia's economic monopoly in the four defeated states. Mr Byrnes has described in *Speaking Frankly* how he 'insisted' on equal economic rights for all Powers in the former enemy countries and demanded equal access for the citizens of all allied countries to their trade, raw materials and industry. It was a pipe-dream. The Russians, who had plundered and economically shackled the ex-enemy states without the least regard for the welfare of their people, now denounced the West for trying to undermine their sovereignty. Britain and America, said Sergeeva in *New Times,* wanted 'to take advantage of the temporary enfeeblement of the vanquished countries in order to deprive them of economic independence'. They wanted to get their 'greedy capitalist clutches' on eastern Europe as they had done before the war. The efforts of the West to keep the economic door slightly ajar were described by *Pravda* as 'attempts to strangle the defeated countries' economy'. The tone had been set by Ilya Ehrenburg, writing of the western allies' attitude to Bulgaria. 'Behind their hypocritical tirades loom the dividends of the tobacco companies, the greedy hands of exporters and middlemen. Business, business and more dirty business!' When America proposed a joint three-Power plan for the economic rehabilitation of Hungary, Chernyavsky commented that by its rejection of the proposal the Soviet Union had 'reaffirmed its policy of excluding any attempt to foist foreign interference on Germany's satellites in their economic life, or any demands incompatible with their state sovereignty and national dignity'. Orlov, broadcasting in Hungarian, said, 'The Soviet Union has taken a firm stand against economically strong countries reducing the vanquished nations to a colonial or semi-colonial status under the pretext of equality of rights.' This was classic Russian technique—to accuse the other side, with a fine show of righteous indignation, of the very offence which Russia herself was committing.

The chief bid to re-write the reparations clauses of the eastern treaties in such a way that there would be some kind of check on Russia's exclusive exploitation of her position was made by Australia. The Australian delegate wanted reparations commissions to be set up to consider the capacity to pay of the various countries and to postpone fixing the sum until six months after the signing of the treaties. He also wanted to know what Russia had already taken; he wanted to end the uncharted drain in goods by insisting that all reparations should be paid in currency and not in kind. The Russians considered this a trick by which the western allies hoped to buy the goods of the eastern countries 'dirt cheap' and make the eastern nations 'dependent on those who have their pockets filled with dollars and sterling'. 'The amendments of the Australian delegation,' reported *Tass* from Paris, 'are obviously aimed at ensuring a predominant position for American and British capital in the economy of Rumania, Hungary, and the other former enemy countries, and at making these countries economically dependent on the Anglo-Saxon *bloc*.'

Whatever the real aims of the West may have been, the point which has to be noted here is that they were not achieved. All attempts to scale down the reparation totals or to set up impartial machinery for controlling the payments were overruled at one stage or another of the proceedings, and the original articles on reparations in the draft treaties were finally adopted. Almost the only matter in which the West had a slight measure of success was in securing a fairer share of Bulgarian reparations for Greece after wearisome hours of haggling.

Not merely did the western allies fail to secure for themselves the equal opportunity in the eastern countries for which they had pressed, but they had the greatest difficulty in obtaining recognition of their reasonable claims for compensation. A South African attempt to prevent Rumania selling foreign-owned property at 'knock-down' prices in order to pay reparations to Russia 'smelt of oil' and called forth a stream of abusive talk about extra-territorial rights and capitulations. Demands for compensation for war damage done to Anglo-American oil installations in Rumania brought from the Russians the retort that Anglo-American bombers had done most of the damage. British attempts to protect the insurance and shipping interests of British nationals were obstructed. Full compensation for the losses incurred by allied citizens was refused.

Closely related to the unsuccessful western attempts to modify the Russian monopoly in eastern Europe was the claim, pressed very strongly indeed by Mr Byrnes and fully supported by Mr Bevin, that a clause guaranteeing freedom of navigation on the Danube should be included in the relevant treaties. The Americans feared, with good reason, that unless freedom of navigation and trade were specifically provided for, the Russians and their satellites would close the river to the West as they clearly intended to close its hinterland. America had a bargaining counter in the fact that she held in her zones of Austria and Germany nearly a thousand Danube river craft belonging to the ex-enemy states.

The Russian view was that the western allies were attempting to restore an imperialist regime on the Danube under the guise of the 'open door'. The control of the Danube, they declared, was the concern only of the riparian States. Did countries not located on its banks participate in establishing a regime for the St Lawrence river, they asked, not mentioning that the St Lawrence was open to navigation by all comers. After long discussions, Russia was prepared to concede the 'principle' of free navigation 'subject naturally to the regulations of the allied commands in the respective territories'—the allied commands being Russian. It would not be proper to incorporate anything in the treaties, it was explained, because there were *allied* riparian countries as well and they, too, must be consulted. Mr Molotov thought it would be enough if the Foreign Ministers expressed their 'confidence' that the riparian States would ultimately allow free navigation. Britain drafted a formula declaring such an intention on the part of the Big Four, requiring the occupation authorities to give appropriate navigational instructions, and laying it down that the Big Four Governments would take the necessary steps to secure the adherence of the riparian States to the principle of free navigation. The full conference, however, took a stronger line. In plenary session it decided by a two-thirds majority that there should be a clause in the treaties providing for international control of the river and requiring a special conference six months later to set up a suitable organization. 'This decision,' said Linetski in a broadcast in Italian, 'served the rapacious lusts of the big foreign monopolies, whose policy is economic enslavement of the Balkan countries.' However, in the final climactic meeting of the Foreign Ministers in New York, the West was obliged to give way. All that Mr Molotov would agree to was a declaration of principle which committed no one to anything and a conference of the Big Four and the riparian States within six months. Naturally, the promised conference was never held.

Once again, in a matter over which they had physical control the Russians had had their way. As a footnote, it is necessary only to add that the Americans, disappointed and defeated, nevertheless released the detained Danube ships to their former owners as a mark of goodwill.

There was one other matter about which Britain, in particular, had a pronounced view. Greece wanted a change in her frontier with Bulgaria at Bulgaria's expense and Britain thought this claim justified. Greece had been the 'poor relation' at the conference and had been consistently insulted by the Russians. By a typically Russian inversion, totalitarian Bulgaria was now a 'democratic' country, while Greece was plainly 'fascist'. The Bulgarians themselves denounced Britain in language which would have suggested to any uninformed person that Bulgaria was a victorious power and Britain a defeated fascist enemy. Britain fought a rather listless battle for her Greek protégé, conscious of divisions at home and of the agreement reached in the Foreign Ministers' Council that the frontier should not be changed. In the crucial divisions she led a large block of abstentions and no decision was taken. Mr Molotov, though annoyed, was not worried. Russia, after all, controlled Bulgaria. He said, 'We confidently tell our friends the Bulgarians: Bulgarians! Do not worry. Your frontier will remain unshakable.' And so, of course, it did. At the final meeting of Ministers in New York, Mr Bevin raised once more the question of changing the frontier, but Mr Molotov blandly advised against pressing the issue 'in order not to provoke passions in the relations between Greece and Bulgaria' and the subject was dropped.

It is now possible to sum up on the eastern European treaties. Because the Russians held the field, they were able to have their way on all matters which they considered vital. Their economic monopoly was maintained intact against all western assaults. Nothing of importance which they wished to include in the treaties was omitted. Nothing of importance was included against their wishes. No Soviet principle, no Soviet interest, was sacrificed. Though the discussions took nearly a year to complete, it is true to say that Russia and Russia alone wrote these treaties and that they would not have been different in any significant respect if the western allies had never been consulted.

* * * * *

We turn to Italy, where the power balance was reversed. Here, Britain and America were in a position to let Mr Molotov talk, and still have their own way in the end. Their plain interest, except on the hypothesis that appeasement would be useful, was to cling to all positions; to concede nothing to violence of language or to threats; to show that stubborn patience which always comes more readily when one's position is impregnable; and finally to impose their will, as Russia had done over the Balkans. Since tough realism was clearly the order of the day, the policy of the West should have been 'What we have we hold'. Instead, it was 'What you have you hold; what we have we give away'.

Let us consider first the respective attitudes of Russia and the West to the question of Italian reparations. The western allies believed that these should be kept very low, not so much because in two years of co-belligerency Italy had gone far to 'work her passage home', but because it was clear that the country was not in a position to meet a heavy war indemnity. Indeed, there were the makings of the same kind of situation as later was to arise over Germany in a much more acute form. By the time the Foreign Ministers settled down to discussions in May 1946, Italy had already received £165 millions in relief from the United States, Canada and Britain, and £100 millions from UNRRA, and before she reached anything approaching solvency she would need many millions more. Any reparations would therefore be paid, in effect, by the western powers and on that ground alone they were entitled to demand that appetites should be restrained.

Russia claimed £25 millions for herself and £50 millions to be divided between Yugoslavia, Greece, and that very dubious ally of the West, Albania. Britain and America, at the Foreign Ministers' conference, would not agree to any fixed sum until a committee of experts had reported how much would be available for reparations after Italy had met her minimum peacetime needs. This was a strong line, but at the next meeting Mr Byrnes expressed his anxiety to meet Russia's wishes as far as possible and suggested that most of what she asked on her own behalf could be obtained from the capital equipment of Italy's war factories, from Italian assets in the Balkans, and from Italian merchant ships and warships. Mr Molotov at once retorted that warships were war booty, not reparations, and doubted whether the value of the merchant ships to be handed over was as high as Mr Byrnes thought.

At the next session, Mr Molotov explained where *he* thought the money should come from. Half of the £25 millions could be met from the assets enumerated by Mr Byrnes; the other half could easily be produced by Italian industry in the course of the next five years. Both the American and the British representatives emphatically disapproved of taking reparations from current Italian production, not least because it might prove to be the thin end of Russian penetration in Italian affairs. Mr Byrnes still thought that Russia could get her requirements in other ways. He reckoned that Italian assets in the three Balkan countries were worth £12 millions; that two large merchant ships offered to Russia were worth £6 millions, and that the balance should be taken out in warships, which might well be booty but if so were western booty, since the West had captured them. Mr Molotov now counter-attacked, bringing his press and radio propagandists into action. Britain, who was seeking compensation for damage to the property of British nationals and requiring the confiscation of Italian assets in Britain, was taking at least as much from Italy as Russia was asking. The United States and British claims were 'the true cause of the difficulties obstructing a solution of the economic problems of the Italian treaty'. Britain and America were imposing on Italy various obligations 'the size and character of which in several cases cannot even be precisely calculated and defined'. Anglo-Saxon 'circles' wanted to destroy Italian competition in the post-war market and turn Italy into a financial colony. There had been, Russia, alleged, a secret transference of industrial, banking, trade and other enterprises from Italian to foreign hands. An Export-Import Bank loan of £6¼ millions in the form of cotton deliveries was intended to strengthen American influence in the Italian textile trade. Commentator Lyontyev talked of the 'plunder and economic enslavement' of Italy by her Anglo-American 'masters'.

To the accompaniment of this propaganda barrage, Mr Molotov proposed that his plan should be accepted as far as Russia was concerned, and that the question of the £50 millions for the other applicants should be decided by the wider conference. Mr Byrnes thought the whole thing should be decided by the wider conference. Before the next meeting, however, he had had second thoughts. He agreed to the figure of £25 millions for Russia; he also agreed that if the named assets were not sufficient there should be reparations from current production. There must, however, be safeguards. The type and quality of goods taken out of Italy should not be such as to be a drag on Italian reconstruction. He agreed that if necessary, Russia should supply the raw materials. Italy should have the option of paying in convertible currency if she preferred, and deliveries should not begin for three years. After further discussion, Mr Molotov cheerfully 'settled' for a two-year moratorium and a five-year 'spreadover', having obtained all he wanted and almost certainly more than he expected. He could now relax, confident that the Principle of Unanimity would carry him safely through the peace conference.

The full conference now met. The correspondent of *Tass* was struck by the Italian Prime Minister's 'quite tolerant attitude' to the claims of Britain and America, but failed to draw the obvious conclusion that these claims, so inflated by Russian propaganda, were not really onerous after all. Once again the small nations went into battle. Australia wanted to refer all claims to a commission for study and to defer any payment for six months, as she had proposed in the case of the Balkans. She was anxious that some neutral buffer should be set up between the Italian Government and possible Soviet demands, but all that Mr Molotov could be persuaded to agree to was that the Big Four ambassadors in Rome should 'supervise' payments. Canada urged postponement of a decision on reparations for Russia until all claims had been considered. As usual, the small countries were voted down. 'In a stiff struggle,' reported the *Tass* correspondent from Paris, 'the Soviet delegation succeeded in upholding with credit the interests of the Soviet Union and the Soviet people.' The chapter of the treaty dealing with reparations to Russia was approved 'without a single letter being changed'. 'In the long run not one of the amendments was accepted.'

As an indication of the reparations which she had voluntarily decided to forgo, Britain had filed a paper claim for £2,880 millions. *Tass,* ignoring the fact that the claim was not being pressed, talked of the 'Anglo-Saxons' unrestrained appetites'. As a result of Russian persistence, the almost negligible British and American claims for compensation for damaged property were successfully whittled down before the treaty was signed.

The question had still to be decided of the amount of reparations for the other claimants and how it was to be divided. Britain proposed a total of £55 millions, of which Yugoslavia and Greece would get £25 millions each and Ethiopia the rest. Russia declared that Yugoslavia should have much more than Greece —twice as much, in fact—but the conference decided against her. However, in New York Mr Molotov worked his old trick. There must be 'unanimity' and how could there be unanimity if the West was obstinate? Yugoslavia was already dissatisfied with her treatment by the conference. Had not the Yugoslavs said they would not sign a treaty which did not give them justice? 'It is hardly desirable to add another complication in connection with reparations,' said Mr Molotov, who has a suave line in blackmail. The West agreed. Russia had her way, and the final treaty gave Yugoslavia more reparations than Greece.

Over reparations from Italy, Mr Molotov had won all along the line. Against the considered judgment of the West, he had compelled Italy to accept obligations which were clearly insupportable. Heavy reparations were to be paid to a country which had suffered comparatively little damage at Italian hands, at the expense of countries like Britain whose losses in fighting the Duce had run into thousands of millions. Mr Molotov was conscious of victory and elated by it, and who will blame him? 'Discussion on the question of reparations from Italy to the Soviet Union,' he said, 'has taken place at 38 meetings, and in all 102 hours have been spent on it. This discussion was terminated by the unanimous decision of the committee . . . which agreed with the correctness of the USSR's proposal of 100 million dollars of reparations in kind, including deliveries from current production. After all these meetings, on which over 100 hours of time were spent in committees and conferences of every sort, the same proposal was arrived at which the Soviet Government had advanced as far back as September last year. The changes in this draft have proved insignificant.' And then, smugly, 'As you see, in order to convince people of the most elementary things the Soviet delegation had to spend no small efforts.' No wonder that people who have not tried to negotiate with the Russians can never quite understand the attitude of the people who have!

*　　*　　*　　*　　*

Another western concession of great potential importance related to the withdrawal of occupation troops from Italy. Both sides knew that one of the main points of clash between East and West would be on the Italo-Yugoslav border, wherever it was ultimately fixed. Russia knew that she intended to bring all possible pressure to bear on Italy once allied troops had withdrawn. Britain and America feared she would do so. Since Italy was to be disarmed by treaty to a degree which would leave her dangerously inferior to Tito's Yugoslavia, it was in the interests of the western allies to maintain at least token forces in Italy until she could rely on her own strength and stability. Russia's interest, on the other hand, was to get allied troops out of Italy at the earliest possible moment. In support of her case, she made sweeping charges that Britain and America had plans for prolonged military control. The Anglo-Saxons were already engaged in 'all kinds of military construction', including the building of military airfields. The story was spread that British representatives had presented a draft agreement to the Italian Government which would have turned the whole of the peninsula into a 'first-class base for the British armed forces'.

A proposal by Mr Bevin that an allied inspectorate should stay in Italy for eighteen months after the signing of the treaty to ensure complete disarmament was opposed by Mr Molotov, who thought it might involve keeping foreign troops in the country. In order to hasten the departure of the last allied forces, he 'offered' to withdraw all Soviet troops from Bulgaria within ninety days after the ratification of a treaty with that country if the western allies would leave Italy on the same terms. This was a typical piece of Molotov negotiation, for he had already agreed unconditionally in London that Russian troops would leave Bulgaria. They had, indeed, no good excuse for remaining. There was some talk of 'lines of communication' with Austria, though only a tortuous diplomat like Mr Molotov would think of travelling from Russia to Austria via Bulgaria. In fact, the Danube route was adequately safeguarded from the Rumanian bank. Nevertheless, the western allies agreed to this preposterous bargain. Ninety days after the treaties were ratified, uniformed Red Army men were out of Bulgaria, leaving the Russian grip on all the Balkan territories not weakened in the slightest degree. Ninety days after the Italian treaty was ratified, the last British and American units had left Italy. If the subsequent danger to Italy proved less great than might have been feared, it was only because American policy towards Russia had so strengthened in the meantime that Moscow felt any overt action by Tito against Italy might well bring American troops back again.

The only important respect in which the West failed to meet Russian wishes was in the matter of the Italian colonies. At Potsdam, Stalin had crudely stated that the Soviet Union 'would like some territory of the defeated states'. The Russians proposed that they should be given the trusteeship of at least one of the colonies, possibly Tripolitania—a plan which, had it come to fruition, would have put Russia—in Mr Bevin's words—'across the throat of the British Empire'. The western powers had gone far in appeasement, but they never seriously considered so damaging a step. However, having taken no trouble to concert a policy between themselves, they were forced in the end to agree that consideration of the whole problem should be postponed for a year.

* * * * *

It is when we turn to the question of the Italo-Yugoslav frontier and the fate of Trieste that we find Anglo-American concession at its most lavish. Let us recall once again that the western allies were in sole possession of the disputed territory and could not have been forcibly ejected. Their troops held Trieste and the greater part of the Julian March. At no time could Yugoslavia seriously have contemplated a *coup* in the face of western firmness. If the West had simply taken a leaf out of Mr Molotov's book and said 'No' to all demands, nobody could have compelled their compliance. It was as easy as that.

There were two related disagreements. One concerned the proper boundary between Yugoslavia and Italy in a territory where there were mixed Slovene and Italian populations. The other concerned the future of the Italian city of Trieste, an enclave in the wider area.

In each case there were two issues to be considered; one of self-interest and one of justice. Russia's interest was that the whole territory, including Trieste, should be handed over to her satellite, Yugoslavia. The area was of the greatest strategic significance. Possession would give Yugoslavia control of the commercial ports of Trieste and Fiume and the naval base of Pola, with their hinterland, and would enable the Slav *bloc* to command the Adriatic and greatly extend its influence in the Mediterranean. Central and eastern Europe would be further cut off from the outside world. Italy would be weakened both economically and militarily.

To the western allies, the problem seemed more complex. Their interest, unquestionably, was to concede no inch of territory to Yugoslavia, but on grounds of ethnic justice Yugoslavia had a good claim to a part of the Julian March.

Trieste was different. Here, from the western point of view, interest and justice did not clash. Its population was eighty per cent Italian; it was of vital economic and strategic importance to Italy, and it was clear that Italy ought to retain it. It would remain valuable as a city and a port for Italy even if—as might well be the case—much of its pre-war European trade was lost through Yugoslav control of its hinterland and Russian domination of central and eastern Europe.

No conceivable solution would leave Trieste Italian and at the same time ensure that it would remain a great international port. Under Yugoslav sovereignty, it would flourish as the outlet for Russia's satellites, but at the cost of justice and western security. Under Italian sovereignty, it would be ostracized by the Slavs. An 'international' solution could be expected to work only on the assumption that Europe would again become an organic and co-operative unit.

It will now be seen what happened round the conference table.

* * * * *

In principle, the Foreign Ministers had agreed at an early stage that the new frontier should follow the best ethnic line. A four-man commission had spent several weeks on the spot. The British, American and French representatives on the commission had drawn very similar ethnic lines; the Russian alone was drawn in quite a different place. The French line was perhaps the fairest—it would have left 130,000 Italians in Yugoslavia and

115,000 Yugoslavs in Italy. Mr Byrnes suggested a plebiscite but Mr Molotov showed an understandable lack of enthusiasm since the Russian line would have left nearly half a million Italians in Yugoslavia.

So anxious was Mr Molotov to have his way that when the Foreign Ministers met in April 1946 he was prepared to make a deal over Italian reparations and colonies in return for the satisfaction of his frontier demands. Mr Byrnes and Mr Bevin were not prepared to bargain with the lives of people. After protracted discussions, in the course of which both arguments and delegates were exhausted, a 'compromise' was reached. From the point of view of ethnic justice, it was not unreasonable. From the point of view of western expediency, it was lamentable. It gave Yugoslavia 300,000 inhabitants and several thousand square miles of territory which she had never possessed before. Twenty-eight thousand Italians and 75,000 tons of household goods had to be evacuated from Pola. The rich mineral deposits of the Pola area went to Yugoslavia and so did the power plants on which the Monfalcone shipyards—the greatest in the whole Mediterranean—depended. An attempt by the West to protect the political rights of Italian minorities in the transferred territories was subsequently described by Mr Molotov as 'insulting to allied democratic states'. There was, he said, 'no reason for apprehension' and at New York the West did not press the matter.

There remained the question of Trieste itself. All the negotiations were conducted against a background of Soviet and satellite abuse. 'The military appearance of Trieste,' said one commentator, 'with the Australian, Scots, Canadian and British troops, conceals intense fascist activity in the political and journalistic field.' Military Government was encouraging the ruthless treatment of Slovene workers by the police and destroying freedom. Nevertheless, 'police truncheons' could not 'dam the powerful stream of the people's hankering for justice'. A Yugoslav newspaper declared that 'but for the USSR and its firm stand another Versailles would have been witnessed, leading to the merciless enslavement of the Slav peoples'. *Pravda* accused Allied Military Government of differing only slightly in its methods from the terrorist regime of Mussolini. The Italian spokesman at the conference was denounced by Vishinsky as 'this notorious mouthpiece of the hopes of the Italian aggressors'.

No argument was too extravagant. Trieste should go to Yugoslavia, Vishinsky solemnly declared, because though its inhabitants were predominantly Italian it 'breathed Slovene air'.

Since the West was still determined to avoid a breakdown, it was obliged in the end to meet Russia 'half way'. The Foreign Ministers agreed that Trieste and its neighbourhood should be made an autonomous Free Territory under United Nations control. The details of the Statute under which the Free Territory would be established were to be discussed by a special four-Power commission and its report referred to the full conference. When the conference met, every argument about Trieste was repeated at length. The Italian Signor de Gasperi warned that the planned settlement would prove to be no settlement at all. 'Do you really intend,' he asked, 'to enclose in the fragile cage of an international statute, with meagre rations and abundant political rights, these two adversaries, and still hope that they will not come to blows?' His warning was unheeded. There were many amendments but the Foreign Ministers remained loyal to their agreement and all attempts to change their decision failed.

The final struggle turned on that part of the problem which had not been settled—the Statute, which would determine the future of the port and city under international control. The trouble arose from the fundamentally different intentions of Russia and the West. Russia had already won the major battle—she had succeeded in taking Trieste from Italy. She had not lost hope that, by indirect means, the Yugoslavs might ultimately be manoeuvred into control. Mr Molotov knew well that there were more ways of obtaining power than through agreements at a conference table. There was always the communist party. 'The time will come,' he prophesied, 'when the national claims of Yugoslavia will win universal recognition, including the unconditional consent of Italian democrats.' His aim was to obtain a Statute which would give the greatest possible power to the people's elected representatives. Once British and American troops were out of the way, the combination of Slovene nationalists and Italian communists, using the methods of 'eastern democracy', should suffice to win control.

The western Powers could read Mr Molotov without difficulty. They had in mind the example of Danzig, where international authority had broken down once the Nazi party had captured the legislature. They knew the danger and wanted to guard against it. Their intention was to set up a Free Territory which would in fact be free and independent and not subject to pressure from outside. In the exceptional conditions which prevailed, they knew that security and stability were a pre-condition of democracy. For the time being at any rate, an impartial Governor must be given sufficient powers to enable him to maintain order in the Territory.

This difference of approach affected almost every paragraph of the Statute. Who was to appoint the Governor? In what circumstances could he call for military aid from the Security Council? How were the fundamental human rights of the citizens to be preserved? Should the Governor be allowed to initiate legislation? What right of veto should he be granted? Should the judiciary be elected or appointed, and if appointed, by whom? Who should control the police? At what stage should Anglo-American forces be withdrawn from the city? Disputes on all these matters could be reduced to one thing: was the Free Territory to be real or 'phoney'? The struggle had its fantastic side. Russia, for instance, wanted the Assembly of the Free Territory to be called the 'People's Assembly'. The analogy with the 'People's Republics' and 'People's Courts' of eastern Europe was more than the western allies could stomach. The French, still at this period astride both camps, thought a satisfactory settlement could be reached by spelling 'people's Assembly' with a small initial 'p'! But the dichotomy was real enough and grave enough behind the burlesque.

The attitude of the West gave the Russians yet another splendid opportunity for propaganda. Britain and America, they declared, wanted to turn Trieste into their colony. Mr Vishinsky taunted the western delegates on the nature of their drafts. 'Genuine executive authority,' he said, 'is surrendered by these drafts to the Governor, who is in no way responsible to the popular Assembly. And you do not object to this! You—the representatives of western and American democracy, who recognize both the division of authority and the responsibility of the government to a popular assembly, a Parliament, a Chamber of Deputies, or whatever it may be called!'

The climax was reached on the night of October 5th, 1946. In the session of the Political and Territorial Committee for Italy, the western Powers determined to end the deadlock. 'At this meeting,' wrote commentator Hofman, 'voting machinery was set in full swing to railroad through the undemocratic Anglo-American-French proposals for the Trieste Statute.' The debate and the voting was completed only at six o'clock in the morning after an all-night session. During that period, fifty-five votes were taken, and the substance of the western proposals was carried—usually by a majority of fourteen to six. For once the West was not bound by a Foreign Ministers' decision, since on the Statute no decision had been reached. It had demonstrated conclusively that if it wished to do so it could carry the conference, and with a two-thirds majority into the bargain.

The Russians were almost beside themselves with anger. *New Times* wrote, 'The proposal to convert Trieste into a Free Territory, with the avowed purpose of protecting the interests of its population, was turned into a scheme virtually to steal away Trieste from its native population and to establish a semi-colonial governorship supported by British and American troops'. Mikhailov, broadcasting from Moscow in English, said, 'Anglo-American reaction wishes to transform this territory into a military base for itself, a stronghold for British and American armed forces in the Mediterranean'. Denunciations of western 'railroading' continued to rumble for weeks in the Russian press.

But that was not the end of the story. The western allies had made a demonstration, but in New York, round the Foreign Ministers' table, they failed to hold their ground. Mr Molotov flatly refused to accept the conference decision on the Statute. Now, for the first time, he did not want a breakdown because he had gained so much, but he did not want the Statute either. There was one more 'compromise'. Once more it gave Mr Molotov most of what he wanted. Mr Byrnes and Mr Bevin might dispute the extent of their surrender, but perhaps the best evidence on the subject is what the Russians themselves said. The *Tass* correspondent in New York reported: 'The stand on principle adopted by the Soviet delegation prevailed against the attempts of the representatives of other powers to force their will upon it. The United States and British delegates, no less interested than the Soviet Union in the conclusion of the peace treaties, were forced to cede some ground, which brought about an agreement.' Mikhailov, with a sigh of satisfaction through the microphone, told his listeners, 'The principles which were laid down by the Foreign Ministers' Council before the fruitless Paris Peace Conference have now prevailed'.

The Council in New York had ended, the Russians were told, 'in a friendly way'. The talks had been 'extremely fruitful', The Soviet press gleefully reproduced foreign press comments on the results. Raymond Gram Swing was quoted as saying, 'The Russians have won—and we have lost'. And in America the *New York Herald Tribune* commented, 'It is hard to say that the Trieste compromise is a good one. In fact, it is probably worse than most other agreements. The western allies had to swallow many things to secure agreement'.

In fact, to secure an agreement which they did not need, the western Powers had put their signatures to arrangements for Trieste which were dangerous, unjust and—perhaps worst of all—impracticable. The Statute of Trieste was born in an atmosphere of riots, strikes and deliberately fomented unrest aimed at discrediting the Free Territory from the very beginning. It was prevented from coming into effective operation because, as might have been foreseen, Russia and the West could not agree on the appointment of a Governor. Without a Governor there could be no elections and no withdrawal of troops. In July 1947 *The Times* correspondent reported that traffic in the port of Trieste was almost at a standstill. Italian traffic was tending to flow through Venice and Genoa. Yugoslavia was sabotaging the use of the port and offering favourable terms to the satellites in the newly-acquired Fiume. The settlement had condemned Trieste to decay, its population to endless strife, and the whole of Italy to lasting resentment. Rarely had there been a worse day's work.

* * * * *

That the signing of the peace treaties as a whole was greeted throughout Russia with the enthusiasm normally reserved for a military victory is not surprising. If Mr Molotov had been a Roman emperor, he would have deserved a 'triumph'. The western negotiators, believing that they were purchasing world peace and friendship, had paid a huge deposit on a worthless contract. To Mr Bevin and Mr Byrnes, it seemed hardly possible to pay too much for co-operation with Russia and if they fought for little else, they fought for that. It is much easier to forgive those who, with the best of motives, made the attempt than it is to forgive those who, with the worst of motives, pretend that the attempt was never made.

CHAPTER V

GERMANY (I)

To the Soviet Union, post-war Germany was just another piece—though a highly important piece—in the mosaic of her world strategy. Her ultimate purpose was to establish a unified communist Germany under her own domination. She hoped that her noisy advocacy of German political unity would offset in the German mind the antagonism aroused by other aspects of her policy—notably, the dismemberment of eastern Germany and her own fantastic reparations claim. The dogma ruled out any expectation of agreement with the West. Such an agreement was neither desired nor sought. To Russia, the many conferences on Germany were merely a means of prolonging uncertainty, of hindering the reconstruction of the western zones and of permitting the unhampered execution of Russian plans beyond the Elbe. The longer the talks could be dragged out, the stronger would be Russia's relative position. While the western allies strained after the dangling carrot of agreement, Russia quietly and methodically imposed her will upon her own zone. From this advanced position, she endeavoured to infiltrate politically into the western zones and to discredit British and American administration in the eyes of the German people and the world. Her whole policy was planned, positive, vigorous and fundamentally consistent.

For two years, Britain and America had nothing that could be called a policy for western Germany. In detail, their administration was conscientious, honest and humane but it floated in a vacuum of good intentions. They did not seek actively to mould and shape and re-create the economy of the western zones with bold initiative and lucid purpose; on the contrary, they were passive and negative. Ignoring the clear and conclusive evidence of Russia's ineradicable hostility, they still believed with simple faith that there would be four-Power co-operation in rebuilding a united democratic Germany and writing a just and workable German peace. Daily and hourly proof to the contrary, spread

105

out on the very doorstep of their zones, was thrust from sight with a fatal obstinacy unequalled since Hitler decided that Stalingrad should fall. Their hands, extended to the Russians in open friendship, failed to grasp the constructive moment in their own domain.

Had the western allies wished to do so, there is little doubt that they could have settled their own considerable differences as readily in 1946 as eventually they would have to do in 1948. The French insistence on security through control of the Ruhr, the American wish for political federation in the new Germany, the divergent views on the speed and extent of acceptable German recovery—all these were problems, and tough ones, but they were never problems which would not fall speedily to a combined assault. Collectively, there was no lack of capacity or knowledge in the West. One thing alone froze effective action by the western allies. They were hag-ridden by the fear of a breach with Russia. It was on that account that for two sterile years Britain and America watched their zones decay; that they accepted a derisory level of industry; that they delayed setting up a separate bizonal administration; that when they did set it up it lacked the political authority to make it work; that throughout the period they vacillated and bungled over denazification and reparations and dismantling. It was on that account that for two years of incomparable opportunity they permitted western Germany to remain an economic wilderness, a creeping desert threatening to inundate and destroy its struggling neighbours.

Let us suppose that a man is critically ill of a disease which, if not checked in time, may start an epidemic. Two doctors stand by. They have diagnosed the illness; they know the treatment which will cure it; they have the necessary medicines. But they also have a distant colleague of uncertain temper who has worked with them on the case and whose presence at the bedside they deem expedient lest they lose his goodwill for ever. So they sit patiently, shaking their heads, listening for the doorbell, waiting for the colleague who fails to come, while the strength of the prostrate victim slowly ebbs away.

That, broadly, is what Britain and America did to Germany in the two years after Potsdam.

*　　*　　*　　*　　*

It was plain from the start that Russia intended to create an eastern Germany as nearly as possible in her own political image. The very secrecy which veiled her activities in the zone, so ominously like that prevailing in the Soviet Union and among the eastern European satellites, was a clear warning that another bit of the world was going behind the curtain. The zone would be administered without regard to other zones, no progress reports would be issued except for propaganda purposes, and visitors would be unwelcome unless they could be relied upon to say the right things when they left. As late as November 1946, American correspondents were being refused entry on the absurd ground that it would be 'dangerous for them to operate'. It was always difficult for the West to have a complete picture of events beyond the Elbe, but there was enough information to leave no doubt about the main features.

Communist leadership in the eastern zone after the war was mainly provided by men taken into Germany by the Russians immediately after victory. Outstanding were Wilhelm Pieck and Walter Ulbricht, both Moscow trainees of long experience. Ulbricht had been a frequent visitor to Moscow before Hitler's rise to power and after 1933 he had made it his headquarters. In 1939-40 he had been a keen advocate of Russo-German friendship, but after Hitler's attack he had taken charge of Moscow's propaganda broadcasts to the German troops and later helped to organize the 'Free German Committee' with which Field Marshal von Paulus became associated. This organization was invaluable to the Russians in the initial post-war period for after political indoctrination many of its members returned to eastern Germany to take up responsible positions in the zone at a time when there was little reliable local support.

At first there were four political parties in the zone—the Communist party, the Social Democrats, the Christian Democrats and a comparatively insignificant party of Liberal Democrats which never gave much trouble. The communists knew they could expect little support unless they could persuade the numerically strong Social Democrats to join forces with them. Many Social Democrats, remembering the disastrous consequences of working-class division in the 'thirties, favoured such co-operation, but on terms which would leave them a measure of influence and independence. At a joint meeting held at the end of

1945, a common programme was drawn up. Enthusiasm for the programme waned when Social Democrats in the West attacked it as a first step to absorption. The Social Democratic leader in the western zones, Dr Kurt Schumacher, when reminded that his own party and the communist party were 'brothers', is reputed to have replied, 'So were Cain and Abel.' Belief in the good faith of the communists slumped badly when they flagrantly cheated their way to victory over the Social Democrats in the trade union elections. Since amalgamation by consent seemed less and less likely, the communists proceeded to compel a fusion with full Russian backing. Socialist workers were asked to vote for the joining of the two parties into one Socialist Unity party at open meetings in the presence of Soviet officers. Communists in possession of membership lists of the Social Democratic party were in a position to check the attitude of every member. Many socialists who opposed unity were dispatched to concentration camps made infamous by Hitler—Sachsenhausen and Buchenwald among them—or were removed to other districts. Social democracy was liquidated as an independent force by methods indistinguishable from those which the Nazis had used.

The Unity party now became, under close communist supervision, the chief political power in the zone. Membership was a civic safeguard and its numbers could soon be counted in millions. By joining Unity, many a former Nazi secured absolution from his past political sins. Unity party members were allotted most of the key administrative positions throughout the zone, taking the place of civil servants dismissed in the big post-war purge. Unity kept an eye on the activities of works councils. Unity dominated the trade unions. The second batch of trade union elections went much more smoothly than the first had done since the chief opponent of the communists among the workers—the Social Democratic party—was now a political Siamese twin. 'Members of the Unity party,' said Moscow radio reporting on these elections, 'worked smoothly with progressive members of the Christian Democrats and with independents. This did not fail to tell.' The unions, as in Russia, became an obedient instrument of the central authority. Their main function was no longer to defend the workers' interests but rather to mould the workers' minds in accordance with the directions they received. Education was largely in the hands of Unity, and more than half the school-teachers in the zone joined the party. Many young people were directed to special political schools to receive a grounding in the dogma. The universities were a Unity preserve—over ninety per cent of the students were party members. It was difficult for anyone with a *bourgeois* upbringing to get anything but menial work.

In close association with Unity, women's organizations, antifascist committees and cultural leagues sprang up overnight to extend and deepen the communist grip. Walter Ulbricht helped to create a Free German Youth movement, patterned on the Hitler Jugend, which marched behind red banners to the roll of drums. Russian and German security police kept the population under close political surveillance; Unity party house wardens with control over ration cards were set to watch over tenants, a custom taken straight from Russia. The usual barriers were raised against the influx of knowledge and ideas from the West. The German people were now given only communist news, as formerly they had been given only Nazi news.

At the same time that the zone was being politically 'coordinated', drastic social and economic changes imposed from above were bringing the territory more into line with the rest of eastern Europe. Many former industrialists, traders and businessmen were swept away, either because they were 'war criminals' or because they were industrialists, traders and businessmen. Bank and savings accounts were blocked and the old middle class was pulverized. A large part of industry and commerce was socialized without compensation. A sweeping land reform, applying to medium as well as to large holdings, distributed millions of acres among hundreds of thousands of families. Many of the resulting farms were so uneconomic that ultimate collectivization seemed inevitable. Many farmers who failed to fulfil their deliveries were imprisoned. Overshadowing this social and economic revolution was the seizure or exploitation by Russia of a large part of the wealth of the zone in the name of reparations.

The Russians knew that they, their communist instruments and their imposed changes were all highly unpopular, and they missed no opportunity to win over support. There could not be much good news in a shattered and defeated country which was being stripped bare by deliberate policy of the occupying Power, but such as there was the Unity party was allowed to convey, thus giving the impression that it was successfully serving the interests of the German people by intercession with the Russians. The party, for instance, was given credit by the Russians for obtaining an increase in ration scales, nicely timed to coincide with the onset of cold weather. Grotewohl, the joint chairman of the party, was permitted to announce to a congress of women that the Russians were about to repatriate 120,000 more German prisoners. From time to time, efforts were made to keep up the morale of the people by promises of more fertilizers, agricultural machines, petrol and livestock or by assurances that dismantling was coming to an end. Coal was to be more efficiently distributed. Hopes were held out of higher industrial and agricultural production and of a greater proportion of the product for the home market. Russian imports of food and raw materials into Berlin were well-publicized. The Russians were particularly sensitive about the ration scales in the zone and the German people were frequently assured, with dubious truth, that their rations were better than those in the western zones. When the food position became really alarming, the Russians announced that the fault lay with some German officials, who would be punished. The cultural interests of the people were encouraged within the tight framework of a communist-controlled society. Special efforts were made to win the support of German intellectuals, and membership of the communist-sponsored Cultural Union carried gastronomic as well as aesthetic privileges. Above all, the Russians gave full scope to those German aspirations which did not conflict with Soviet intentions. A propaganda speech made by Mr Molotov at the Paris Peace Conference was 'plugged' throughout the zone. Revenge, it appeared, was not a good counsellor. German industrial strength was an important link in world economy. There must be no thought of annihilation, of separation of the Ruhr, of federalism, of any kind of political division. The Unity leaders spread the glad tidings. 'We cannot but be thankful,' said Grotewohl, 'when at the end of this horrible war one of the belligerent Powers comes to us and says that it is actuated by no revengeful feeling or design of retaliation against us. We would welcome it if similar words came to us from the other side.' The political parties of the zone were allowed to make a public demand that the Saar should remain in Germany, and in November 1946 the Unity party was permitted to produce a draft constitution for a united German Republic.

It is unlikely that these Russian attempts to win over the Germans had much success. They were too blatant and naïve. It is true that the Germans all wanted a united Germany but they did not want a communist Germany. Nor had they forgotten the dismemberment already carried out east of the Oder, the Russian failure to account for hundreds of thousands of German prisoners, the bottomless pit of reparations. This, at least, appeared to be the case when elections were held for the five provincial Governments in the zone. In spite of the great electoral privileges it enjoyed, the Unity party nowhere succeeded in obtaining a clear majority. The communists were therefore obliged to resort to a well-tried method. Coalition Governments were formed, and unanimous decisions were ensured by holding preliminary committee meetings at which the trade unions were brought in as a make-weight. With the support of the unions, the Unity party could always be certain of having its way. Despite its minority position, Unity appointed four of the five Prime Ministers and all the Ministers of the Interior. Conditions were made so unpleasant for the opposition Prime Minister of Thuringia, Dr Paul, that he fled to the West. The Christian Democrat party was subjected to increasing pressure and arrests were frequent. The leader of the party, Jakob Kaiser, declared that the two non-Marxist parties were only 'a fig-leaf for eastern democracy'. After the final unsuccessful meeting of the Foreign Ministers in London just before Christmas, the Russians announced the dismissal of Kaiser and his deputy from the leadership of the Christian Democratic party, and eastern Germany began to move more rapidly in the direction of open one-party rule.

From the beginning, the western allies could hardly have failed to see the drift of Russia's purpose, but they were obsessed by the dangers of division and consequently refused to draw the logical conclusions. The fact was, not merely that Russia did not want a Germany united and free, but that she had already created an eastern zone which was so transmuted that it was no longer capable of taking part in a free union with the western zones. Politically, eastern Germany was oil and western Germany was water. To expect an ultimate unity was hardly

more sensible than to expect a federation of the United States
and the USSR on a basis of common principle. Henceforth, German
unity could become a reality only if all Germany became
communist or if Russia were driven from the eastern zone. Since
the one alternative was undesirable and the other impracticable,
the West should have made the best of division. This was precisely
what it neglected to do.

*   *   *   *   *

Having insulated their own zone as far as possible against outside
influences, the Russians began to interfere in the political
life of the western zones, hoping in the end to capture western
Germany for communism under the very noses of the occupying
Powers. The plan was to extend the fusion of communists and
Social Democrats already accomplished in the east, to the western
zones. In their own zone, they had achieved the merger by
coercion; in the West, it would have to be by persuasion. At an
early stage, therefore, we find communists busily engaged in
spreading Unity propaganda in the western zones. The very
name of the new organization—the Socialist Unity party of
Germany—declared its nation-wide ambition. At the joint conference
in the Russian zone where Unity was founded, a high
proportion of representatives from the western zones were elected
to the executive. For purposes of political infiltration, if for
no other, it was evident that Germany was to be treated as a
whole.

The authorities in the western zones were disturbed by the
activities of Unity, and with reason, for if the Russian project
succeeded and a united, communist-directed opposition to Military
Government in the west were created, administration might
soon become impossible. It was laid down that a Unity party
would not be licensed in the western zones unless there proved to
be a spontaneous demand for it. Moscow radio complained that
Pieck and Grotewohl, invited to attend an organizational meeting
at Essen in the British zone, were refused admission. The
Russian assumption that the west should be open to Unity propagandists,
though the eastern zone was firmly closed to independent
Social Democrats like Dr Schumacher, was characteristic.

The western authorities, however, were anxious not to offend their Russian friends. In August 1946, Unity party representatives from the eastern zone were conducting something like an offensive in the western zones by permission of the British and American military governments. Leading communists like Pieck, Ulbricht, Franz Dahlem and Anton Ackermann, and ex-Social Democrats like Grotewohl, Fechner, Mayer, Lidtke and Frau Kern, were found crusading in many of the largest cities of the west, the ground having been previously prepared by special organizing committees. Great audiences were addressed at Düsseldorf, Essen and Cologne. At Brunswick nearly 20,000 Germans heard the communist leaders. It was only after this damaging broadside that the British authorities clamped down again on the unreciprocated free travel of Unity members from the Russian zone, and the Americans on the formation of Unity committees.

However, no bans could wholly defeat communist persistence. Unity 'cells' were organized secretly with the help of 'activists' smuggled across the zonal border. Thinly-disguised Unity meetings could still be held in the west under the auspices of the Communist party, which was legal. Many circumnavigations of the law were attempted. In Bavaria, for instance, the Communist party tried unsuccessfully to get permission to merge itself with Unity. Frustrated in this, it asked if it might change its own name to the Unity party. Though branches of Unity could not be formed in the west, organizations were set up calling themselves 'Circles Friendly to Unity'. Nobody could accuse the communists of lacking either ingenuity or persistence, and their propaganda efforts had a modicum of success. In Rhineland-Westphalia, for instance, the Social Democratic party was persuaded to enter into a close working agreement with the communists. But because the element of coercion was absent, the Social Democrats in the west were able to retain both their identity and their independence.

Some of Unity's proselytizing efforts were made at a much higher level than the 'cell' or the soap-box. In June 1947 a conference of all-German Prime Ministers was held at Munich to consider various common problems. Though it had been made clear that the conference would not be allowed to discuss politics, the five Prime Ministers from the Russian zone arrived with

113

a long document covering many political matters including the centralization of party problems—a transparent attempt to get the subject of the Unity party on the agenda. When they found that the political ban was to be enforced, they walked out of the conference and left for the Russian zone the same night.

Perhaps the most ambitious effort to popularize Unity in the western zones and represent it as the voice of all Germany was made in November 1947, while the Foreign Ministers were conferring in London. The Unity party called in Berlin a 'German People's Congress for Unity and a Just Peace' and invited all other parties to attend. The Social Democrats and the Christian Democrats recognized the enterprise for what it was—a communist manoeuvre—and refused to have anything to do with it. The Foreign Ministers, by three to one, refused to receive a delegation, and it was left to thirteen Labour Members of Parliament to send to the Congress a message of support and encouragement.

While Unity was representing itself as the authentic voice of the German people, Mr Molotov was trying to clear the obstacles from its path by urging, at the various meetings of the Foreign Ministers, the early establishment of a central German government. He believed, probably correctly, that if the political frontiers of the western zones were once thrown open to the full impact of communist methods, Unity would win. His advocacy of a unified, as opposed to a federal, Germany was pressed with demagogic cynicism. In March 1947 he was even prepared to put the question to the test of a German people's plebiscite—a suggestion which reminded Mr Bevin of Hitler and compelled the amiable M. Bidault to point out that the result would naturally be a foregone conclusion. 'What was left after that,' asked Yermashev in a Moscow broadcast, 'of the claim that the western Powers were defending Germany's interests? To condemn the German people indiscriminately and identify them with the Hitler regime is a dangerous mistake.' Now that Russia believed she could use the German people for her own purposes, the time had clearly come to trust them!

Closely associated with the Unity party's efforts to establish itself on a four-zone basis were the activities of the Free German Youth movement. The western authorities were equally suspicious of this organization, which had soon enrolled nearly half a million Germans, mostly in the 14-18 age group, under communist leadership and was trying to extend its influence in the west. Theoretically, like the World Federation of Democratic Youth, the Free German Youth movement was anti-fascist and non-party, but the storm of applause which greeted the appearance of communist leaders at the first Youth Parliament held in the Russian zone in 1946 showed unmistakably where its political sympathies lay. At this conference, there were present more than a hundred delegates from the western zones who had succeeded in crossing the 'green' frontier illegally and would no doubt return in the same way. The communists complained of the restrictions imposed on the organization in the west. 'In the Hanover area,' said the Russian-licensed *Berliner Zeitung* in December 1946, 'a district organization of the Free German Youth is permitted only in the city itself,' and the British authorities were condemned for favouring small youth clubs and frowning on the creation of a strong youth movement. Again, it seems, the West relented. When the Movement's second annual conference was held at Meissen in the Russian zone in May 1947, the Free German Youth of the western zones was strongly and legally represented. Some interesting facts about the Movement were given, including the information that in Germany as a whole there were 12,000 groups of which nearly 3,000 were in factories and nearly 1,400 in schools. 'Leadership schools' had been established in the Russian zone and more than 6,500 trainees had already passed through courses there. In the British zone, it was claimed, there were now 35,000 members compared with 40,000 in the Social Democratic party's youth organization. Slight progress was being made even in the French zone, where the Movement had been illegal until three months before. The communist leader Pieck, in a militant address, reminded his audience that the Movement was an instrument of Unity. 'Do your share,' he urged returning delegates, 'in the merging of the two socialist parties in all parts of Germany.'

The third prong of attempted communist penetration in the western zones was the trade union movement. Unlike the Russians, the western Powers had made no attempt to establish a huge, centralized and subservient body of trade unions in their zones immediately after victory. They had preferred that the unions should grow from the bottom upwards, and that they

115

should have industrial rather than political aims. The communists had represented this caution as a sign of western hostility to all workers' organizations. Their own proclaimed intention was to set up a Federation of Trade Unions with centralized control and leadership for all Germany, since they knew that in such a Federation the large regimented membership of the eastern zone would carry the day. The project withered when a British trade union delegation reported on it unfavourably in November 1945 and the Allied Control Council withheld its sanction. The best the communists could do was to establish a United Association of Free German Trade Unions in the eastern zone and to hope that it would gradually win adherents in the west.

Russian attempts to get a political foothold in the western zones were backed up by a stream of propaganda designed to bring the western administrations into disrepute. Loyalty to allies in the presence of the common ex-enemy was less than perfunctory. In October 1946 Stalin told Alexander Werth that the Soviet Union was precluded from making use of Germany against the West because she was bound by treaties and because it would be against her national interest. Yet in practice the Russians rarely missed an opportunity of using the German people as a counter against the western allies. At a very early stage they were found attacking the actions of the western Powers before German audiences. Criticisms of western policy voiced by the Russian representative in the Allied Control Council were repeatedly released to the Soviet-licensed German press. The British and Americans deeply resented the breach of etiquette, but in the main refrained from following the Russian example. 'We have no wish to compete for the role of champion of the new Germany,' said the British C-in-C, General Robertson, in February 1947. In the British zone, such powers of press control as existed were used by Military Government far more to protect the Russians than to protect itself.

In Berlin, particularly, the Russians did all they could to discredit and humiliate the West. They made it clear, by such actions as the abduction and arrest of people nominally under the protection of their allies and the retention in power of communist administrators after the defeat of the party in the city's elections, that in their view quadripartite control of Berlin was nominal and temporary. In December 1947 a German meeting which had been banned by the British was held in the Russian-controlled radio station *in the heart of the British sector* under Russian protection. Many plays and films permitted to be shown in the Russian sector were deliberately aimed at bringing the western allies into hatred and contempt. A film exhibited in the Russian sector towards the end of 1947 opened with a commentator saying that the Soviet Union and 'You'—the members of the audience—wanted peace, but that everywhere the warmongers were at work. Shots were then shown of British troops in training, of American warships in the Mediterranean, and of British landing craft setting down commandos on beaches. 'Recognize your enemy' was the commentator's final injunction.

On the whole, the Russian attempts to undermine the authority of the western administrations and to establish their own political institutions in the western zones were a failure. They failed in spite of, or perhaps because of, the large amount of latitude given to them. Within limits, the western authorities consciously adhered to their fundamental principle of permitting the Germans to choose their new political path for themselves. As a result, it was shown once again that communism could expect to win power only if it were backed by force and terror. Had the western zones not been under military occupation, those instruments would no doubt have been used.

The error of the British and American authorities was not in their handling of the problem of Russian infiltration, but in their failure to draw the inescapable conclusion. They continued to talk of co-operation and joint purpose, while the Russians busily tunnelled and excavated in the foundations of the western zones with the evident purpose of bringing the structure down.

* * * * *

It is emphatically no part of the function of this book to attempt a general assessment of western administration in postwar Germany. Two aspects of it, however, throw much light on the respective attitudes of Russia and the West. The first is 'denazification'; the second is 'demilitarization'.

One of the most difficult tasks the western allies had to face after Potsdam was the carrying out of their undertaking to 'denazify' and 'democratize' western Germany. No promise was ever more easy to give or more troublesome to execute. It was a comparatively simple matter to dispose of the top-flight Nazis, but where was the line to be drawn through the rest of the population? Practical considerations suggested that it should be drawn high up. It was all very well to say—as a World Federation of Trade Unions delegation was quoted by *Tass* as saying in July 1946—that 'no Nazi should be considered indispensable'. The fact was that in Hitler's Germany practically everyone in a position of responsibility had felt it wise to join the Nazi party, and an undiscriminating purge would make the task of administering and restoring Germany quite impossible. How could a modern State function properly if its best engineers and scientists and civil servants were set to clean the streets before new men had been trained to do their jobs? That was one problem.

Then there was the moral question. 'Denazification' was bound to develop into a 'witch-hunt' and for that reason was repugnant to western feeling. The sifting, over a period of years, of perhaps millions of cases would poison the moral atmosphere and rot the social fabric. There was real danger that the simple, the obedient and the unpolitically-minded would be roped in, while the clever scoundrels would escape. It was also extremely doubtful whether the process of 're-education' and the cause of democracy would be advanced by the creation of a vast army of degraded citizens.

Finally, there was the administrative problem. Who was to do the purging? How could Military Government, with its exiguous personnel, cope with the swollen dossier of cases and guarantee to treat each individual with even-handed justice? It would take a generation to complete the job. Moreover, what would be the ultimate value of a purge which the German people did not themselves recognize, by their participation, as right and necessary? Yet if the Germans took charge, was it not likely that there would be local vendettas and unwarranted exonerations? Could the Germans be relied upon to do a swift clean job? All these and many other considerations weighed heavily upon the minds and consciences of the western zone administrators.

Their task was not eased by the exhortations and criticisms which flooded in from the east. The Russians had everything to gain from demanding the maximum denazification in the western zones. If the western German economy collapsed through lack of competent German personnel, so much the better. The

West, with one ear tuned to Moscow radio and the other to principle and commonsense, hesitated. The eradication of all active Nazis was apparently not enough. From the communists came a nagging demand for further measures. 'There is only one way of truly denazifying Germany,' said Melnikova in June 1946, 'and that is by resolutely encouraging genuinely democratic parties and forces and by waging determined struggle against all manifestations of fascism and reaction.' But who was 'genuinely democratic'? Not great representative organizations like the Christian Democratic party—they were definitely 'reactionary'. Not the German trade unions in the West, two million strong— they were 'undemocratic', for they refused to surrender themselves to communist wooing. Certainly not the Social Democratic party. Dr Schumacher, who had spent ten years in Hitler's concentration camps, was high on the Russian purge list. *Pravda* called him 'a traitor by choice and calling'. According to Zaslavsky, he was 'a demagogue, blackmailer, persecutor of communists and follower of the fascist school', 'a new Führer', 'a puppet Hitler under Anglo-Saxon influence'. When a man like Schumacher was so categorized, what possibility was there that the Russian appetite for purges in the West would ever be satisfied? The answer, of course, was 'None'. They were insatiable, for in their view only communists and their co-workers were 'democrats'.

Nevertheless, as long as the western Powers cared at all what the Russians thought, they were very vulnerable. Their zones were an open book, and the German communists were tireless in supplying the Russians with propaganda ammunition. If important Nazis were overlooked, if less important ones were temporarily retained in service, if useful men were given the benefit of the doubt, if the process of weeding-out was slow, if the authorities showed any signs of flagging, the Russians always pounced. Reasons or excuses were brushed aside. The West was not attacked, as it might fairly have been, for lack of clear directives, for lack of a consistent policy, for lack of resolution; its motives were attacked. According to the Russians, denazification and democratization were proceeding so unsatisfactorily because the western allies were mentally in league with Nazis, fascists and reactionaries. They were not really trying to make Germany democratic.

There was a scheme, said commentator Hofman in May 1946, to turn over political power in the west of Germany to the armaments combines and the banks. Reactionaries and imperialists were thriving. Viktorov quoted with approval an allegation that Britain and America were deliberately holding up denazification because they wanted to keep a strong Germany. As in the days of Munich, it was hoped that Germany would become a useful ally of the West. In June Moscow radio named several big German industrialists who were 'not behind iron bars but in their directors' offices'. In Hanover, for a time, a 'Nazi war criminal' was chief of police. His subsequent dismissal was given less publicity. 'The democratic reconstruction of Germany,' said Mikhailov in June 1946, 'is being undermined and discredited by the leniency, in some cases the positive encouragement, German diehards are getting from the occupation authorities.' *Tass* said that Hitlerites expelled from the Russian zone were being welcomed in the West and that good jobs were being found for them. A *Red Star* correspondent in July, while compelled to admit after a tour that the Americans had issued 'strict anti-fascist orders and instructions', said that they nevertheless very often encouraged fascist elements. The American decision to pardon all Nazis up to the age of 27, said the Russians in July 1946, 'cannot but fill all liberty-loving people with misgiving'. In August 1946 Mikhailov said the Americans had 'released about 25,000 SS' and the British were about to release 33,000—'about half the war criminals they have in their camps'. The remaining internees were living a life of leisured ease—'a real rest cure'. *Tass* in December 1946 denounced a western plan to acquit young men and women who were children or adolescents when Hitler came to power. The venomous Zaslavsky, writing in *Pravda* in April 1947, said 'the German fascists are keeping a watch on the British authorities, though it is doubtful whether the latter are keeping a check on them'. *Trud* assured its readers in November 1947 that the Anglo-American administration was conducting a 'debauch of police reaction' against democratic organizations. *Izvestia's* Berlin correspondent wrote, 'An industrial police has been formed of SS men.'

To disentangle this mass of charges, to sift the grain of truth from the chaff of distortion and invention, is a task beyond the knowledge and competence of this writer. Though some day, no doubt, a faithful account of the western stewardships will be given to the world by those who know all the facts, the contemporary chronicler of the two post-war years has little to work on but shreds and patches. What the world would have welcomed, and what it did not get, was an early, detailed and authoritative statement of western denazification policy and a comprehensive reply to the charges made. Unlike the 'ill-disposed animal' of fable, the West was slow to defend itself when attacked.

Enough facts emerged, however, to show that western denazification was by no means the hypocritical farce that the Russians alleged. Many western observers would say that it went too far. Consider, for instance, a progress report made to the House of Commons in January 1946 by Mr John Hynd, the Minister responsible for the British zone. The Potsdam agreement, he said, had provided for the exclusion from office of members of the Nazi party who had played more than a nominal part in the organization. In consequence, some 72,000 former Nazis in the British zone alone had been removed from office by the end of 1945. A further 41,486 had been excluded from holding office. The more dangerous were held under arrest and others were directed into suitable employment. A few days later Mr Hynd said that ex-Nazis removed from employment were directed mainly to manual work and that about 40,000 were held in internment camps. Special efforts had been made to eradicate Nazism where it might be most dangerous. In February 1947 a *Times* correspondent reported on the widespread purge which had taken place in the educational system in the British zone. 'There are hardly any textbooks,' he said. 'Nearly all those in use were destroyed as displaying Nazi or militarist tendencies. Perhaps the purge went rather far. One wonders if a child's mind is contaminated by doing a sum about two armoured cars travelling at different speeds along an autobahn.' Anyway, the administration had taken no chances. 'Over 16,000 teachers,' the report went on, 'nearly a quarter of the pre-war number in the zone, have been removed from their posts or refused permission to teach. . . . Schoolmasters who carried out their normal social activities in a village found membership of some Nazi organization inevitable and now suffer for it.' In October 1947 a Member of Parliament, Mr Birch, described the total purge which had been effected in the British zone as 'colossal'. By August 1st, he

121

said, 334,000 persons had been dismissed from office and there were still 23,000 Germans in concentration camps. The plain fact was that, rightly or wrongly, an enormous class of social pariahs had been created. Even the Americans, uneasy though they were about the extent of denazification, had been far from idle. After a period of uncertainty, they had made denazification tribunals responsible to a special German ministry in each of the provincial Governments. In November 1946 the deputy Military Governor in the United States zone was telling Prime Ministers that he was 'thoroughly disappointed' by their failure to rid their ranks of Nazis, and that unless a substantial improvement took place within sixty days, Military Government would itself resume the task of denazification. In March 1947 Mr Marshall told the Foreign Ministers that some two million persons had been registered for investigation.

Contemporary records show many specific charges falling to the ground upon investigation. In December 1945, for instance, Mr D. N. Pritt, KC—whose considerable forensic abilities were frequently devoted to popularizing the Russian cause—was actively questioning Mr Hynd about the employment by Military Government in Hamburg of a number of German Nazis, whom he named. A summary of the answers is illuminating. The first man, Herbst, had been dismissed on October 18th; Kröger had been dismissed on November 12th though there was no evidence that he had been a member of the SS, as had been alleged; Westring had been dismissed and had since been prosecuted. A certain Major Hennigsen had not, as was alleged, been in charge of important political appointments and in any case had been dismissed on November 12th. A Major Schröder had been dismissed on September 22nd. Behind these exchanges it is possible to see many of the elements which made the problem of denazification so difficult—the political nature of the attack; the hearsay charges which often turned out to be erroneous or exaggerated; the difficulty of sifting individuals where so many were necessarily involved; the evident desire to do the right thing once the facts were discovered.

Charges made by Mr Molotov himself, of great propaganda value, were shown to have little substance when the truth was known. During the March conference of Foreign Ministers in Moscow, Britain was specifically accused by Mr Molotov of em-

ploying five named, leading Nazis in the British zone. Mr Bevin
dealt in detail with each of the five cases. Hermann Buecher, he
said, had been chairman of the Allgemeine Elektrische Gesell-
schaft until he had been removed by the British authorities;
Alfred Hugenburg was in a civilian internment camp; Ernst
Poensgen, formerly a director of Vereinigte Stahlwerke, Düsseldorf, was believed to be in an Austrian sanatorium; Wilhelm
Zangen, formerly a director of Mannesmann Röhrenwerke, had
been due to be arrested in May of the previous year but had been
too ill to be moved and was still in hospital; Heinrich Dinkel-
bach, now German head of the North German Iron and Steel
Control, had been given a clean bill of political health by a denazification panel the previous year. Such explanations, of
course, did not result in any modification of the general Russian
charges which were made, not to bring about an improvement
in the administration of the western zones but simply to embar-
rass the administrators.

Particularly unscrupulous were the Russian attacks on the
western zones for allegedly serving the interests of wealthy German industrialists of the Nazi era. *Tass* itself had reported in
August 1946 that the British delegate on the Control Council
had announced that he intended to take control of the whole
metallurgical and steel industry in the British zone until the
question of ultimate ownership was settled. Mr Bevin on several
occasions made it quite plain that whatever happened to these
industries they would certainly not be restored to their former
owners, who had abused their power. Yet Russian propaganda
ceaselessly sought to give the impression that the great industrial
magnates were still controlling and enjoying their property.
When a peat-bog was handed back to the firm of Krupps, the
interest in which had passed for ever from the family, it was reported in the Russian-licensed *Neues Deutschland* that 'such a
war criminal as Krupp is receiving back some of his possessions'.
In March 1947 Mr Molotov himself denounced Britain's
failure to break up the big cartels, completely ignoring the fact
that the process of breaking them up was already far advanced.

All these Russian charges had to be considered in the light of
what the Russians themselves were doing in their own zone. Denazification beyond the Elbe had been carried out on a strictly
empirical basis. No mass-trial of a nation had been attempted.

The worst of the Nazis had been quickly weeded out, but the Russians had not allowed the administration of their zone to be crippled by too many dismissals. On the contrary, realistic as ever, they had forgiven the bulk of former Nazis who were willing to work for them, and many of them held high posts. The western Powers had not in the Soviet zone a puppet party which could be relied upon to keep them abreast of all the facts, and in any case it was not their policy to make counter-charges. But at the Moscow conference of Foreign Ministers Mr Bevin was provoked into producing his own list of employed Nazis—Nazis who were holding high rank in the Soviet zone. There were, he said, thirty or forty such names in his possession. Unlike Mr Bevin, Mr Molotov had no reply to the charge, then or later. All he said was that the accusation would be 'checked and examined'.

Sometimes a particularly flagrant incident would illumine the brazen front of Soviet propaganda. Such a case occurred in Berlin in April 1947 and was reported in some detail by the Berlin correspondent of *The Times*. Communist metal-workers had called a strike as a protest against the re-employment at Siemens works, Spandau, of a certain Dr Wolf Dietrich von Witzleben, a director of the company, who had been denazified on a reversed judgment. When the works council met at Siemens to consider the case, the men showed more interest in another Siemens director, Georg Benkert, whose application for denazification had been dismissed by the same court which cleared Witzleben. The day after his denazification had been refused, Benkert entered the employment of the Russian-controlled No. 20 constructional and technological office of the Saxon Ministry for the Electrical Industry at Niederselitz. The Siemens works council took the opportunity to urge the communist-controlled union to see that in future men dismissed from one post because of their former Nazi activities did not get another 'in German or foreign industry'. 'There is every reason to believe,' said *The Times* correspondent, 'that Benkert's case is by no means unique, and that in spite of violent Russian criticism of denazification in the western zones, a man's political antecedents take second place in the Russian zone to his technical ability and usefulness.'

* * * * *

The Russians were more strident over the alleged failure of the western allies to 'demilitarize' their zones of Germany than over any other single topic. The war had hardly ended before Soviet propaganda began to represent the western zones, and particularly the British zone, as an armed German camp, with the British maintaining German military strength for sinister purposes. The Soviet member of the Control Council was complaining that 'large formations of the German armed forces, and navy, army and air force authorities, continue to exist in the British occupation zone'. Five German military areas had been set up, it was alleged, and 25 district *kommandaturas*. In Schleswig Holstein there were nearly a million officers and men not on a prisoner-of-war basis who were carrying on a programme of military training.

A few days later, Mr Hynd replied briefly to the charge in the House of Commons. German units totalling about 520,000 men had been retained for essential work. This had been necessary because of shortage of British manpower. German staffs had had to be retained to see that British orders were carried out. The units, he explained, had no armament.

After further attacks, the Control Office for the British zone issued, in May 1946, more particulars. By that time there were only 120,000 Germans retained, of whom 75,000 were employed on mine clearance, heavy labour and transport; 23,000 were engaged in ground duties for the RAF, and about 23,000 were employed by the Royal Navy on minesweeping. The units were organized under foremen; their dress was a loose green working garment bearing no resemblance to German field grey. No badges of rank were permitted, but foremen wore two-inch strips of black tape on the upper arm. The employment of these men was still necessary because of the shortage of mobile labour. Surrendered enemy personnel amounting to about $2\frac{1}{2}$ millions had been disbanded, and a further 400,000 had been transferred to other zones. All German headquarters had been dissolved.

This frank and comprehensive statement had no effect whatever on the Russian propaganda campaign. *Pravda,* noting the British admission that 120,000 Germans were still retained of whom 75,000 were engaged in de-mining, declared that the British were forming 'a sort of Black Reichswehr'. The fact that the German formations were engaged in de-mining and servicing transport 'in no way changed the position'. A Moscow broadcast referred to reports of 'organized formations of the former German army numbering hundreds of thousands of officers and men in the western zones'. By November 1946, *Pravda* was quoting reports that the 'Black Reichswehr' was being trained as a punitive body for use against the German people. It was like the parlour game where a sentence like 'The clinic has a long waiting list' is whispered along a row of people and emerges as 'Mr Churchill is a communist'. By January 1947 the Russian-licensed *Berliner Zeitung* had the new German army lined up on the quay at Wesermünde 'for dispatch on foreign service'—'some of them suspect it is intended they should serve in Indonesia'. In February 1947 Moscow radio told a German audience there was evidence that certain British and United States circles were forming an army of mercenaries from foreign cut-throats.

The picture of the western allies conspiring with reactionary German militarists received a damaging blow in February 1947 when allied Intelligence, having patiently held its hand till the moment was ripe, exposed a far-reaching if unpractical SS plot and made a large number of arrests. However, one looks in vain for any word of congratulation or pleasure from the Russians, or any recognition of the anti-Nazi policy which the West was so patently pursuing. The fact was, said Yermashov in a churlish broadcast to the Finns, that 'the western zones offer a good refuge for Germany's reactionary forces'.

At the March meeting of Foreign Ministers in Moscow, Mr Molotov was still complaining about the 81,000 Germans organized as 'auxiliary detachments' in the British zone. Mr Bevin agreed that that was about the number. There were, he said, roughly 20,000 still sweeping and lifting mines. The other 60,000 were cutting timber, repairing roads and so forth. They were 'labour battalions' pure and simple, and in no sense military formations. The men were not in their original units or with their original officers and they were unarmed. They worked with and under the supervision of British units. They were doing highly useful work and saving British lives, and Mr Molotov's whole charge was just a bogy. In any case, the Germans were steadily being replaced by ordinary labour. The intention was to dissolve the labour battalions by the end of the year, and if it was found necessary to keep the mine clearance men on after that, the other Powers would be notified.

Even the Russians now realized that this rich vein of propaganda ore had at last ceased to be payable, and the subject was dropped.

There had, in fact, never been any mystery about the retained German units in the west, where developments were fully reported by British, American and Russian correspondents. The same could not be said about events in the Russian zone. The western allies had studiously refrained from making counter-allegations on the subject of demilitarization of German personnel. There had, however, been some intriguing reports from Berlin about the existence of armed German units in Russia, working in close association with the Red Army. The gist of the charge, transmitted by allied correspondents in Berlin, was that General von Seydlitz, former head of the officially-disbanded League of German Officers in Moscow, had organized a strong German military force in Russia with Russian encouragement and with the co-operation of about eighty former Nazi generals made prisoner during the war. It was also reported that the Russians were quietly recruiting former Wehrmacht officers, particularly skilled technicians, for service with the new cadres.

It was impossible to know how much truth there was in these reports. The evidence, such as it was, was indirect and sketchy. It was significant, however, that when at the March conference of Foreign Ministers Mr Molotov was at last persuaded to say how many German prisoners were still left in Russia, many hundreds of thousands were left unaccounted for. It was, of course, quite possible that they had just died off in Russian hands; it was equally possible that they had not. In any case, what had happened to the large number of German generals and high officers captured by the Russians? Some were back in Germany, holding key posts, like the Russian-appointed Berlin chief-of-police Colonel Paul Markgraf, who had received the Knight's Cross from Hitler during the battle of Stalingrad. But the majority had not been repatriated: what were they doing? It seemed most unlikely that they could still be held as prisoners. Altogether, there was a very large question mark over the demilitarization of Germans in the east.

Though the Russian mirage of a 'Black Reichswehr' in the

127

West faded away through sheer lack of substance, another charge relating to demilitarization was pressed. The western allies, it seemed, had failed to destroy German military potential, as was required by the Potsdam agreement. Britain and America were trying to keep German armaments factories intact, presumably for ultimate use against Russia. As early as April 1946, Orlov referred in an English broadcast to the 'frank programme for the revival of the military economic might of the Rhine-Ruhr region'. In October 1946 *Izvestia* published a report from Copenhagen that many German munitions factories were continuing production in the British zone. Tanks and aircraft were being repaired and spares for tanks, aircraft and warships were still being manufactured on a large scale. V-weapons were being made and shipped to England at factories the names of which were given. After this broadside, an officer of the British Control Commission told the press that all newspapermen were welcome to 'come and see for themselves that the charges were not true'. The Russians did not avail themselves of this opportunity—on the contrary, they decided that this was the opportune moment to recall eight leading correspondents on the ground that they had been denied adequate opportunities to see what they wanted. The propaganda offensive continued. *Pravda* reported in July 1947 that the Wilhelm Schultze factory in Hamburg, an aircraft factory in Hameln, a motor works in Oldenburg and the Deutsche Werke in Kiel were producing armaments and other war supplies for the British army. Flying bombs, it was asserted, continued to be made in Schulenburg, Siegburg, Cuxhaven and Kiel.

All these stories were flatly and officially denied. A British progress report to the Control Council in June 1946 declared that no armaments or warlike stores whatever were being produced in the British zone. What was true was that the destruction of war potential was being held up, chiefly by the wider failure among the four Powers to agree on the complex problem of reparations. Much plant could obviously be turned to civilian purposes, and until it was known what capital reparations would be required for shipment to Russia, demolition in some cases would have to wait. Even so, the work of destroying German war potential had proceeded far in all the western zones. At the March conference in Moscow, Mr Marshall said that 80 out of 117 war

plants in the US zone had been completely liquidated; work on dismantling all remaining top-category war plants was in progress and would be virtually completed in the course of the next few months. The position in the British zone was described by the C-in-C, General Robertson, in August 1947. There were, he said, 198 war plants in the zone. Of these, twenty-nine had been completely liquidated. In sixteen more, demolition of the buildings would complete the liquidation. Forty-three were occupied by British civilian or military personnel and would be destroyed when conditions permitted. In the remaining 110, complete liquidation could not take place until equipment offered in reparations had been removed.

When we turn to the subject of arms plant destruction in the Russian zone we find, once again, a question mark. In the summer of 1946, long lists of German factories alleged to be producing armaments and war supplies for Russia were published in the British press from semi-official sources. It was known that the Russians had found the physical removal of plant to their own country a wasteful process, and it seemed quite likely that they had decided to exploit the German arsenal where it stood. In this connection an interesting paragraph appeared in the *New Statesman and Nation* in September 1946 over the signature of 'Critic', a contributor whose record would acquit him of any anti-Russian bias. 'I have recently been talking,' he wrote, 'to two friends just returned from lengthy periods of service in Munich and Berlin. The first told me that the most remarkable development in Bavaria has been the trek of skilled workers, army officers and managers into the Russian zone where they are offered secure employment and special rations. Many of the jobs, my friend says, are in German armament factories such as Junkers at Dessau, which is now working twenty-four hours a day for the Russians. I was inclined to discount this story until my other friend told me that just before he left Berlin he had actually read a letter which a German socialist had received through the post from the Russian zone. It came from an old party comrade who had worked in a secret armament factory during the war. He wrote that all the old gang are now together again, on secret work.'

Reports of arms production in the Russian zone could not be directly checked. Where the facts could not be physically hidden,

the Russians were found in serious default on their demilitarization undertakings. In March 1947, for instance, Mr Molotov had to admit that the former German aircraft carrier *Graf Zeppelin*, the pocket battleship *Lützow* and the heavy cruiser *Seidlitz* had not yet been destroyed 'owing to the technical nature of the work'. Destruction, he said, would take place by August 1947. The rest is silence.

* * * * *

In view of the heavy suspicions which the Russians harboured, and the ignorance in which the West was kept about the Russian zone, the obvious course was to open up all zones to the impartial inspection and report of a four-Power commission. In December 1945 the Russians suggested that an allied commission of inquiry should visit the British zone to investigate the existence of German military formations. The western allies were in favour of such an investigation provided it applied to all the zones and was expanded to cover war plants as well as personnel. The Russians objected, and a long wrangle followed. In the end, as so often happened, the western Powers accepted a compromise which was really a defeat. The commissions would go to all zones, and would investigate war plants as well as personnel, but *only plants designated by the occupying Power*. Since it was perfectly obvious that no plant in active production of war materials would be designated, the investigation would have no value.

It did, however, result in a remarkable *Tass* report from Berlin in January 1947—a report which seemed to justify the Russians' claim that their press showed 'rare objectivity'. The commission, it seemed, had visited nine former German war plants in the Russian zone. On the basis of this carefully canalized inquiry it was 'able to satisfy itself' (said *Tass*) 'that not a single plant which formerly produced war materials remained in the Soviet zone'. The American representative, Mr Davis (according to *Tass*) 'stated to the press that the Soviet military administration in Germany had brilliantly coped with its task'. The British representative, Mr Richards (according to *Tass*) 'noted that by signing the record he confirmed the actual destruction of German war potential in the Soviet zone'.

Stage management in the western zones was absent. The western allies, with nothing serious to hide, appear to have given the commission its head. Anyway, *Tass* was able to report that a very different picture had emerged in the western zones, and that in their report the commission had noted unanimously that in these zones, particularly in the US zone, liquidation of factories was proceeding in a very unsatisfactory manner. At one factory there were no documents on the amount and nature of equipment destroyed and at another the commission was unable to examine dismantled equipment because the American representative had no key. Two of the factories examined were working for the US army—though it was not alleged that they were producing war material. In the British zone, also, destruction was proceeding slowly. Out of seven factories examined, only one had been destroyed.

If, from the beginning, there had been full four-Power inspection in all zones, the complete picture could have been made public and the long and barren dispute about demilitarization could have been avoided. The Russians, and the Russians alone, opposed such a procedure, and it is reasonable to suppose that the Russians, and the Russians alone, feared such an investigation.

* * * * *

When the Russians accused the western allies of failing to demilitarize their zones, it was presumed by the West that their motive was anxiety about the possible re-emergence of a strong and aggressive Germany—an anxiety which was certainly shared by the West and which in all the circumstances could only be considered right and natural. One of the excuses the Russians had repeatedly advanced for their domination of eastern Europe was that they needed a protective cushion against a resurgence of German militarism. It was to set these anxieties about Germany finally at rest that Mr Byrnes, as early as September 1945, suggested a four-Power treaty guaranteeing the demilitarization of the German state for twenty-five years—a period later increased to forty years. The proposal had at first been well-received by Molotov and Stalin and in February 1946 the Americans had followed it up by sending a draft treaty to Moscow.

Historically it was a document of unique importance. Here was the United States of America finally shaking off the shabby rags of isolationism and stepping forth in shining armour as the guarantor and co-guardian of European peace for forty years to come. Like the later Marshall plan, the offer was the product of clear vision and goodwill. The draft treaty itself was brief and simple. It specified the joint measures to be taken for the complete demilitarization of Germany, it provided for four-Power inspection after the end of the occupation, and it promised swift four-Power sanctions in the event of any violation of the disarmament provisions.

The Russian reaction was hostile. Mr Molotov, after a long delay which the Americans attributed to apathy, harshly criticized the draft treaty. The gist of his criticisms was that the proposal left many aspects of the German problem unsettled, including reparations, cartels and monopolies, democratization, and half a dozen other disputed but irrelevant matters. He produced an alternative draft treaty which appeared to show that he wanted to broaden the proposal into something like a general peace settlement—the very thing which for the time being was visibly unattainable. In vain did Mr Marshall point out that the American treaty was 'against one thing which can be identified and which is most feared; namely, the military re-armament of Germany', and that it would be unwise 'to fail in this task because we cannot agree on a long list of controversial matters'. The Russians had different ideas about the best way to safeguard their security. 'The United States draft,' said Yermashov in April 1947, 'creates the illusion that to safeguard the world against renewed German aggression it is enough merely to disarm Germany without troubling with denazification and demilitarization. . . . That is why the Soviet draft points out that the task of preventing German aggression cannot be accomplished in full without the elimination of German militarism and Nazism and a radical reconstruction of the public life and state system of Germany on a broad democratic basis.'

In the light of the taut American proposals, all this seemed like so much double-talk. In fact, it made absolutely clear that the Russians had no desire for a treaty of guarantee against Germany and indeed were determined to prevent any such thing. They were no longer afraid of Germany. In May 1947 Oleshchuk, deputy chief of the Russian Communist party's propaganda organization, said in a lecture that democratic circles no longer believed that another world threat would come from Germany. And why should they? Russia had already dismembered Germany and was confident of her ability to capture and dominate the whole. It was now the western allies who were the enemy. As for an American guarantee, the sooner United States troops were out of Europe the better. Then it would lie at Russia's feet.

For a brief moment, it seemed that the West was about to see the light. Russia's attitude, said Mr Marshall, 'seems to throw doubts on our common determination even on this basic point'. *The Times* correspondent at the Moscow conference in March wrote, 'the only question in many observers' minds was whether Mr Molotov was deliberately postponing concluding a treaty'. Editorially, however, *The Times* refused to acknowledge so conscious a purpose and preferred to blame 'the peculiar ineptitude of Russian diplomacy'. Stepping carefully over the thread of Soviet intention, it called for 'a supreme effort to avoid a breach, to open up new possibilities of genuine co-operation'. No lover pressing unwelcome attentions upon a lady had ever been more impervious to rebuffs. What *The Times* took for diplomatic ineptitude was simply the consistent execution of a world plan which so far was moving with smoothness and precision towards the end which the dogma had appointed.

CHAPTER VI

GERMANY (II)

In general, the deficiencies of the western allies in their treatment of post-war Germany were due to weakness rather than to stupidity. There is, for instance, no doubt at all that Mr Bevin and his experts knew just what the German problem was as the war ended and pretty well how it should be dealt with.

Germany—and particularly its industrial core, the Ruhr—was at one and the same time Europe's greatest asset and Europe's greatest danger. Without the coal and steel and technical skill of Germany, post-war Europe would have no chance of quick recovery. A prosperous Germany was the *sine qua non* of a prosperous Continent. A Germany abandoned to starvation and ruin would eventually bring Europe to economic disaster. This was elementary. Everyone knew it—even the French.

Yet Germany had repeatedly shown that she could not be trusted with great industrial power. The Ruhr was her arsenal as well as her workshop. If she were allowed to build up her industries once more, would she not again misuse them? This was the anxiety of Europe and the nightmare of France.

The dilemma was obvious, and so was the solution. Prosperity lay in raising German production as fast as possible—which could not be very fast anyway. Security lay in maintaining, perhaps indefinitely, a technical inspection and control of her industrial activities, with allied sanctions in the background. This, too, was elementary. It was also feasible and foolproof.

A corollary was that there could be no substantial reparations for anyone from the western zones. Provided no one cared what happened to Germany, of course, reparations could be taken. Factories could be removed, raw materials looted and half the population allowed to starve to death, with the direst consequences for Europe. But on the assumption that Germany was to recover and play her full part again in the European economy, she would need to keep everything she had and receive a great deal of help from outside into the bargain. If reparations were taken out, that merely meant that more help would have to go in.

Russia was not interested in German recovery. She certainly would not dream of helping to subsidize it. She insisted on reparations, which could be paid only by America and Britain. She opposed the industrial revival and the economic unity which alone could make Germany solvent. Having in these various ways sabotaged essential reconstruction, she put the blame for the whole situation on the western Powers.

The western allies knew they were wrong not to build up Germany, knew they were wrong not to repudiate the whole concept of reparations for Russia, knew they were wrong not to go ahead in their own zones as soon as it became clear that Russia would not treat Germany as an economic whole. Conscious of their economic errors, for the best part of two years they persisted in them. Pulled in one direction by material self-interest and plain horse sense, and in the opposite direction by their determination not to break with Russia, they were half-hearted about everything. Rarely has there been a more pitiful and costly abdication of responsibility. Mr Bevin himself confessed everything in one short sentence when he told the House of Commons in October 1947, 'We have not been free agents in dealing with the problem'.

*   *   *   *   *

The first thing to note is the nature of the zonal division. Germany's main industrial concentrations were in the west; her granary was in the east. The post-war arrangements gave the best of the granary—the part of Germany which before the war had enjoyed a large food surplus—to Poland. Since the Poles were busy expelling the indigenous German population and were themselves short of settlers, many of these rich fields soon became a wilderness. The Russian zone, with considerably more industry, was nevertheless well-balanced and able to feed itself comfortably. The western zones, and particularly the Ruhr, could feed the people only if there were large food imports. Poland sent nothing, and Russia only very small quantities on a barter basis. A great and inescapable burden, therefore, fell upon Britain and America.

This burden was aggravated by the swollen population in the

135

west. Not merely had the Russians and their Polish satellite acquired the areas of food surplus; they had also been active in dispatching unwanted Germans into the western zones. As a result of the spate of refugees, legal and illegal—chiefly elderly people and children and prisoners released by Russia in such a condition that they were unfit for heavy work—the population of the British zone was soon $2\frac{1}{2}$ millions greater than it had been before the war. The population of the British and American zones combined had been increased by something like a quarter. There were, in short, far more mouths to feed than ever before. The Malthusian view that 'with every mouth God sent a pair of hands' had never been more misleading, for the hands were for the most part those of unproductive dependants or 'green' labour needing training. The humanitarian west accepted the influx of homeless people because there was nowhere else for them to go. Callously deported from the east, they must now stay. 'Millions of people,' said Chernaya in a peculiarly nauseating broadcast from Moscow, 'are not a ball to be thrown backwards and forwards.' It was all right, of course, if they were just thrown forwards.

America and Britain shouldered the burden. Ignoring communist propaganda which ceaselessly insinuated that the western Powers were pursuing a 'strategy of starvation' and were deliberately seeking to kill off masses of Germans, they together provided the food necessary to keep forty million Germans alive. Mr Marshall in December 1947 put the cost at £175 millions a year. It had to be done; it was right to do it; what was sent barely sufficed. But let no one think it was easy to do, particularly for Britain. It represented an appreciable and conscious sacrifice.

Russia's contribution was, as usual, criticism and abuse. Part of the trouble in the western zones—though only a small part—was the difficulty of extracting food from the country districts for the towns. A greater measure of centralized political authority for western Germany—ruled out by Russian opposition—would have helped to overcome this difficulty. So would better administration. A census taken in North Rhine-Westphalia in June 1947 showed that only thirty-five per cent of the farms visited had returned their livestock correctly. The Russians chose to see a political policy rather than an administrative shortcoming. Writing in *Izvestia* in March 1947 Moran referred to the hypocrisy of the British in complaining about being unable to feed Germany when actually they were 'reserving food for land-lords'. Ignoring the fact that western Germany never had fed itself and never could, Melnikov wrote in *Izvestia* in April 1947 that the grave food shortage in the western zones was 'actually entirely due to the failure of Britain and the United States to implement land reform'. Moreover, said the Russians, the western Powers were actually importing unnecessary things into Germany with the deliberate purpose of increasing the German debt to them and so consolidating their grip on the country. In December 1947 the Russian-licensed *Neues Deutschland* was allowed to make the fantastic charge that sixty-two per cent of the goods imported into the British and American zones in the second quarter of 1946 had consisted of non-essentials. The Russians talked of 'cakes and wine', unmoved by Mr Bevin's statement that the import programme was on the basis of requirements listed by responsible German authorities. Not for the first time, one feels the lack of a hundred synonyms for the word 'unscrupulous'.

It was the mounting burden of necessary imports into western Germany which finally and belatedly determined the western attitude to Russia's reparations claims and to Germany's industrial rehabilitation. For it soon became clear that unrequited imports would have to continue for many years, even though Germany's export capacity was raised as fast as possible. The distance to be covered was shown by a report of US Military Government for 1947, which said, 'it is unlikely that exports will reach one-tenth of the £500 millions which has been estimated as the minimum necessary for a self-supporting economy'. The most favourable prospect was a long and weary drag to a bare balance of imports and exports at a subsistence level, and even that could be realized only by the withholding of all reparations and the single-minded pursuit of industrial recovery.

*   *   *   *   *

Before the Russian view of reparations is considered, one thing must be made clear. If a nation can rightly be held responsible for the misdeeds of its rulers—and the judgment of the world is that it can—then the Russians were entitled to all the reparation they could get for the immeasurable injury which the German invasion had done them. This writer, who during the war had exceptional opportunities to see for himself the unbelievable devastation to which western Russia was subjected, would be the very last to underrate her moral claim. But the exaction of reparations is not simply a moral question. It is a practical question. The size of reparations has to be determined not merely in the light of the guilty party's capacity to pay but in the light of its effect on general prosperity in an economically-interdependent world.

It is relevant to note in the first place that apart from reparations Russia had acquired assets of considerable value as a result of the war. No one outside Russia can say what was the worth of the booty which she seized during her conquest of eastern Germany. President Berut of Poland told correspondents in December 1945 that he valued Russian removals of equipment, factories and livestock from that part of Germany which subsequently became Polish at £125 millions. The territory which Russia had taken from Poland in the east he valued at £900 millions—a loss for which Poland had been more than compensated by the acquisition of German lands east of the Oder-Neisse line valued at £2,250 millions. These figures, of course, were rough estimates. In addition, Russia had annexed a periphery of valuable territory from Finland, Czechoslovakia, Rumania and East Prussia, including the port and city of Königsberg. In the Far East, although she had suffered no war depredations at the hands of Japan, she had acquired a great deal of territory, some good ports and much booty.

As soon as the fighting was over in the West, Russia began to help herself to reparations from her zone of Germany, both in capital and consumption goods. She never accounted to her allies for any of these reparations. Mr Molotov once undertook to account for 'every kopeck' but the promise was never honoured. At first the Russians concentrated on dismantling plant and equipment and removing them to the Soviet Union. The scale of this operation was perhaps best shown by a report from the Berlin correspondent of the *Manchester Guardian* in March 1947. His figures were of especial interest because they were derived from material used by the German authorities in the Soviet zone and were to some extent official. They showed dismantlings totalling 100 per cent for the plywood industry; 80 per cent for iron foundries and rolling mills; 80 per cent for soda; 60 per cent for the electrical industry; 60 per cent for precision instruments; 60 per cent for nitrogen; 55 per cent for motor vehicles; 55 per cent for heavy industry. Of metallurgical and mining plant, only 7 per cent was left for the use of the Germans. The picture was one of 'almost complete denudation'.

Later, it was decided that the dismantling process had gone far enough. It had proved uneconomic and wasteful. Stories of factory equipment looted from Germany standing rusting in the open air in Russia were almost certainly true. Moreover, the plant was of minor value without the German technicians who knew how to get the best out of it. In October 1946 the Russians were arbitrarily deporting considerable numbers of German specialists to the Soviet Union from their zone of Germany and their sector of Berlin. The Berlin correspondent of *The Times* reported on October 24th that about 700 express train coaches had been assembled at stations in eastern Berlin, that workers were being allowed to take their families, and that the families were being allotted a compartment each. Many of the deportees were technicians in the electrical, radio and precision instrument industries; some were experts in radar, jet propulsion and V-weapons. The element of compulsion varied. In some cases contracts were signed before departure. Men taken from the Zeiss works at Jena received a document stating that they and their families must hold themselves in readiness to go to Russia where new contracts, initially for five years' work in the Soviet Union, would be concluded. The Russians, challenged in the Control Council, declared that 'a few groups of German specialists' had left gladly and voluntarily, 'most of them' under contract. On November 3rd the Russian-controlled Berlin radio blandly announced that the Soviet Government's requirements of skilled German workers were covered for the time being. No more need apply!

Having dismantled and removed to their hearts' content, the Russians settled down to exploit what was left of eastern German industry on the spot. Early in January 1947 Berlin radio announced that 200 large undertakings earmarked for dismantling would be turned instead into Soviet companies. In March 1947 foreign correspondents invited to the Leipzig Trade Fair were able to make some fruitful inquiries about this new development. They found that the large Russian-owned sector of German industry was working at full capacity and covered a wide field. One report estimated that Soviet concerns were controlling 100 per cent of the zone's remaining output of iron and steel, rolling stock and cars; 80 per cent of rolling mills, and 50 per cent of locomotives, machinery and bicycles. A German-owned socialized sector of industry was sending a large part of its output to Russia at low prices, while the small private sector was finding difficulty in keeping going at all for lack of materials.

The correspondent of the *Manchester Guardian* reported from Leipzig that the Drune firm's total output of 300 refrigerators a year was being sent to Russia at £8 apiece. All Mercedes typewriters had been sent to Russia at £4. 12s. each. Ninety per cent of Standard Para rayons and 80 per cent of the Weimar porcelain output was on reparations account. It was difficult, said the report, to find a firm of any size which was not contributing to reparations.

In the absence of official data, no one could say with certainty just what proportion of eastern Germany's post-war output was taken by Russia. But in October 1947, Mr Bevin—who might be supposed to have all the information available—estimated the proportion exported or consumed by Russia at 70 per cent of the whole and thought £1,750 millions was a reasonable valuation of the reparations which Russia had already received. In effect, eastern Germany had become an economic preserve of the occupying Power; almost an economic extension of the Soviet Union. Exports from the zone to foreign countries were included in Russian trade statistics as Russian exports.

The Russians were not content to denude the zone of its plant and industrial output. They stripped the public utilities and 'balkanized' the railways. *The Times* correspondent in Berlin, quoting the Central Traffic Administration of the Russian zone in September 1947, said that 4,375 miles of railway track had been taken up for reparations since 1945 and that all but three main lines were now but a single track. Branch lines had been removed wholesale and train services on many sectors were cut down by three-quarters. In June 1947 orders were received in the Russian zone and sector for the immediate delivery of two million tons of scrap iron. The Russians were locusts.

From the western point of view the whole proceeding was reprehensible mainly because the Russians had undertaken to treat Germany as an economic unit and under that provision were clearly not entitled to strip their own zone bare without regard to what was happening in the other zones.

*   *   *   *   *

Exasperated by the reluctance of the western allies to dispatch additional reparations to Russia and fully conscious of their unrestrained exploitation of their own zone, the Russians adopted a familiar tactic and accused the West of doing precisely what they were doing themselves. Britain and America, the story ran, were making 'a good thing' out of reparations from their own zones. 'The United States and Britain are not showing the slightest intention of renouncing their own share of reparations in favour of Germany,' said *New Times* in January 1947. 'They are actually taking care of their own reparations at their own discretion.' Melnikov, in *Pravda* in February 1947, declared that the western Powers were 'most intensively satisfying their reparations demands' and alleged that Britain and America had already received from Germany sums exceeding the £2,500 millions demanded by the Soviet Government.

First, there was coal. 'Britain,' said Viktorov in April 1947, 'has to all intents and purposes monopolized the Ruhr coal.' She exported it and sold it, and between the purchasing price and the selling price there was a tremendous difference which went into the pockets of British exporters. The Ruhr coal had in effect become a source of reparations to Britain.

The fact was, as had often been explained to the Russians, that because of the uncertain value of the mark, the coal was sold in dollars at world prices, and the difference between the buying and the selling price was credited to the German economy. In this as in all other cases, explanations made no difference. The Russians did not argue about the explanations; they did not seek to investigate or expose them, to challenge or disprove them. They merely went on repeating the same falsehoods as though no explanations had been given. Even as late as December 1947, Mr Molotov was himself to declare that Britain was making 'enormous profits' out of Ruhr coal. Moscow radio

141

told the Germans in January 1947 that 'a considerable portion of the Ruhr coal is being exported to Britain'. In fact, none was being exported to Britain. Hofman in April 1947, having repeated that coal exports 'brought in a very pretty sum to those who had monopolized them', proceeded to build a fantastic superstructure on his original error. The fact that Ruhr output was only 53 per cent of the pre-war figure, he said, was the result of a definite policy of deliberately holding back the increase of coal production so as to keep prices up and make extra profits. This policy was also designed to keep the German coal-mining industry out of the running as a competitor for a long time to come, as Britain's coal industry was experiencing a severe crisis. Vishnyakov, broadcasting in August 1947, embellished the story. 'The Anglo-US masters of the Ruhr,' he said, 'are directly interested in reducing its coal exports, thus creating a coal shortage in Europe and particularly in France. This shortage will contribute to maintaining high prices and compel European countries to buy coal from the United States, which reaps enormous profits in this way.' Such propaganda must be considered in the light of facts which were well known everywhere—that Britain, later assisted by the United States, was making desperate efforts to raise Ruhr output, that Britain's coal crisis was one of acute under-production and would remain so for years, and that demands for American coal so far exceeded the supply that Britain at the height of her need was reluctant to put in a claim for the diversion of shipments.

At a memorable press conference held in Moscow in April 1947, Mr Vishinsky himself told foreign correspondents that Britain had been drawing reparations from her zone in the form of coal. W. N. Ewer, the diplomatic correspondent of the *Daily Herald*, asked, 'Is Mr Vishinsky aware that Britain has not received a single ton of coal from Germany since the war, and if he is aware of this will he be good enough to explain his motives in making charges of this kind?' The question brought no answer, and after a short pause Mr Vishinsky switched his attack and spoke instead of the money which Britain was making out of selling German coal. Ewer asked if Mr Vishinsky was not aware that every penny received by Britain for German coal had gone to pay for German imports. Again, Mr Vishinsky failed to find an answer. Commenting on this remarkable incident, Edward Crankshaw, representing the *Observer,* wrote, 'If this is the best that can be done by the Deputy Foreign Minister and the chief lawyer of the Soviet Union in defence of one of his government's first-line propaganda stories, it suggests very strongly that the British Government is at fault in meekly sitting down under the perpetual barrage of charges from the press and radio of a late ally which crumple up at the first breath of fresh air'.

But this was only the opening shot of the Russian propaganda barrage. In general, it seemed, we were helping ourselves to reparations from Germany's current production on a vast scale. 'Fifty per cent of the current production of some industries is going to Britain, said *New Times* in January 1947. There had been wholesale removal of equipment from 444 German factories on account of British reparations claims. Melnikov said we were confiscating the entire output of some industries. Leonov, writing in *Pravda* in March 1947, conceded that certain sums of Anglo-American money were being spent on imports into the western zones but 'huge sums exceeding these expenditures dozens of times' were 'flowing out of western Germany to Britain and the United States'. In vain did Mr Bevin declare in March 1947 that no reparations from current production were being taken from the British zone. Only four days later Zhukov was writing in *Pravda* that Britain and America were receiving 'regular reparations deliveries out of current German production'. The allegation was not dropped even when Mr Bevin repeated his denial in December 1947 in terms so clear and emphatic that there could be no possibility of misunderstanding. 'I wish to repeat,' he said, 'that all exports from the British zone prior to fusion and from the combined zones since fusion have been charged for at world prices or the closest estimate we could make of world prices, and that the full proceeds of such exports have been devoted to the financing of essential imports into Germany for the benefit of the German economy.'

We were not merely draining Germany of her current production, it appeared—we were also seizing much of her capital—'buying it up for a song' as Leonov put it in March 1947. 'There is no doubt,' wrote Leontyev in *Pravda* in January 1947, 'that as a result of new investments made—which run into millions —American and British capitalists will own far more enterprises than they did before the war.' Stocks and shares of German concerns were being handed over to Americans and Englishmen. Anglo-American measures to bring about the de-cartelization of German industry by putting it under public trustees—measures for which the Russians had pressed and which were adopted in accordance with a four-Power agreement in the Allied Control Council—were deliberately misconstrued as 'appropriation'. 'Such well-known industrial associations as I. G. Farben, Vereinigte Stahlwerke, Opel and many others,' said Leontyev, 'have already passed into the hands of Americans and Englishmen.' Siemens, said the Russian-licensed *Neues Deutschland* in February 1947, had been 'confiscated' by British Military Government. Feingardt, broadcasting from Moscow in German in the same month, said, 'The British have acquired the coal, steel and big arms industries and the Americans have taken over the chemical and light metal alloy industries'. 'British investments in Germany have reached £600 millions,' said *Izvestia* in February 1947. The greedy capitalists were hard at it again. Was it not typical of them, asked Korolkov after a visit to Cologne, that a factory with the word 'Ford' inscribed in white brick on the chimney had been magically saved from destruction by the allied air forces? It may be recalled that in the case of damage to the foreign-owned Rumanian oilfields, the western allies—in the Russian view—had only themselves to blame since they had dropped the bombs. As Prosecutor Kirillovitch said in *The Brothers Karamazov,* 'We are able to accommodate every possible contradiction'.

These stories of allied acquisitions of German capital were repeatedly denied at the official level. Sir Brian Robertson said in February 1947 that no German industries or plants had been sold, given, or made over to any British concerns. In March General Clay, the United States C-in-C, said, 'Investments by the United States in Germany have not been increased by one penny during the occupation'. Mr Bevin, in December 1947, said, 'I wish to repeat my previous denial that any German industry or plant in the British zone has been taken over by either the British Government or any private British or foreign interest'. It might have been a soliloquy for all the good it did.

Then there were the German patents. In the last months of the war, *Tass* explained in November 1946, the allies had set up on the western front special commissions to ascertain the possibilities of the technical and economic exploitation of Germany. By January 1947, *New Times* was writing of the huge income the Anglo-Saxon Powers had derived from 200,000 German patents. *Neues Deutschland* declared that £250 millions could hardly cover their value. Soon the number had risen to 245,000 patents. The value, together with confiscated gold, was £1,250 millions said Melnikov in January 1947. For the truth, we have to go to the measured rebuke delivered by Sir Stafford Cripps at a meeting of the Chartered Institute of Patent Agents in May 1947. It had been constantly suggested, said Sir Stafford, that Britain had derived some exclusive benefit from patents and knowledge acquired in Germany. 'This is a complete misunderstanding. We have made the knowledge available not to our own nationals but to the world. The Russians benefit from it as much as we do; this is made clear by the fact that the Russians have been the best and most consistent purchasers of reports on German production methods. We are delighted that they can and have shared this knowledge, but we are not so pleased when we are accused of deriving an enormous and exclusive advantage from it.'

Early in 1947, *Pravda* started a hare of its own. The British and Americans, it alleged, had helped themselves to German shipping to which they were not entitled. In fact, German shipping had been distributed in the first place by a tripartite commission on which Great Britain, the United States and Russia were represented. This commission had distributed tonnage in roughly equal shares between the three countries, but subsequently Britain and America had voluntarily surrendered their shares for redistribution by the Inter-Allied Reparations Agency among the western nations, and in this redistribution both nations had finally received a small allocation. The British share of ships of the former German Navy and mercantile marine, said Sir Brian Robertson in February 1947, was substantially less than that received by the Soviet Union. *Pravda* found it difficult to nourish this hare, which subsequently died.

Finally, there was gold. The Anglo-Saxon forces, said Zhukov in *Pravda* in March 1947, had seized all the gold in western Germany. The facts, as explained by Mr Bevin in March, were that no gold found in Germany had been or would be made available to the United Kingdom. Gold captured, amounting to 235 tons —the Russians naturally queried the figure—was being held on behalf of those allied countries represented on the Inter-Allied Reparations Agency whose gold had been looted by the Germans. The United Kingdom was not among those countries. Subsequently Mr Marshall made it plain that America also was not an interested party.

The actual reparations taken by the western allies were no secret. In March 1947, Mr Marshall gave details of total reparations amounting to £68,750,000, a figure which included a substantial sum for German assets in America. Mr Bevin gave the corresponding British figure as £22 millions and emphasized again that Britain had taken nothing to which she was not entitled.

The Russians had, or could have had, access to information disproving every one of the allegations which they made. They did not want the information. They preferred to go on repeating their symposium of cock-and-bull stories, undisturbed by facts.

*　　*　　*　　*　　*

It was over reparations for Russia from the western zones that the worst trouble arose in the two years after the war. To understand the dispute, we must go back to the Yalta conference. There, it will be remembered, the Russians staked their 'extremely modest demand' for £2,500 millions of reparations for themselves, and suggested a total of £5,000 millions altogether. The Russians proposed to take a part of their share from the produce of German factories—'reparations from current production' was the phrase.

Both President Roosevelt and Mr Churchill had grave doubts. The British view, in particular, was realistic. Mr Churchill had received from the War Cabinet at home a telegram the gist of which was subsequently revealed by Mr Bevin. The Cabinet 'considered it quite inadmissible to state any figure for German reparations until the possibilities had been properly investigated on the spot'. It pointed out that the reparations total suggested by Russia—£500 millions a year for ten years—was equal to the whole of Germany's pre-war gross exports. 'It was not to be thought that this should be paid by Germany, bombed, defeated, perhaps dismembered, and unable to pay for imports.' The consequence of accepting any such figure was clearly foreseen.

Priority must be given, said the telegram, not to reparations but to Germany's ability to pay for her essential imports, 'otherwise we shall find ourselves paying for the imports to keep Germany alive while others obtain the reparations'. This was indeed prophetic.

Neither Britain nor America accepted at Yalta either the Russian figure or the proposal that reparations should be taken from current production. But the proposals were taken, in whole by the United States and in part by Britain, as a basis for further discussion, and thereafter the Russians continually reverted to them and claimed that agreement to discuss was tantamount to acceptance. 'For the Soviet Union,' Leonov wrote in *Pravda* in March 1947, 'Yalta was no less than a bond sealed with blood and the word of gentlemen—in the Slav meaning of that word.'

The Potsdam agreement of 1945, which since it came later in time was held by the western allies to supersede Yalta, did not mention either a reparations figure or the possibility of collecting reparations from current German production. What its reparations clauses did—and this was their essential vice—was to accept the underlying but incompatible purposes of both Russia and the West. On the one hand, it was taken as basic that Germany, regarded as an economic whole, should be left with enough resources to pay her way. 'Payment of reparations,' said clause 19, 'should leave enough resources to enable the German people to subsist without external assistance.' At the same time, heavy reparations were clearly contemplated. Russia was to be allowed to make 'removals', quantitatively unspecified, from her own zone. In addition she was to have a considerable proportion of the industrial capital equipment to be dismantled in the western zones—equipment 'unnecessary for the German peace economy'. In short, Potsdam assumed—in spite of all the evidence of history and of commonsense—that post-war Germany, broken in spirit and in health, with shattered industries and towns, neglected fields and denuded farms, no mercantile marine, and a swollen, unbalanced and half-starved population, would in some miraculous way have a 'surplus' for distribution as reparations.

It was a wholly unwarranted and disastrous assumption in any conceivable circumstances. The British and Americans were quick to discover their error—their economic advisers can hardly have been unaware of it at the time—and in the two years which followed laid more and more emphasis on making Germany self-supporting and less and less on reparations. It rapidly became clear that western Germany, far from being an asset and the source of a 'surplus', was in fact a colossal liability, and that if any reparations at all went to Russia from the western zones, America and Britain would have to pay them. Russia, on the other hand, was reluctant to admit the error. In April 1947, *New Times* could still write, 'There are ample opportunities for reasonably recovering occupation expenditure and reparations removals simultaneously'. Mr Molotov suggested one way at a meeting of the Foreign Ministers—a further reduction of the rations on which the German people were already practically starving in the west. In any case, the Russians insisted that reparations should have priority. It was on this issue that the Foreign Ministers finally broke in London in December 1947. But in the meantime, the western allies were to give a deplorable exhibition of irresolution. Their path of duty and interest was clear, but repeatedly they were to turn aside, postponing the inevitable breach.

*   *   *   *   *

One of the first tasks after Potsdam was to decide the level of industry which it would be necessary to allow to Germany to enable her to satisfy her minimum peacetime needs. Only after that would it be possible for the West to undertake on any substantial scale the dismantling and removal of 'surplus' plant and equipment. The level of industry, it must be repeated, was to be such as to enable Germany to pay her way and not be a burden on anybody.

The key to the level of industry was steel production. Given a certain annual output of steel as a framework, the main details of the rest of Germany's economy could be filled in without much difficulty. How great a steel production, then, was she to be allowed? Early in 1946 the four Powers reached an agreement. Germany was to be allowed an output of 5,800,000 tons a year, and a capacity of $7\frac{1}{2}$ million tons.

This agreement was a calamity. The permitted level would not enable Germany to subsist unaided and the British, before

signing the agreement, said so. But the French wanted to keep
the level low because France was terrified of German steel production anyway; the Russians wanted to keep it low because at
this time they still feared the industrial revival of western Germany and appeared to have little understanding of the broad
economic issues involved; even the Americans wanted to keep
it well below the 10-12 million tons advocated by the British.
America, indeed, was only now beginning to emerge from the
stage of the Morgenthau plan, which had proposed the virtual
destruction of German industry and the 'pastoralization' of the
country.

The Russians seemed satisfied with the figure agreed upon.
'This measure,' said Linetsky in *Izvestia,* 'is aimed at the reor-
ganization of the German economy on new foundations and the
prevention of the revival of German economy as a base for aggressive war.' The level was 'quite sufficient' to satisfy Germany's peacetime requirements, and *The Times* was sharply
criticized for suggesting that it was too low. 'Concern for German steel is the continuation of a politically dangerous and economically erroneous policy.'

The British, with a clear conscience, soon abandoned any attempt to justify the new level. American support of the figure
hardly survived the signing of the agreement. Nevertheless, for
eighteen months the British—and for many months the Americans—continued to base their dismantling and reparations
plans on a level of industry which they knew to be unworkable.
The British Economic Sub-commission in Germany went on re-
stricting and earmarking and decimating the key industries of
Germany as though the discredited figure were still valid. Meanwhile, the burden on the West steadily mounted. The worst of
both worlds was achieved. German industry was hampered, yet
Russia received next to no plant in reparations. Potsdam was
bearing its fruit.

The continual drawing up of new dismantling lists, the index-
ing and the making of inventories, the destruction and the
threatened destruction had a disastrous effect upon German
morale. Retrospectively, it seems that every conceivable mistake
was made. Small quantities of irreplaceable machinery were removed from some factories, crippling their vital production.
Others worked listlessly under a stay of execution. Decisions

149

were made slowly and changed quickly. So inadequate was the co-ordination, so faulty the planning, that in June 1947 the British Regional Commissioner for Hamburg was appealing to the zonal authorities to withdraw an order for the dismantling of the Blohm and Voss engineering firm, as it was engaged on important repairs to the electricity power station of Hamburg. Everywhere there was dislocation, frustration, and something very like chaos.

The Russians were restive. A first list of dismantlings had been endorsed by the Control Council in December 1945 and a second in April 1946. After that advance deliveries had been interrupted for a time. By November 1946, according to the Russians, the Control Council had assigned only 145 factories to recipients, and assignment was a far cry from transfer. Only one-eighth of all the factories in the British zone had been valued. They complained that some factories earmarked for dismantling were being blown up and that others were being stripped of their equipment, which was being sold to the Germans. In May 1947 the Berlin correspondent of the *Manchester Guardian* reported that of 444 plants scheduled to be dismantled in the British zone, only four had in fact been dismantled and roughly 100 prepared for dismantling. The slowness was in part due to repeated failures to agree upon allocations in the Control Council in Berlin, but most of all it was due to a total lack of faith in the whole basis of the reparations plan. The western allies were marking time.

In December 1946 the British and American zones were fused, for reasons which will be discussed later, and by August 1947—two years after Potsdam—Britain and America had agreed upon a revised level of industry with the unenthusiastic consent of France and in the teeth of Russian protests. The upper level of steel production was now fixed at 10,700,000 tons— roughly the figure which the British had urged in the first place. On this basis, it was believed, German industrial production could be raised from the then existing level of 38 per cent of the pre-war figure to the level of 1936. The western allies were still chasing the chimera of a 'surplus' which could be used for reparations. Even the new high level of permitted German industry would leave room for the dismantling in the British and American zones of 682 enterprises, compared with some 1,636 formerly listed. Time would probably show that these new plans were as wrong-headed as the earlier ones—that by the time 30,000 German workers had actually taken the plant to bits, and transport had been found to move it, and more labour had been found to set it up outside Germany's borders, there would be little advantage to anyone. Time would probably show also that even the new level of industry was insufficient for Germany's minimum peacetime needs. It would probably be seen before long that the only sensible policy for Germany was to set no limits and to press ahead towards a self-sustaining economy at the greatest possible speed. But such a policy, with its frank corollary of no 'surplus' and no reparations, would have meant still more trouble with Russia. There was an important Foreign Ministers' conference ahead, and agreement was still hoped for.

Russian propaganda against the revised level of industry rode off in all directions. The Russians were against it, that was all that was clear. There was not enough dismantling, there was too much dismantling, there was the wrong sort of dismantling. Melnikov, in October 1947, said the new dismantling list was designed to treat Germany's war industry (which under the plan was to be destroyed) 'as an appendage of the war industries of America'. Many of the plants to be dismantled were, it was alleged, essential to the development of German civilian production. The dismantling policy was meeting the 'full resistance' of the German people. Though the plan envisaged the immediate destruction of 302 war plants, there was to be 'next to no dismantling of plants suitable for war production' which had to all intents and purposes been 'totally discontinued'. For propaganda purposes, Russia was now against dismantling—perhaps suspecting that her reparations dream was over. At the 'People's Congress' held by the communists in Berlin in December 1947, there were a conspicuously large number of representatives from firms due to be dismantled in the western zones and—more cynically still—there were even delegations from Germany's forbidden shipbuilding industries.

*　　*　　*　　*　　*

As has been suggested already, the Potsdam assumption that in a post-war Germany shorn of its eastern provinces there would be a 'surplus' from which reparations could be paid was unfounded. But the inevitable deficit in the west would certainly have been much less if, as Potsdam had provided, defeated Germany had been treated as an economic unit. It is emphatically not true of economic affairs, as it is of Euclid, that the parts are equal to the whole. The economic life of a country is like a living organism which functions healthily only when all the limbs are working in unison and all the arteries are free. For that very reason, the Potsdam agreement laid it down without qualification that 'during the period of occupation Germany shall be treated as a single economic unit', and specified the joint economic agencies that were to be established. The French, fearful of any centralization, must take a share of the responsibility for undermining this provision in the period which followed Potsdam. But it was the Russians whose uncompromising rejection of economic unity finally compelled the western allies to go their own way.

In the view of Britain and America, the intention of Potsdam had been that there should be free movement of goods and people throughout the four zones; that all Germany's resources and all Germany's essential requirements should be pooled; that any 'surplus' should be shared in reparations and that any deficit should be jointly borne. The zonal boundaries, in their view, were intended merely to delimit the area in which the common policy would be carried out by each of the four occupying Powers. Economic unity, vital in itself as an aid to German recovery, was all the more necessary for the western allies when it became clear that their zones were going to be a heavy financial burden. Finally, as the deficit mounted, they demanded that Russia should share the load and that reparations payments should be deferred until the large sums already expended on western Germany had been refunded from German exports.

Russia, on the other hand, had never intended that there should be economic unity. Her treatment of the whole eastern zone as her private and exclusive perquisite was plainly incompatible with such a concept. Her purpose was to seize everything which lay within her grasp, and for the rest to put her faith in western appeasement and the skill of Mr Molotov. The western allies, she hoped, would continue to irrigate the German desert so that she could draw refreshment from it. America, from

whom there was no hope of a direct loan, would help to rehabili-
tate Russia's shattered economy with an indirect one. If western Germany could not afford reparations, then America and
Britain would have to pay them. In no circumstances would
Russia contribute to the feeding of the western zones.

Russia's rejection in practice of the principle of economic
unity could not escape the attention of the western allies but for
more than a year they shut their eyes to its implications. In May
1946, Mr Byrnes was raising the question at the meeting of
Foreign Ministers in Paris and receiving no satisfaction whatever. About the same time came the first reaction from the West.
The Americans announced that, until there was economic unity,
there would be no more reparations deliveries from the United
States zone except for factories already allocated. This step,
taken 'to safeguard the economy of the zone' (and incidentally
soon retracted) was at once denounced by the Russians as 'a
crude and flagrant violation of the decisions of the allies'. In
July 1946, Isakov in *Pravda* attacked the whole western position on economic unity. 'The German occupation zones,' he
wrote, 'according to the letter and the spirit of the Potsdam conference decisions, are independent not only in the military and
administrative spheres but also in the economic. This means that
each occupation zone must be regarded as an independent economic unit.' Nothing could have been plainer than this. With all
the authority of the Russian Communist party's chief organ, the
western allies were being told that their hopes of economic unity
were illusory. From that moment, if not earlier, they should have
ceased to nourish them.

Sheer economic necessity, rather than any change of heart,
compelled the West to take a first step to reduce the deficit in the
western zones. America and Britain would in any case have to
continue their heavy subsidies, but a union of the two zones—in
some ways economically complementary—would improve the
prospects of economic revival and reduce the cost to the Anglo-
American tax-payer. Without such a union—and the accom-
panying impulse towards recovery—the cost would probably
grow. In December 1946 an agreement to merge the British and
American zones for economic purposes was concluded, and
'Bizonia' was born.

To say that the western allies took this step regretfully would be to perpetrate a gross understatement. From this moment, indeed, dates a new diplomatic parlour game with which British and American statesmen, military governors and journalists were to divert themselves for at least twelve months. It was called Keeping the Door Open. There was not the least intention, they explained, of shutting Russia out as a result of the bizonal agreement. If she would only change her mind, everyone would be positively overjoyed to welcome her back to the fold. It would always be a pleasure to hear from her. And in the meantime, just to reassure her, the West would proceed very, very cautiously with its reforms.

The Russians, naturally, had no intention of changing their minds, since their course had long since been charted to their satisfaction. However, fusion in the West provided them with a splendid new propaganda peg. There was no real economic need for Bizonia at all, they said. The whole thing was a dirty capitalist plot. The idea was to dismember Germany and so pave the way for an anti-Soviet western *bloc* the political policy of which would be dictated by big landlords and monopolists. German industry in the west—which everyone knew had 'not suffered much war damage'—had been neglected on purpose. 'The production standard lags behind to such an appalling extent,' Marinin wrote in *Pravda* in February 1947, 'because it answers the interests of certain Anglo-Saxon circles.' He proceeded to develop this fascinating argument with spirit. For eighteen months, it seemed, the British and American occupation authorities had been deliberately retarding the development of German industry as a 'definite strategy'. The idea was 'to compromise the regulation of industry on Potsdam lines and so prove the necessity of economic and therefore of political division and achieve the subordination of Germany's western zones to Anglo-American domination'. An additional reason why the British and Americans had worked for disorganization was in order to bring pressure on German industrialists to yield up their enterprises for next to nothing. In this attack, Marinin was backed up by Cherniavsky who, in an English broadcast from Moscow, said the aim of fusion was 'to impose on the western zones an artificial regime of economic stagnation that would send nice profits to Germany's protectors on the other side of the Channel and the Atlantic'.

154

A special paragraph must be devoted to a certain Leonidov, who contributed to *New Times* what can only be described as a farrago of nonsense. There were, it appeared, three groups of conspirators working to dismember Germany and turn it into a 'colony of monopoly capitalism'. They comprised 'leaders of heavy industry in the north of England and the group around the monopolist Birmingham circles connected with finance capitalists of the City and the leaders of the Conservative party', the 'Guest Keen and Nettlefold Trust' connected with 'the Chamberlain family', 'the Berry brothers', 'Sir John Anderson'—all working for 'an arsenal of Birmingham on the Continent of Europe'—the 'powerful United States Catholic group' linked with 'the Vatican' and 'the Morgan bank in New York', 'Dr Bruning' and 'Cardinal Spellman', the 'American steel trusts', 'Rockefeller', the 'steel magnates of Lorraine'—in fact, old uncle Tom Cobleigh and all. They were all united in one great plot.

The western allies, far from dreaming of a political western *bloc*, were so terrified of dividing Europe that they failed to take the minimum measures necessary to make Bizonia a success. The political power of Germans in the fused zones was so slight, responsibility was so divided and liaison so defective that the expected economic benefits conspicuously failed to materialize. In March 1947, Sir Sholto Douglas was at pains to deny that there was any thought of political fusion and General Clay said that American and British Military Government had deliberately refrained from even planning political unification since such a step would lend itself to misinterpretation. The Foreign Ministers were about to discuss the German problem and the Door must be Kept Open.

Before the conference, the Russians took out and dusted the Principle of Unanimity. There was no ground for pessimism, they declared; results could unquestionably be achieved if all parties were ready to collaborate. Had not the satellite treaties shown what could be done when no one tried to impose his will on anyone else? Then the conference assembled, and the Foreign Ministers patiently traversed all their old disagreements. The western allies were unable to meet the Russian demands, notably for the unconditional abandonment of fusion, without dipping still deeper into their pockets, and at last they stood firm.

155

Because this was the first international conference at which they were resolute, it was also the first which ended in total deadlock on every crucial issue. Retrospectively, perhaps the high-light of the talks was Mr Molotov's cool demand for a share in the control of the Ruhr while refusing any share in the cost of its upkeep. Having toasted each other, the Ministers parted with virtually nothing accomplished. However, the Door was Still Open. They would meet again in November.

Statements made after the conference reflected the dispositions of the participants. Mr Bevin stoutly refused to be pessimistic. After weeks on the diplomatic treadmill, he was still not disposed to give up. It was true that on the surface the results might seem disappointing, he said, but the Ministers had actually made more progress towards agreement in many ways than he had dared to hope when he arrived in Moscow. After such a frank exchange of views as had taken place, the conference might well turn out to be a basis for building peace and security. 'I ask the British people to have patience,' he said, 'as we have had to exhibit it.' It was now nearly two years since Potsdam.

Mr Marshall was less cheerful. The conference had clarified the issues—that was about all. 'Critical differences were for the first time brought into the light and now stand clearly defined, so that future negotiations can start with the knowledge of exactly what the issues are that must be settled.' After this piece of wordy flannel, his innermost feelings exploded with the force of a thunderclap in one terse sentence. 'The patient is sinking while the doctors deliberate.'

Even *The Times,* absorbed in the new parlour game, had a moment of realism. 'Not even the failure at Moscow,' it wrote, 'justifies closing the door on hopes of political and economic unity for Germany as a whole, but it justifies an end to the policy of holding it so scrupulously wide open that the resulting draught blights all hope of recovery.'

As for the Russians, they simply refused to admit that the conference had been a failure. They foresaw, of course, the final deadlock; they knew that Mr Molotov's magic was no longer as effective as it had been in Paris. But Russia could still win a little time before the final 'show-down'; could still bring western Germany and western Europe a little nearer to the edge of the economic abyss. So Russian tones were soothing. 'It is natural,' said *Izvestia*, 'that the resolution of such problems cannot be easy and rapid. It demands time first of all. It is quite understandable that the major and complicated problems could not be resolved as the result of one session of the Foreign Ministers' conference.' Stalin seemed quite satisfied, even pleased. The Moscow meetings, he told Mr Marshall, 'were only the first skirmishes and brushes of reconnaissance forces'. One can almost see the avuncular hand resting affectionately on the Foreign Ministerial shoulder.

For the next six months, vitally urgent changes in Bizonia were held up in deference to the diplomatic fiction that the Moscow conference had not been a failure. All concerned were falling over backwards in their efforts to make it clear that four-Power loyalty came before efficiency. The overdue concentration of all the bizonal economic agencies at Frankfurt—a very minor reform—led the Berlin correspondent of the *Manchester Guardian* to say, 'It is stressed that these bodies represent only an interim stage and that there is absolutely no hint of cutting off the other occupying Powers by creating a west German State'. Yet something drastic had to be done, for the economic chaos was alarming. In May, the western Powers set up a bizonal German Economic Council with the task of reconstructing Bizonia as an integrated economic area. The decision was hailed by *The Times* as marking 'the end of the hand-to-mouth arrangements of the past two years and the beginning of planned reconstruction'. Lord Pakenham, now the Minister responsible for the British zone, said that Germany stood 'on the threshold of a new era'. Dr Schumacher, more cautious, called it 'the last chance'. In fact, because political authority was still withheld, the new Council proved a feeble and ineffective body. It was powerless even to compel the province of Bavaria to share its surplus of potatoes with its neighbours. A special correspondent of the *Manchester Guardian* wrote, 'British and American statesmen have never tired of pointing out that the fusion of their zones of occupation is so far an economic fusion only. Their statements have often been received with scepticism, if only because it is not easy to see how economic fusion could possibly work without political unification. But they are true—and in token of the fact, economic fusion has not worked yet'. There had been just sufficient improvement in the economic position of Bizonia to indi-

cate what might have been achieved with greater resolution. But
that was all.

Urgent measures were consciously postponed. In August 1947
Sir Brian Robertson, admitting that the results of fusion were
not very encouraging, said that one of the most serious brakes
on economic recovery was the failure to reform the German currency. But, he added, the British and Americans could not reform the finances of the two zones independently of the rest of
Germany. Such a step would mean the division of Germany, and
the two Powers were quite unwilling to take it unless and until
they were forced to.

Everything must now wait until November; nothing must be
allowed to jeopardize the prospects of November. In August,
the bizonal authorities discussed plans for improving the economy of the Ruhr. 'It is to be hoped,' said *The Times* anxiously,
'that the present talks will leave the door open for Soviet adherence, if the Russians on their side should show a new willingness,
and that the present talks, whatever they may decide, will not
prejudice whatever prospects there may still be of four-Power
agreement in November.' In September Lord Pakenham joined
breezily in the parlour game. 'The British Government,' he said,
'have not held the door open for $2\frac{1}{2}$ weary years in order to bang
it at the eleventh hour. I doubt if Mr Bevin has ever mobilized
greater energies than those he is summoning for November to
prevent a definite split of Germany and Europe.'

The November conference came and went. On the evidence
available to all, there was never the least chance that it could
be anything but a total failure. Mr Molotov produced the Principle of Unanimity, gave it a rather sickly glance, and put it away
again. He knew that the end had come. But he could still put on
an impressive display of propaganda pyrotechnics. Not the least
of his ranging accusations against the western Powers was that
they had come to the conference bent on failure and armed with
a cut-and-dried scheme for setting up a western German State.

General Clay subsequently described this accusation with a
word which has been kept out of these pages only by constant
vigilance. He said, 'It is a flat lie'. And so, incredibly, it turned
out to be. The western allies, paralysed by their loyalty, had
nothing cut-and-dried at all. It would be some weeks before they
announced even the next step on the road to the final and in-

evitable creation of a separate western Germany. And still there was a hankering for the impossible. 'Neither government,' said *The Times,* 'has quite given up the hope of some measure of agreement with the Soviet Union.'

It is not easy to do impartial justice to the political leaders, British and American, who for two and a half years—at enormous cost to their own countries—allowed western Germany to stagnate in a futile attempt to stave off the division of Europe. They could no longer be considered 'first offenders'. They and their predecessors had already offered up many sacrifices—the freedom of eastern Europe, the just claims of Italy, the well-being of millions of deportees—on the same unresponsive altar. Was it really necessary that they should have to come so near to slitting the throat of European revival?

It has been argued that once again the price they paid was worth while 'to get the record straight'—to make it clear, beyond all possibility of doubt, where the responsibility lay for the final breach. It may be so. But it is the task of statesmen to know when the time has come to draw two red lines under the record and make a fresh start. In the case of Germany, it is difficult not to feel that the moment was unduly postponed.

*　　*　　*　　*　　*

To avoid the dullness of a twice-told tale, we can pass quickly over Austria. In many respects, Austria was a Germany in miniature. Here were the four zones and the four sectors of the capital. Here were all the old Russian criticisms of the western allies—that they were supporting Austrian reactionaries, that they were slow in seeking denazification, that they were giving shelter to anti-Soviet elements, that they were trying to turn Austria into a financial colony, that they were planning to make it a strategic bastion against Russia. Here, too, was the same Russian determination to exploit the eastern zone to the limit, the same attempt to capture the Government for communism. It was the West that was anxious to conclude a peace treaty, to restore the economic unity of the country and to end the paralysis brought about by occupation; it was the Russians who wanted delay.

As far as their political designs were concerned, the Russians

159

had no success. It is true that during the 'black-out' which followed their invasion, they had succeeded in installing a provisional Government under the elderly and fanatical pan-German, Dr Karl Renner, without consulting or informing their allies. But at free elections held in November 1945 the Catholic People's party became the strongest political force, and the communists failed to dominate the coalition Government which resulted. Most conspicuous was their lack of success in persuading the Austrian socialists to unite with them. The fact was that the Red Army soldiery had been more than usually brutal and licentious in Austria and its deeds were not forgotten. Nor were the thousands of tons of wheat, meat and fodder which had been looted, or the thousands of head of livestock driven away. The communists reaped the whirlwind of that sowing. The Russians used wooing tactics similar to those employed in Germany. It was, for instance, to the Austrian Communist party that Stalin sent a letter in 1947 saying that all Austrian prisoners would be repatriated by the end of the year. But the results were negligible. From the communist point of view, Austria was politically a total loss.

Economically, things were much brighter. True, it was not quite clear whether the country had been 'conquered' or 'liberated' and on that account the four Powers had agreed that no reparations should be claimed for themselves. The western allies, however, had blithely agreed that it should be permissible to impound 'German assets'. The term 'German assets' had not been defined. One does not seek a written definition of 'love' when a honeymoon is in prospect.

Russia, determined to control the future economy of eastern Austria as she controlled that of the other eastern European countries, would have preferred the old method of setting up joint stock companies for the main enterprises on a 'fifty-fifty' basis and in September 1945 had proposed such a plan for signature by Dr Renner's government. The Austrians, however, had refused as a result of pressure from the West. The Russians thereupon began to take over most of the key plants of the eastern zone under the heading of 'German assets'. By the end of 1947 they controlled some 250 enterprises, including—according to a statement made by Mr Marshall at the March conference of Foreign Ministers—100 per cent of Danubian shipping,

100 per cent of steel production, glass, sulphuric acid, rayon and tobacco, and 50 per cent of hydraulic tools. Moreover, they considered themselves entitled to plants of which foreigners were the beneficial owners. They seized the Zistersdorf oil wells, which had been started as a risky undertaking with the help of British, Canadian and other foreign capital and subsequently enormously developed by the Germans for war-time purposes. In August 1947 Soviet troops occupied a large oil refinery at Lobau in the Soviet zone just outside Vienna which was the property of British and American interests. Earlier they had taken over an edible-oil factory near Vienna which belonged to a British firm.

Though at Moscow in 1943 the Big Three Powers had announced their intention of restoring a 'free and independent' Austria, and the new Austrian government had in fact considerable authority, the Russians treated the factories they had acquired as though they enjoyed extra-territorial rights. Increasingly, these enterprises were isolated from the Austrian economy. Raw materials were imported and the products exported without regard for Austrian law. The bulk of the output went to Russia. Only half the oil was allocated to the home market and the Russians were always in arrears with their deliveries to the western zones. At the Russian factories, where managers had to acknowledge Russian command and ownership, there was plenty of fuel for the machines, plenty of food for the employees. The economic organization set up by the Russians to control their new assets—the 'Administration of Soviet Property in Eastern Austria'—behaved as though it were a State within a State. Statistics of production at Russian-owned plant were consistently withheld.

To the western allies, all this was a lamentable development. They had themselves no claims on Austria—the bulk of the German-owned factories in their zones had been given into the 'trusteeship' of the Austrian Government pending a settlement of the general problem. From 1947 onwards they undertook to bear their own occupation costs. While the Russians were busy milking eastern Austria, the United States in two years gave or loaned to the Austrian Government nearly £70 millions. It was the old game of 'put-and-take' with the West 'putting' and the Russians 'taking'. Because of the industrial development which had occurred in the country during the war years, there was a good chance that post-war Austria could at last become economically viable if she were allowed to keep and control the bulk of her own wealth. Her oil was now sufficient to supply all her needs and to leave a substantial amount for export. But if the Russians insisted on skimming the cream of her economy, it was unlikely that she would ever pay her way. If there were no treaty, and the country were permanently partitioned, 'Austria' would survive only as a geographical recollection.

At all the discussions of the Foreign Ministers, it was the problem of 'German assets' and of Russia's economic intentions that claimed most time. The Russian view, developed over many sessions, was that 'German assets' meant all property that had belonged to Germans before the invasion of Austria in 1938 and all property that had been acquired subsequently unless 'direct forcible action' had been employed or no compensation had been paid. The Russians also claimed all enterprises which had emerged or been developed after the German invasion. They naturally refused to take over any of the liabilities which went with the assets. They refused all suggestions of arbitration. Under their definition, they would retain two-thirds of the oil installations, three-quarters of the refineries and all the reserves of the industry, and as a result would be in a position to exercise complete economic control of the country. They were particularly insistent that their property should not come under Austrian law—while denying, of course, that they sought anything like 'extra-territoriality'—and pressed this demand right up to the final breakdown of negotiations.

To the West, the definition of 'German assets' involved complicated questions of equity and law. It was known that the Nazis, on entering the country, had at once taken steps to transfer all the important industries, utilities and financial institutions into German hands. Every gradation of force and chicanery had been used. Compensation was often nominal. Frequently the Germans entered into sales contracts, paid at low prices, and confiscated the money later. There was a good deal of intimidation short of force. On the whole, the western allies were inclined to believe that the Russians were entitled to only two-thirds of the 'assets' they had seized and that if they took any more it would mean that the Austrians would have been—in Sumner

162

Welles's phrase—'twice robbed'. In any case, the western Powers were wholly opposed to Russian enterprises being worked regardless of Austrian law, though they were prepared to make provision against expropriation.

As can be imagined, here was a complex and highly technical issue capable of providing the Russians with interminable opportunities for 'filibustering'. When the Foreign Ministers themselves failed to agree in March 1947, an Austrian Commission and a fact-finding commission were set up to carry on the task. For five months they wrestled without result. The Russians did not want a result, since any agreement could only mean that they would be required to return a part of their gains. They preferred the *status quo*. Like a first batsman in a 'timeless Test', they stone-walled happily, undeterred by barracking from the western boundary.

When the Foreign Ministers gathered for their final meeting in November 1947, a new French proposal came up for discussion. It sought to get away altogether from the barren attempt to define a 'German asset', and suggested another method of allocation. A substantial part of the oil wells and the shipping would be distributed immediately, and other claims would be commuted into ten yearly payments by Austria of £2½ millions. The western Powers, eager for a settlement, approved this plan in principle, but Mr Molotov made it as plain as anyone could that he would not consider any settlement which required Russia to give up anything. As he would not say what Russia was getting already, there was no alternative but to drop the subject for the time being.

There was one other dispute of substance on which a settlement was found impossible. The Yugoslavs had demanded that what they called 'Slovene Carinthia', a territory in southern Austria rich in iron and lead and containing a valuable rayon industry, should be incorporated in Yugoslavia. Tito backed his case with organized riots. Russia supported Yugoslavia and the western Powers opposed the transfer. A plebiscite in this territory after World War I had gone in favour of Austria and there was no reason to suppose that a new one, unless conducted under the flag of 'eastern democracy', would reverse the decision. Mr Molotov was as persistent on this matter as on all others and in April 1947 he was still appealing for a 'further examination' of a subject which had been exhaustively ventilated. He proposed, on that occasion, that the Foreign Ministers' deputies should be allotted three days for new discussions. 'Why?' asked Mr Marshall. 'They can disagree in two hours.' That summed up the position.

It is not suggested that this brief review of the Austrian question has done more than brush the surface of a complex picture. Considered in isolation from the world scene, there was a good deal in the Russian attitude which might have commanded sympathy. Austria's natural market for the industrial output of her newly-developed oilfield was the Danube valley, and it was proper that economically Russia should expect her to look to the east. The Russian complaint that denazification was perfunctory and inefficient had some foundation, and it was certainly questionable to what extent the country had undergone a change of heart since the Nazi regime. The strategic importance of Austria at the heart of Europe inevitably made it a battleground, and neither side could claim to be wholly disinterested.

The fact is, however—and this is basic to our argument—that what Russia did and wanted in Austria could not be judged except in relation to its world context and particularly its European context. Russia wanted permanent economic control of Austria, and eventual political control, as a part of her own grand design everywhere, and that was the framework in which her claims had to be rejected. It was perhaps fortunate that the question of Austria was always discussed by the Foreign Ministers together with Germany, and that western firmness on the greater problem of Germany automatically involved firmness on the lesser one of Austria as well.

CHAPTER VII

RUSSIA'S SOUTHWARD DRIVE

The end of World War II found Great Britain in anything but an imperialist frame of mind. She was drained of wealth, and knew that she could no longer afford—even if she desired— to hold her positions everywhere against the flood-tide of aggressive nationalism. But to suggest that shortage of men and materials was the only factor in her post-war imperial attitude is to ignore the steady trend towards enlightenment which, with ups and downs, had marked the pre-war years. The plain truth was that Britain no longer wished to hold colonies and dependencies by force against the will of their peoples. The war had strengthened her determination to renounce the old imperialism for ever and to follow a path of constructive conciliation. The election of a Labour Government in 1945 was a sign of the times. Most statesmen and the majority of the British people viewed with pleasure rather than apprehension the prospect of a Commonwealth free from any element of coercion. Hopefully, they looked forward to the transformation of the imperial heritage into a voluntary union of independent States joined only by bonds of friendship and mutual assistance, and relying for their ultimate security on the power and prestige of the United Nations.

Loyal to this ideal, the British Government after the war set to work with firm and conscious purpose to expand the area of self-government in its vast overseas estate and to encourage rather than to repress colonial aspirations. For the first time, public opinion at home was ahead of the nationalist movements and the initiative came from London. In less than three years, India was free; Burma had been allowed to leave the Commonwealth and become an independent sovereign republic; Ceylon had been given self-government; so had Malta. Malaya was moving steadily in the same direction. Measures were hastened to prepare the more advanced colonies for responsible government. There was a great recoil from strategic positions which

165

had long been regarded as vital to the safety of imperial communications and interests. The new Britain felt uneasy about the system of client states and puppet rulers, and about the chain of bases held with the dubious consent or active disapproval of the local inhabitants. Aware of the risks, it still preferred to retire from many advanced positions rather than incur the odium of continued forcible occupation. In the Middle East, particularly, there was a great retreat. The legions were called home from the Levant; Iraq was evacuated; proposals intended to lead to the evacuation of Egypt were pressed. In 1947 the evacuation of Palestine was announced. The whole complex security system from India to Greece, the historic bastion against northern pressure, was being broken up as an act of deliberate policy. There could have been no clearer demonstration of British confidence in the friendly intentions of the Soviet Union.

Russia, however, saw in the great withdrawal the fulfilment of the dogma rather than an act of enlightenment. Here was a magnificent opportunity for a frontal attack on what she conceived to be the disintegrating British Empire. She saw, or thought she saw, the beginnings of a power vacuum which she must occupy before the Americans woke up. The prospects seemed good, for an influential body of American opinion still thought of the British Empire as dangerously imperialistic and likely to lead the United States once again into conflict. For Russia, here was the chance to divide her two enemies and to seize invaluable spoils from the less powerful before help came.

Success would mean not merely the furtherance of ideological ends but the realization of historic Russian aspirations. Before the German attack on Russia Mr Molotov had made clear to Hitler the far-reaching ambitions which Russia entertained in the Middle East and the Persian Gulf. In the post-war period, Russian interest in the Mediterranean was not hidden. When Mr Molotov asked for trusteeship over Tripolitania in September 1945 he said, 'The Soviet Union should take the place that is due to it and therefore should have bases in the Mediterranean for its merchant fleet'. His assurance that 'we do not propose to introduce the Soviet system into this territory apart from the democratic order that is desired by the people' was more sinister than silence would have been. At home, the Russians were reminded of bygone achievements in the Mediterranean. Reviewing a book by Professor Tarle in June 1946, Moscow radio told its home listeners, 'By her three early expeditions into the Mediterranean, Russia once and for all firmly announced that in no circumstances was she prepared to regard the Mediterranean as either a British, French or Turkish lake and that she would in the future stand up for the interests of the Russian people and Russian rights on this most important European sea artery'.

The first objectives of Russia's southward drive were Greece, Turkey and Persia. If these three countries could be brought under communist control, it would be difficult for any part of the Middle East to withstand Soviet pressure. At the same time, Russia would seek to hasten the withdrawal of the British from the bases which still stood in her path. Propaganda from outside or agitation from within would help to clear the Levant, Palestine and Egypt. Nor must the enemy be left in peace to settle down elsewhere and re-form his ranks. If possible, the British must be prised out of Cyprus; their plans to set up bases in Libya must be opposed; their strategic schemes in East Africa must be undermined. There was no contented colonial community which Russian propaganda could not in the end stir into disaffection. Finally, the periphery of Britain's imperial power must not be neglected. No opportunity must be lost to scheme and plot against British rule in every part of the world, or to discredit by propaganda British methods and intentions. After all, Britain was only an ally.

*   *   *   *   *

High up on the list of priorities in Russia's post-war grand strategy was the incorporation of Greece in the eastern European *bloc*. The outline of the plan was to detach Greek Macedonia and include it in a Slav federation which would give Russia control of Salonika, and to bring the rest of the peninsula, together with its strategic islands, under the rule of a Greek communist dictatorship. If this project could be carried out the collapse of Turkey would be expedited, Russian domination of the Aegean would be achieved, and the possibility of an eventual western counter-offensive through the Balkans would be removed.

167

At no time did the Russians seek to honour the understanding reached with Mr Churchill at Moscow that they would keep out of Greek affairs. At no time was there a moment when either British or Greek conciliation could have brought about a satisfactory settlement with the Greek communists. Backed by Russia, the communists aimed at one thing and one thing only— absolute power. Even while the war was on and Bulgaria was an enemy, they were conspiring with Bulgarian communists for the partition of Greece and its transformation into a vassal of Russia. Their fiercest opposition was reserved not for the Germans but for the Greek Nationalists. They always intended to strike for power once the German grip relaxed, and in December 1944 they thought the moment had come. The military arm of the party, ELAS, tried to seize Athens, displaying in the process a brutality which the Greek people never subsequently forgave. The attempted *coup* was frustrated by British troops. Had the rising not been crushed, Greece would at that moment have become a satellite of Russia. Even at the time, the communists knew that they were fighting something more than the battle of Greece. Later, they were to boast in their Athens newspaper *Rizospastis* that they had been the first to fight against Anglo-Saxon imperialism.

Temporarily worsted, the ELAS forces withdrew into the hills to nurse their wounds and prepare for the next round. Russia carried on their fight in the Foreign Ministers' Council, where a campaign was launched against the Greek Government in Athens and efforts were made to bring about the earliest possible withdrawal of the British forces. The British devoted themselves, conscientiously but with little success, to the task of healing the violent political quarrels in Athens, inducing a little cooperation and tolerance, and training a Greek army and gendarmerie for the defensive battle which lay ahead.

Elections in March 1946 were supervised by an international team which Russia refused to join on the ground that it involved 'intervention' in Greek affairs. They were boycotted by the Left and a right-wing and royalist Government was returned to power. 'The elections were held,' said *Tass,* 'in an atmosphere of extraordinary terror.' The view of the supervisors was that they were as fair as any elections could have been in the tense political atmosphere that prevailed. The same thing was true of a plebiscite in September which rehabilitated the Greek monarchy. The fact was that the bulk of the Greek people, increasingly fearful of communism and its threat to the nation, were instinctively moving to the Right.

In August, the Russians had transferred their propaganda offensive to the United Nations. Mr Manuilsky said that a situation had arisen in Greece 'threatening peace', and that all the blame lay with the Greek Government and the British. It seemed that Greece, with her population of seven millions, was deliberately trying to provoke the northern Slav *bloc* of two hundred millions. She was causing frontier incidents; she was systematically firing on Albanian frontier posts and 'peasants in the fields'. She was trying to start an armed conflict with Albania with the intention of annexing Southern Albania. She was persecuting the Slav minority in Macedonia and that was why there was a guerilla movement. The reason all this was possible was that there were still British armed forces in Greece supporting the 'aggressive Royalist elements'. The right of the Greek people to 'free self-determination' was being prejudiced. 'Democrats' were constantly disappearing, and special tribunals of a fascist type were passing death sentences almost daily.

The Security Council held nearly a dozen meetings to discuss the charges. The Russians, who were so eager to ventilate the dispute before the world, as usual refrained from allowing their own people to form a judgment on the facts. After a typical day's hearing in the Council, Soviet newspapers carried many columns devoted to the case against Greece and dismissed the Greek defence in the single sentence: 'Manuilsky was followed by the Greek representative Dendramis who again defended the reactionary policy of the Greek government'. The outcome of the discussions—a decision to take no action—was the first of many UNO deadlocks over the Greek question. The exchanges, said Moscow radio, had 're-emphasized to the whole world the support which the Anglo-Saxon *bloc* is giving to the aggressive policy of Greek reactionaries'. And it praised 'the glorious warriors of ELAS'.

In spite of the 'unbridled repression' which the Greek government was alleged to be using against 'democratic elements', it was noticeable that the Greek communist newspaper *Rizospastis* was still appearing and was regularly to be found in the van of the strident and subversive propaganda campaign. Indeed, one of the remarkable features of this whole period of 'monarchist-royalist-fascism' was the fact—apparently undetected by well-meaning liberals at home—that the tiny and seditious communist minority was seemingly unhampered in its destructive task. The din of accusation was incessant. In September 1946 *Tass* quoted *Rizospastis* as saying that the British were inspiring and organizing civil war and that the first condition of a normal solution of Greece's internal problem was the withdrawal of British troops. In October a renewed British effort to bring about a broadening of the Greek Government by the inclusion of moderate elements was described by the Moscow commentator Hofman as an attempt to split the Greek Opposition. The British Government was itself very unhappy about political developments. It did not like the right-wing regime and constantly sought to liberalize it. But the Greek Right was disinclined to make overtures to anyone. It pointed to the fact that the Yugoslav communist newspaper *Borba* had just published a map of Greece which included Salonika and all Macedonia in a Slav federation. In vain did the British argue that national unity on a broad programme of social and economic reform would be the surest way of warding off the threat to the independence of the country.

By now, the forces of ELAS had rallied. They had been reorganized, trained and re-equipped in communist Yugoslavia during the summer of 1946 and were ready to resume the struggle under the title of 'The Democratic Army'. In the early winter, communist forces took the field under the leadership of Vafiadis or 'General Markos', into whose hands the Germans had delivered Salonika two years before. Ranging the 750-mile long mountain frontier of northern Greece, the rebels soon controlled hundreds of villages in wild and inaccessible country. Using Albania, Yugoslavia and Bulgaria as their base and sanctuary, they successfully defied encirclement and destruction by Greek regular forces. Still, in this 'fascist' state, the Communist party remained legal and its Moscow-trained leader Zachariadis was at large.

The Russian propaganda offensive grew shriller as Greece's northern lands were devastated, her villages burned, her crops destroyed, and more than two hundred thousand of her people put to flight in the face of rebel atrocities which broke new ground. Though it was the rebels who all the time had taken the initiative, though it was the northern communist neighbours whose connivance and support were making that initiative possible, it was the British who were to blame. The British, said Moscow radio, had 'destroyed freedom and democracy in Greece'. Mikhailov, broadcasting from Moscow in English in November 1946, said, 'The Greek Fascist-Royalist gang is in power against the will of the people, backed by British bayonets and British diplomats'. 'The reactionary Greek government,' said *Trud,* 'aims to drag British forces into the war it is conducting against the Greek people.' Yet the truth was that the Greek people, in spite of their political dissensions, were being steadily drawn and knit together by their all but unanimous hostility to what they regarded as a thinly-disguised foreign invasion.

In December 1946, the scene shifted again to the Security Council. Prime Minister Tsaldaris formally complained that the rebels were using the territory of Greece's northern neighbours as a base for their incursions, and the United Nations decided to send out a Commission to investigate the position on the spot.

British efforts to obtain a more representative Greek Government were untiring. They still met with little success and received no thanks from anyone. A change in the administration in January 1947, described by the *Manchester Guardian* as 'a very slight broadening towards the Right and Centre', was the result, said *Tass,* of the 'backstage machinations of the British'.

Then the Americans appeared on the scene. The British Government had spent nearly £100 millions, not one penny of which it could afford, on trying to preserve the independence of post-war Greece. It could spend no more. In March 1947, President Truman announced that help would be given to countries threatened by communist aggression and Greece headed the list, with Turkey a close second. The Truman Doctrine was a defensive measure; a belated defensive measure. Denounced by communists and fellow-travellers everywhere as an open manifestation of rampant American imperialism, it was in fact nothing but the first step to a policy of 'containing' communism. To soften its impact, the Americans themselves provided that the planned aid would be discontinued if the General Assembly of UNO or the Security Council expressed disapproval. The flag

171

of liberalism was publicly nailed to the Doctrine. 'We have condemned in the past,' said President Truman, 'and we condemn now extremist measures of the Right or Left. We have in the past advised tolerance and we advise it now.'

Mr Gromyko did his best to exploit American uneasiness. The Truman Doctrine had gravely weakened the United Nations, he said. It had pre-judged the findings of the UNO Commission. The alleged threat to Greece was properly a matter for the Security Council (where effective action could always be blocked by Russia's veto). Aid to Greece should properly be provided by the United Nations (which had no money). But American opinion recovered its stability and the Truman Doctrine was finally approved. A slow trickle of American aid began to move towards the eastern Mediterranean, accompanied by a show of naval and air strength.

The UNO Commission of investigation was meanwhile hard at work investigating charges and counter-charges. It had set out with vigour and enthusiasm, but hardly had it reached the Balkans before its nine members split into two hostile factions. Seventy-three meetings were held, and almost every one involved passionate debate. The Commissioners travelled hundreds of uncomfortable miles, many on mule-back. In Greece, all facilities were provided and communist witnesses—strangely unaware of the 'fascist terror' around them—appeared openly to give their evidence against the Greek Government. In Yugoslavia and Bulgaria, however, there was a significant lack of opposition to the policies of the two Governments. All witnesses favoured the rebels. 'On-the-spot' investigation in the territory of the northern neighbours was discouraged. In rebel territory, the Commission met nothing but obstruction. Commissioners made a fantastic journey on mule-back in an attempt to see 'General Markos' by appointment. After waiting at the rendezvous for several days, the majority decided to return to their base. The Russians and Poles, with their Yugoslav, Bulgarian and Albanian liaison officers, decided to wait. Miraculously, 'General Markos' at once appeared and an enjoyable party meeting was held by all. Shortly afterwards, the Russian group returned to the commission with a 285-page memorandum of 'evidence'.

Naturally, the final report of the Commission was not unanimous. The Russians and the Poles put all the blame upon the Greek Government. The view of the majority was that Yugoslavia and to a less extent Bulgaria and Albania had supported the rebels; that Yugoslavia had established a camp at Bulkes where Greek refugees were given political and military training before being sent back to fight in Greece; that Albania had provided similar facilities at Rubig near Tirana, as well as guides and liaison assistance; that Bulgaria had provided hospital facilities and arms as well as help in crossing frontiers; that Yugoslavia and Bulgaria had openly supported a Macedonian separatist movement, though Greek persecution of Macedonian Slavs had offered a fertile breeding ground. Both sides were blamed for frontier incidents, with Greek persecution a contributory factor. The majority commented on the considerable measure of political freedom existing in Greece, but declared there was evidence of brutalities by Greek gendarmerie and right-wing bands.

In July, Moscow radio said the object of the majority report was to confuse the issue and save the Greek Government from the just charges brought by Yugoslavia, Bulgaria and Albania. When the Security Council came to consider the report, the Russian delegate vetoed further action, thereby showing the nature of the authority which the Truman Doctrine was alleged to have undermined.

The Commission had left behind on the frontier a subsidiary group to continue to watch events. Russia had opposed this step in the Security Council; she had also tried to sabotage the work of the sub-commission by suggesting that it should not be allowed to investigate anything without consent of the parent body and that its headquarters should be shifted from Salonika, which was near the scene of the fighting, to Athens, which was not. This move, also, was defeated. Nevertheless, the northern neighbours, backed up by Russia, refused to recognize the authority of the subsidiary group and henceforth flouted every decision of the Security Council on the subject of Greece. Repeatedly, the Commissioners were turned back by frontier guards when they attempted to pursue their inquiries across the northern borders. Yugoslavia, refusing permission for the investigation of two 'incidents', coolly declared that she had carried out her own investigations and was satisfied that the 'incidents' had not taken place. On one occasion the Commissioners sought to get to the bottom of an 'incident' on the Bulgarian border after informing Bulgaria of their intention. On this trip they took with them four guerillas prepared to testify that they had been led across the frontier to a 'rest camp' north of Sofia. At the border, Bulgarian guards turned the sub-commission back. It was Bulgaria, incidentally, which had announced a few months earlier that 'Bulgarian public opinion calmly and confidently awaits the investigation'. After this 'insult' from Bulgaria, the French delegate suggested that the sub-commission should abandon its task. The Soviet representative eagerly supported the proposal, which was not accepted. No criminal had ever been more anxious to divert the attention of the police from the scene of a crime.

When the Greek question was raised in the General Assembly of UNO late in 1947, the Russians and their satellites maintained their attitude of defiance. Russia opposed at every stage a proposal—finally carried—that a permanent Commission should be kept on the frontier and subsequently the Slav countries all made it clear that they would give the Commission no facilities.

In Athens, meanwhile, the American Mission had been proving a good deal tougher than the British had been, perhaps because it had more to offer as a reward for good behaviour or perhaps because it had fewer inhibitions about 'intervention'. In May 1947 it was urging an amnesty of political prisoners under international supervision. 'World opinion,' said a stiff American Note, 'formerly well-disposed towards Greece, is now feeling that the Greek Government is not dealing with justice and fairness in the amnesty question.' The Americans were also anxious to proceed with the complex and urgent task of economic and financial reconstruction and required the more active co-operation of the Greek authorities. The Greek Government, visibly chastened, acknowledged a long list of duties including the improvement of administration and the encouragement of democratic organizations. It was, as the *Manchester Guardian* said, 'as much a confession of things left undone in the past as a promise to do better in the future'. Increasing American pressure was applied to bring about the formation of a broader-based Government. A one-party Government was stated to be 'inadmissible'. In September the Americans had their way. A

Government was formed by the veteran Liberal leader, Themistocles Sophoulis, who earlier in the struggle had been in Russian good books for his denunciations of right-wing 'terror'. Behind Sophoulis, all Greek elements rallied except the communist fringe. The Government was so broad, said one correspondent, that it sagged in the middle. The measure of agreement certainly surpassed all expectations. The Royalist-Republican feud was laid aside; ancient antagonisms between the historic Liberal and Populist parties were buried. In the Chamber, the new Government received an almost unanimous vote of confidence. At last, the communists had united everyone against them. If any Government could stop the civil war by liberal and conciliatory measures, this one could. The claim of the Left that 'rebellion' had been evoked by 'reaction' was about to be put to the test. That was why the communists attacked the new Government even more savagely than they had attacked the old one. It was, said *Rizospastis,* 'a monster brought forth by American midwives'.

The new Government, urged on by its American and British advisers, declared an amnesty, and though the civil war was at its height proceeded to set free half its political prisoners. Earlier, the rebels had protested that reconciliation was what they most desired and that an amnesty would bring rebellion to a halt. Yet in two months only 5,000 men took advantage of the amnesty. In the rebel areas, men found reading the amnesty proclamation were shot. The claim that right-wing terrorism was responsible for the civil war had been finally exploded.

While the governmental change was in progress, the struggle in the north had taken on a sharper aspect. With the stream of American aid steadily mounting, a popular Government in power in Athens and a growing unity among the Greek people, it was clear that the communists must win quickly if they were to win at all. In the summer, the Greek delegate to a French Communist party congress at Strasbourg had foreshadowed the establishment of a 'free Greek Government' in the territory held by the rebels. In August 'Markos' announced from his radio station in Albania a 'constitutional charter' for the rebel districts. 'People's committees' were to be elected. As though to emphasize the nation-wide ambitions of the rebel movement, King Paul was declared dethroned. At the end of 1947 'Markos' took the logical step and proclaimed his 'free Greek Government', which consisted almost entirely of communists. Simultaneously he launched a full-scale offensive in an attempt to seize the town of Konitza as his 'capital'. He was backed by all the weight of Russian and Cominform propaganda, and more materially assisted by some newly-acquired heavy artillery with which he pounded the town from the security of Albanian territory. The offensive failed, but the prospects for Greece remained dark. The rebels could not be pursued and destroyed as long as the Greek regulars were obliged to respect the frontiers of the northern neighbours, and it seemed likely that 'Markos' would receive increasing and more open assistance from the Slav states. At best, the protracted frontier battle would be a 'running sore', draining Greece of the strength she so badly needed for peaceful reconstruction.

No post-war event produced more soul-searching or more muddled thinking in the West than the Greek civil war. Understandably critical of many aspects of Greek government, western liberalism failed to see to the heart of the problem. Not for the first time, a situation which formed part of the pattern of Russian world strategy was judged on its local merits. Western liberals would not see that Moscow was pumping poison into the body of the world and that of the boils which erupted in consequence, the Greek civil war was one. It could be argued that Athens was full of black reactionaries, that the Islands were crowded with political internees, that atrocities were committed on both sides, that the Greeks were illiberal to their northern minorities, that the Greek political parties were uncompromising and intolerant, that there was graft and privilege and a marked disinclination to carry out economic and social reforms. But, true or not, these things were largely irrelevant. The thesis of *The Times,* that 'a radical change of policy by those in power in Athens will alone bring the fighting to an end', was exploded when a 'radical change of policy' brought nothing but an intensification of the northern invasion. A better Government in Greece, a less repressive attitude to the minorities, might have reduced by a handful the total of the rebel forces. But if Greece had been a democratic paradise, a political Garden of Eden, the civil war would have occurred just the same. Had there been no grievances, the communists would have had to invent some.

176

For this civil war was planned and ordered in Moscow and its success was considered a vital Soviet interest.

* * * * *

If the Russians were to succeed in their aim of expanding southwards and breaking up Britain's Middle East positions, Turkey—like Greece—was an obvious objective. It lay across the path of advance like a felled oak. Once Turkey was reduced to subservience by infiltration or pressure, there was every prospect that the rest of the Middle East would crumple.

Russia opened her offensive against Turkey by indicating in March 1945 that she was not prepared to renew the pre-war Russo-Turkish treaty of friendship on the old terms. Mr Molotov outlined his new requirements to the Turkish Ambassador. Russia, he explained, wanted bases in the Straits and the cession of three Turkish provinces. These demands, had they been accepted, would probably have sufficed to destroy the integrity of the Turkish State.

Turkey's flat refusal to pay so high a price for 'friendship' called forth a Soviet war of nerves on lines made distressingly familiar by Hitler. Day after day, Moscow radio blared its hostility. Turkey was a pro-Nazi and undemocratic State, relying on force to crush all popular movements and institutions. Its elections were riddled with irregularities. It was serving foreign interests and putting its territory at the disposal of the British and Americans for such provocative purposes as the building of anti-tank fortifications and the construction of coastal defences. Had the Turks forgotten that only a quarter of a century ago British and American imperialists had 'tortured the nationalist revolutionaries and assaulted Turkish women'? The Turkish government was persecuting its national minorities, withholding lands which rightfully belonged to Russia and refusing Russian co-operation in the defence of the Straits. Behind the din, and not far behind, there was the ugly threat of force.

The Russian campaign for the dismemberment of Turkey was pressed with ingenuity and persistence. The resources of what passed in the Soviet Union for scholarship were quickly mobilized. In the early summer of 1946, a Professor Dakaishivili published in the Tiflis newspaper *Zarya Vostoka* an article en-

177

titled 'Georgian Lands Seized by Turkey'. 'Within the borders
of Turkey,' wrote the Professor, 'is a part of the southern territory of Georgia. . . . These lands are an inseparable part of
Georgia and prospered thanks to the labour and cultural efforts
of her sons. The Georgian nation is not reconciled and never will
be reconciled to the seizure of these lands by the Turkish usur-
pers.' Now that the war was over, said the Professor, 'the time
has come to right many historic injustices'. Georgians had contributed to victory, therefore 'the legitimate demands of the
Georgian people must be satisfied'. But this campaign, which
would have transferred a considerable tract of Turkey to Russia
including the towns of Trebizond and Kerassund on the Black
Sea, was not regarded as very promising and the demands were
soon put into cold storage.

The Russians were more hopeful about an attempt to create
a division in Turkey by stirring up the Turkish Kurds against
the central government. 'Is There a Kurd Question?' asked *Trud*
in June 1946, and decided that there was. It appeared, however,
that there was no Kurd answer, for the Turkish Kurds showed
little disposition to respond.

The claim which the Russians pressed most vigorously was
for the cession of the Turkish province of Kars and district of
Ardahan, which they described as 'the most fertile lands of the
Armenian republic'. These territories, long a part of the Turkish
Empire, were given to Russia by the Treaty of Berlin of 1878 to
ensure the payment of a Turkish war indemnity. After the Russian Revolution, Lenin revoked this piece of imperialist annexation and returned them to Turkish sovereignty. A plebiscite held
at the time, and recognized as valid by the Soviet authorities,
resulted in an overwhelming majority in favour of Turkey. The
greater part of the inhabitants had always been Moslem and the
preponderance had been increased by Turkish massacres and
Armenian flight during and after World War I. 'The whole
world knows,' said the Turkish Foreign Minister in 1945, 'that
there is not a single Armenian living in these territories', and even
Russia had to admit the fact. For regrettable historical reasons,
there was no longer an Armenian minority. On ethnic and juridical grounds alike, Russia had not the vestige of a case. However, she devised a plan which even Hitler had lacked the wit to
think of. There was no pressure of population in Soviet Armenia

178

anxious to overflow into new lands, so one must be created. A head of nationalist steam would be deliberately built up; the population would be increased first, and the demand for *lebensraum* would then be greatly strengthened. In 1946, therefore, the Russians began to comb the world for Armenians willing to return to the Soviet motherland in return for lavish promises. Reception centres were set up with much publicity on the Soviet side of the Persian border. Immigrants would be allowed to practise their chosen professions and would be granted house-building loans which they could repay in instalments. Communist-sponsored repatriation committees were established far afield. In July 1946 a committee in Sao Paulo, Brazil, applauded 'the great and humane act of the Soviet Union in permitting the repatriation of Armenians scattered all over the world'. It was clear, however, that the motive was not purely humanitarian, for in July 1946 an American Committee for Armenian Rights was protesting against a United States loan to Turkey and in May 1947 a World Armenian Congress in New York was defining its main aim as 'the liberation of lost Armenian territory' and its annexation to 'our now beautiful Soviet Armenia'. In July 1947, *Tass* reported that American Armenians had requested the United Nations 'to settle the Armenian question by restoring to Soviet Armenia the districts wrested from her by Turkey'.

The campaign had its colourful aspects. Immigrants arriving from Syria, Persia, Bulgaria and Greece displayed their enthusiasm in such identical terms that their suitability as immigrants to Russia could hardly be doubted. One body of Greeks sent a telegram to Moscow expressing its 'gratitude to the great Stalin for his fatherly solicitude'. *Tass,* not usually gravelled for lack of matter, said in July 'The joy of the Armenians on treading Soviet soil defies description'.

Still the build-up went on. In November 1946 *Tass* declared that 800,000 of the million Armenians residing abroad had asked for visas. Let them all come! 'Half a century ago,' *Tass* said, 'over one million Armenians lived in that part of Armenia which was seized by Turkey.' Meanwhile, the head of steam in Soviet Armenia was rising nicely. An itinerant representative of the British-Soviet Society—that non-political body which was always so much more Soviet than British—broadcast from Moscow in August 1946 that the reason feeling about the ancient lands was so intense in Soviet Armenia was that the country could not easily absorb its population. In 1946, 51,000 Armenians were repatriated and in 1947 a further 60,000.

With equal vigour, though by more direct means, the Russians pressed their claims for control of the Straits. What they wanted was to be left to negotiate a new arrangement with an unsupported Turkey. They would be backed up by their dutiful Black Sea satellites. Turkey would be isolated. As long ago as 1939, when the Russo-Turkish non-aggression pact had been signed in Moscow, Stalin had suggested to the Turkish Foreign Minister that Russia and Turkey could settle the Straits question quietly and amicably between themselves. At Potsdam, it had been agreed by the Big Three that as a first step to securing the revision of the Montreux Convention, which regulated Turkey's guardianship over the Straits, each Power should approach Turkey individually and directly.

The gist of Russia's case was that in World War II, as in most previous wars that had threatened Russia, Turkey had granted the opposite side the use of the Straits. She demanded that the establishment of a new regime should be regarded as the affair solely of the Black Sea countries; that Turkey and Russia, as the nations chiefly interested, should jointly devise a defence plan, and that this should provide for Russian bases and fortifications.

On grounds of security and fair dealing, Russia could make a good case on paper for the control by herself of a waterway which led nowhere except into a closed sea in which she had a predominant interest. But Russian command of the Dardanelles and the Bosphorus would mean the bisection and could easily mean the disruption of Turkey. The claim was flatly rejected by Turkey, Britain and America, who did not believe that it was a purely defensive measure. Only their combined firmness prevented Russia from imposing her will by force.

*　　*　　*　　*　　*

In the post-war period, Russian pressure was nowhere exerted more flagrantly than in Persia. The immediate and avowed objective was the right to exploit the oil-bearing region of Azerbaijan in Northern Persia. Subsequent events suggested that

Russian ambitions were more far-reaching and that oil—though no doubt valuable in itself if Azerbaijan should prove to contain it in payable quantities—was regarded also as a convenient lubricant for Soviet southward penetration. Whether or not the Russians believed that they would succeed in taking over suzerainty in the Persian Gulf from a decaying British Empire, they certainly made a determined attempt to bring the whole of Persia under their control.

Russia had first raised the question of a northern oil concession in the autumn of 1944. Her demands, backed by 'spontaneous' demonstrations organized in Teheran by Soviet agents, had resulted in what Moscow termed 'a defiant refusal'. The Persian Government had said that it could not give a final decision until the war was over, and it was plain that a good deal of coercion would be necessary.

The instrument of 'persuasion' which the Russians forged was the 'Democratic Party' of Azerbaijan, an area then under the physical occupation of the Red Army. This party had no roots in the soil but it soon had many branches, tended and trained by a communist from Russia named Pishevari. By November 1945, 'disturbances' and 'incidents' were occurring in the north, aimed at undermining the Teheran Government's already much-diminished authority. At first, Russia tried to cover up the activities of its puppet. *Tass* talked of 'crude falsifications' in the Persian press about a 'revolt' in the northern provinces. 'Persons not above suspicion in the capital,' it said, 'continue to spread rumours about a non-existent separatist movement among the Azerbaijanians.' At the same time, the central Government at Teheran was having to complain to the Russians that the Democrats were inciting the Kurdish tribes to revolt, that the transport of food to the south was being obstructed, and that the appointment of gendarmes and officials was being taken out of its hands. It asked to be allowed to send troops to restore the position. The Russian refusal was characteristically couched. 'Believing it necessary to avoid any complications undesirable for both the Persian and Soviet Government . . . the Soviet Government finds this measure inexpedient at the present time. It should be considered that if more Persian troops are brought into these districts . . . this will cause disturbances and possibly bloodshed in northern Persia and consequently the Soviet Government will

181

be compelled to bring into Persia additional troops of its own to maintain order and ensure the security of the Soviet garrison.'

All the developments in the early months of 1946 took place against a background of Russian military force. There was need for haste, for by an agreement with the western Powers the Russians were committed to withdraw their troops from Persia by March. In February the Persian Prime Minister, Qavam-es-Sultaneh, was persuaded to visit Moscow for friendly talks. He had been brought to power in Teheran as a result of Russian pressure and was regarded by the Russians as malleable. The atmosphere in Moscow was 'cordial' and Qavam expressed his readiness to be reasonable. In April, he concluded an agreement with the Russians. The plan was to form a joint Soviet-Persian oil company to exploit the deposits of Azerbaijan. Russia would have a 51 per cent interest in the concern. Qavam could not, of course, sign such an agreement without the approval of the Persian Majlis (Parliament). Unfortunately, he pointed out, there was at present no Majlis and under Persian law there could not be elections for a new one until all foreign troops had left Persian soil. He would see, however, that the agreement was brought before a new Majlis within seven months. He would also recognize what had happened in Azerbaijan as a 'purely internal affair' of the Azerbaijanians. The Russians, who felt confident that they would be able to engineer a complaisant Majlis into being with the help of the Democratic Party, agreed in the circumstances to withdraw their troops from Persia, which they had omitted to do in early March as their international commitments required.

Qavam's hand in these negotiations had been weakened by events in Azerbaijan, where Pishevari had been steadily consolidating his position and where the writ of Teheran was now ignored. In April Tabriz radio, the mouthpiece of the Democrats, announced that a 20-year treaty had been signed between the 'National Governments' of Azerbaijan and Kurdistan. The two 'nations' promised each other mutual assistance against aggressors. Pishevari and other 'Ministers' signed for Azerbaijan, which evidently regarded itself as a sovereign State. Nor was Azerbaijan's *de facto* autonomy Qavam's only worry. It was becoming apparent that the Democrats were looking beyond autonomy to the capture of the central Government itself—a plan

182

which would be assisted by the Russian-sponsored Tudeh party in the rest of Persia. Demands put forward by the Democrats in May required not merely that Azerbaijan should have the right to reject central government legislation, guard its frontiers with its own army, appoint its own Ministers and keep three-quarters of its taxes, but also that it should be allotted one-third of the seats in the central Majlis. This proportion, together with the seats the Tudeh party would win, would probably give them control. Pishevari himself made it plain in a broadcast on May 15th that autonomy was only a means to an end. 'We are not going to separate from Persia,' he said. 'I told Qavam-es-Sultaneh that if a constitutional Government for Persia were formed, we would dissolve the Tabriz Majlis and forget self-government.' His idea of a constitutional Government was, of course, one controlled from the north. Teheran was no longer a suitable capital, said Tabriz radio. Only the 'spirit of Tabriz' could lead the Persian people. The 'spirit of Tabriz' was already speaking with the authentic accents of eastern democracy. At one Democratic Party meeting, it was reported, 'the beloved leader of our people, Pishevari, entered the hall amid prolonged applause and the faces of those present radiated with boundless love'.

If Qavam's hand was weakened by Russian proximity and the threatening attitude of Azerbaijan, it was somewhat sustained in this trying period by the Security Council. Realizing that his negotiations with Moscow for the withdrawal of troops would be assisted by a little outside support, he had lodged a complaint with UNO over Russia's failure to withdraw on the required date and her interference in Persia's internal affairs. Russia blamed Britain and America for the fact that the subject appeared on the Security Council's agenda, but there is plenty of evidence to show that both countries had repeatedly urged Russia to avoid such a disagreeable outcome by honouring her obligations, and none whatever to show that they encouraged Persia to bring the dispute before UNO. Once the matter was raised, Russia's treatment of UNO was cavalier. The Soviet representative, before he walked out, referred to the dispute as 'this so-called question'. Negotiations were proceeding satisfactorily between the two parties, so what was all the fuss about? 'The attempts,' said Linetsky in April, 'to foist upon the Soviet Union and Iran other ways of dealing with the questions of interest to both became particularly inept when an understanding had already been reached on some of these questions and talks were continuing in a satisfactory manner.' The Security Council, unconvinced that undue pressure was not being exerted, continued to discuss the matter from time to time in spite of a Russian boycott and after May 9th, when the last Russian troops left Persia, kept the subject on its agenda.

With the Red Army out of Azerbaijan, Qavam could breathe a little more freely. There was still pressure from the north, however. When it seemed that the negotiations on Azerbaijan's claims might break down, Tabriz radio declared, 'The Azerbaijan nation will not submit to the tyranny of the central Government. The Azerbaijan national army is now ready to fight against the enemies of freedom'. Qavam did not like such language. In June he resumed negotiations and an agreement was reached. The Democrats were content with only a part of what they had asked. They were now looking to the Majlis elections and a wider power. Qavam, still anxious to appease Moscow, reached a friendly understanding with the pro-Russian Tudeh party, jettisoned his pro-British advisers and appointed an ardent Russophile as army Chief-of-Staff. Moscow radio sang his praises.

The Russians, with an oil agreement in their pockets, a trusted friend in Prime Minister Qavam, and elections ahead, now felt they could carry the battle into southern Persia. Under instructions, the Tudeh party began to stir up trouble in the Anglo-Persian oilfield, with radio support from Moscow and Baku. Strikes and disorders were fomented. The company, said Belinkov from Moscow, paid no attention to the sorry plight of its employees, who were forced to work in intolerable conditions for wages insufficient for a bare existence. 'Labour conditions,' said Moscow radio, 'are worse in the concession territory than in similar enterprises in other countries.' Trade union activity and democratic organizations were forbidden—indeed, the whole concession had an 'enslaving character'. A broadcast in German quoted a Persian report that the British were establishing a corps of supervisors from Palestine who were treating the workers with 'unheard-of brutality and cruelty'. Lurid details were given of soldiers being ordered to fire on women and children. By July, *Tass* was quoting the demand of a Persian newspaper that the British concession should be annulled. In the middle of that month a general strike was organized in the oilfields and political demands directed against the British were sent to the Teheran Government.

It is important to note that so far in the Persian story the whole of the aggressive initiative had come from Russia. In the face of political developments which were calculated to undermine and finally destroy a vital British interest, no counter measures had yet been taken, no action threatened. There was, however, a limit. Early in August Britain announced that troops were being sent from India to Basra, in Iraq, 'in order that they may be at hand for the protection, should circumstances demand it, of Indian, British and Arab lives and in order to safeguard Indian and British interests in southern Persia'. Actually a brigade was sent. The Russians talked of a division of 10,000 men and quoted local rumours of 80,000 men. In its home service, Moscow quoted Iraq press reports to the effect that two British colonels were preparing an act of provocation, the murder of an Englishman, to create a pretext for bringing Indian troops from Basra into Persia. *Tass* quoted reports that Britain was plotting the annexation of Persian territory. Serezin in *New Times* wrote, 'Events go to show, all declarations and charters notwithstanding, that Great Britain's foreign policy continues to be determined by selfish interests which are pushing her towards further expansion, towards acts that endanger the peace of the world'. Vladimirov wrote in *Pravda* that the management of the British oil concession was 'deliberately trying to aggravate the situation in order to create "justification" for the concentration of the British troops in Basra'. Meanwhile, the British Minister in Teheran had sent a quiet but firm note to the Persian Government denying reports that the troops had been instructed to enter Persian territory 'in any case', expressing appreciation of the Persian Government's quick and successful efforts to re-establish order and security and agreeing that the re-establishment of law and order was the duty of the Persian Government forces exclusively.

Qavam, who reacted to any demonstration of power like a seismograph to an earthquake, noted the new tone. He was encouraged to do so by one of those coincidences which make history so interesting. Just as the British were beginning to get 'tough', some of the southern tribes started a revolt against the central Government at Teheran and themselves put forward political demands. The Teheran Government, they required, should be reconstituted without the Tudeh elements which Qavam had taken in to placate Russia; provincial councils should be formed in the south, and there should be greater representation of the tribes in the Majlis. Moscow blamed the British for stirring up the trouble, for resorting to methods 'well-known in the days of Lord Curzon'. It accused the British consuls in Ahwaz and Isfahan of having organized the rebellion—a charge which Mr Bevin described as 'baseless'. Whoever organized the revolt, it was very successful. The rebels occupied Bushire and the central Government troops suffered a sequence of severe reverses. Moscow talked of 'alarming developments'. There were people inside the Teheran Government, it said, who supported the rising; the Government was not acting firmly enough. All that was necessary was a bomb or two on Bushire. Military action against Azerbaijan a month or two earlier would have been fratricidal strife, but in the south no suppression could be too bloodthirsty.

Qavam, correctly reading the political omens, re-formed his Government without the Tudeh party and quickly made peace with the rebels on mutually satisfactory terms. In November he announced that elections were to be held all over Persia, including Azerbaijan, with the supervision of central Government forces, 'to ensure freedom of voting'. Moscow now turned upon Qavam. 'The nearer the date of the Majlis elections,' wrote Viktorov in *Pravda,* 'the more unbridled becomes the terror of reaction against the democratic elements.' Qavam's Government was now 'a refuge for sinister reactionary groups'.

The balance of forces had shifted and the days of 'democratic Azerbaijan' were numbered. The Democrats were ill-equipped for a war of nerves but Tabriz radio put on a bold front. The Azerbaijan workers would fight for their freedom, it said. A meeting of 50,000 people had demanded immediate general mobilization. The Azerbaijan Government was distributing arms. But in the second week of December, Teheran troops entered Tabriz almost without opposition. As they approached the town, the radio said, 'We have agreed to the arrival of the troops'. The Governor sent a telegram to Qavam saying, 'The Persian army is welcome in Azerbaijan'. The people openly rejoiced. Pishevari fled to Russia, a few Democrats were hanged, and a chapter of Persian history was closed. From beginning to end, 'democratic Azerbaijan' had been nothing but a Russian invention.

Slowly, very slowly, Qavam prepared for the elections. The Tudeh party had decided not to contest them, and when eventually the new Majlis met it was solidly anti-Russian. Moreover, it felt confident. The Russians had been so busy exposing imaginary British plots in the south that they had failed to notice an event of much greater significance in Teheran—the intensification of American diplomatic activity. A Persian newspaper wrote in April, after the announcement of the Truman Doctrine, 'Our fear of the Russians has now gone, thanks to the Americans who have firmly opposed the Russians in all the Middle East countries'.

Russia now concentrated on trying to get the oil agreement signed. For some reason, she thought the chances of ratification would be improved by a campaign of unrestrained abuse. Qavam, the Shah, the Majlis, the 'Persian reactionaries', the 'stranglers of the working-class' were all attacked with impartial ferocity. In September, a Note accused the Persian Government of 'returning to a policy of discrimination and hostility towards Russia'. Qavam was practically ordered by the Soviet Ambassador to secure immediate ratification. The American Ambassador said that America would defend Persia's freedom to make her own choice over the oil question. The British counselled moderation—it would be better if the Majlis were to Leave the Door Open and not just return a blank negative. But in October the Majlis rejected the oil agreement by 102 votes to 2, and forbade all further foreign concessions. It decided that prospecting in the next five years should be carried out by Persian or neutral experts and that any surplus oil might possibly be sold to Russia. A Note from Moscow in November accused the Persian Government of 'treacherously violating its undertakings' and held it responsible for any consequences. There, for the time being, the matter ended.

This Persian story is not a very pretty one but Russia had only herself to blame for the course of events and for the rebuff which she suffered. If she had really wanted only a 51 per cent interest in oil, and had gone about getting it in a friendly and civilized way, she might have succeeded. But what she wanted was a 51 per cent interest in Persia. If her crude and brutal plans had not in the end been countered by diplomatic firmness and a show of force from the West, there is little doubt that Persia today would be under communist control.

CHAPTER VIII

THE ATTACK ON THE EMPIRE

In a broadcast in Spanish in January 1948, Moscow radio used the phrase 'the twilight of the British Empire'. That metaphor was the frank expression of the hope, belief and intention which had dominated a large part of Soviet policy since the end of the war. There was nothing in the dogma about any peaceful transition from brutal colonial exploitation to free and fraternal association. Doctrine demanded a cruder view. The British Empire, going the way of all previous empires, had reached the point where it no longer had the power to hold down its conquests; now, therefore, was the time for the vultures to gather. Communism would soon tear the flesh off the old bones.

There was no attempt to conceal the purpose. Moscow's radio assaults on British policy in all parts of the globe could not have been more savage if the two countries had been at war. No temperate reference was allowed to escape the censor's vigilant eye.

Strangely enough, this Empire whose end was so near had never—according to Moscow—been so aggressively imperialistic. It might be on its last legs, but they were still strong enough to kick a native in the teeth. It might seem to be withdrawing everywhere, but in fact it was advancing everywhere. This, at least, was what the Russians told the world. In November 1946, Galaktionov wrote in *New Times,* 'Britain's purpose in maintaining a large peacetime army is to perpetuate and strengthen the yoke on the peoples of India, Malaya, the Netherlands Indies, Egypt, Palestine and Iraq and to extend British domination over other peoples in the Near and Middle East'. *Trud* wrote in December, 'British leading circles are infected with a fever of imperialist expansion. They are taking the dangerous road of imperial conquest'. No charge was too fantastic. The Empire, in this period of its greatest retreat, was getting not merely 'wider still and wider'; it was getting more and more repulsive in its methods. 'It is plain,' said Moscow radio in August 1947, 'that the British taxpayer can expect no lightening of the burden of

189

Empire. On the contrary, he may be asked to pay still heavier taxes to equip the colonial police for a gas war against striking workers.' Remarkable allegations were made about the number of British troops engaged in the protection of imperial interests. In September 1946, Lutski wrote in *Izvestia* that Britain still had 200,000 officers and men in Egypt, over 100,000 in the Sudan, Ethiopia and Libya, 60,000 in Palestine, 150,000 in Transjordan and no fewer than 100,000 in Iraq, with new reinforcements constantly arriving. This was a total of 610,000 officers and men! Had Britain been in a position to deploy even half that number, the Cabinet in London would have been saved much anxiety.

As the British imperialists fell back to unprepared defence positions, giving up whole chains of airfields and historic naval bases, Russian propaganda pursued and hounded them, lest they should come to rest too soon. Moscow was particularly sensitive about Cyprus, which—it was hoped—would eventually be restored to a communist Greece. Russian propagandists followed with solicitude the progress of 'Enosis', the movement for the reunion of Greece and Cyprus. The activities of Cyprus 'democrats' were given publicity. In September 1946, *Trud* printed a report from Nicosia that during 'a week of protest' over 700 meetings had been held demanding the annulment of harsh laws and the liberation of trade unionists. In January 1947, *New Times,* describing the efforts of the Cypriots to rid themselves of foreign rule, pointed out how cold had been the reception given in London to a delegation which had arrived to discuss the island's fate. Lynx eyes watched the unfolding, or supposed unfolding, of other British plans. Schemes for the creation of a 'Greater Syria' or the establishment of an Arab Union in the Middle East capable of withstanding pressure from outside were regularly attacked. A project to set up a military base in East Africa was pounced upon by Byelskaya in October 1946. 'The new proposed plans for military measures in East Africa,' she said, 'will only lead to an extension of the centre of unquiet and disturbance and to a strengthening of the centrifugal forces which are characteristic of the British Empire today.' In the same month, *Trud* was complaining about the presence of British troops in Ethiopia. In January 1947, Moscow radio gave a talk in Arabic denouncing British plans to establish bases in Libya. While

British demolition squads methodically pulled down the pillars of the old Empire, the Russians struggled to prevent the masonry being used for new construction anywhere else.

* * * * *

To appreciate the full impact of the Russian attack, it is necessary to make a quick tour of the main trouble-spots in the imperial heritage. Let us start with one of the worst of them—Palestine. Only one aspect of the Palestine problem really interested the Russians—how to bring the British mandate to an end and get British troops out of the country at the earliest possible moment and with the maximum of discredit.

On the specific question of Jew and Arab, Russia's attitude was cautious and contradictory. Her propaganda was persuasive only when it dwelt on the demerits of British rule. She refused for a long time to admit that the Jew-Arab feud was anything more than the artificial creation of British policy; it would die down, she said, when the British left. She purported to see a solution in the creation of an independent Palestine in which Jews and Arabs would eagerly co-operate once the British ceased to prod them into strife. In UNO it was difficult to maintain this thesis, and in the end Russia, like almost everyone else, was obliged to accept the necessity of partition. Her statements, however, made it clear that she was more interested in setting up what she called a 'democratic' Palestine, free from imperialist interference, than in the establishment of two stable sovereign communities. Her desire seemed rather for a period of unsettlement from which she might profit, and all the omens were bright. With an eye to the future, she endeavoured at all stages to avoid committing herself to one side only. Her long-standing antagonism to the Zionist cause—reaffirmed in July 1946 when a Moscow lecturer, Lutski, declared that Zionism was 'reactionary' and could be realized only through the 'oppression' of the Arabs—was modified in 1947 when Mr Gromyko declared that the desire of European Jews for a state of their own was 'natural and justified' and gave partition his blessing. But the adjustment of the Russian attitude in the face of contemporary facts and inescapable UNO responsibilities was a matter of tactics rather than of conviction. Russia's policy—as commentator Pfeffer

191

made clear in June 1947 in a broadcast in Yiddish—was a 'Leninist-Stalinist policy' which supported 'all nations in their struggle for a better life'. Once the mandate was ended and Palestine was independent, Russia would do her best to bring the 'better life' to both Jews and Arabs with stern impartiality. She could not feel that the Jew-Arab problem was very serious because she knew that if she could get her hands on Palestine and give it a little medicine from the 'eastern democracy' bottle, the problem would soon disappear.

But the first thing was to create a vacuum into which, one day, she might hope to move. The British must be evicted. Scurrilous abuse, subversive propaganda and quiet intrigue were the weapons with which Russia hoped to hasten the event. British policy, wide open to criticism for its post-war weakness and vacillation, was attacked by Moscow as inherently vicious. The theme was simple. Palestine, explained Mayev in *Izvestia* in May 1946, was of immense strategic importance to Britain. It was a great military base designed to guard the Suez Canal and the approaches to India. It followed that the British would not willingly leave. For years, said Mikhailov in June 1946, they had been trying to make mischief between Arabs and Jews, to get them fighting one another, and so retain their hold on the country. Moscow radio declared in Arabic that signs of possible collaboration between Jews and Arabs had increased the British imperialists' uneasiness and every attempt was being made by the British authorities to prevent such collaboration. Another Arabic broadcast said that the smell of petroleum was saturating the atmosphere and that the thing the imperialists feared most was that their underhand manoeuvres might fail to increase the gap between Jews and Arabs.

'Britain does not want and cannot find the correct solution,' said Leontyev in December 1946. 'The Arabs and Jews can attain their lawful democratic rights only on the condition of the withdrawal of British occupation troops.' 'The people of Palestine,' said *Trud* (before Russia had agreed to partition), 'in defence of the independence and indivisibility of their country, demand the evacuation of British troops and the transfer of the Palestine problem to UNO. Only this course can save the country from deliberate division and put an end to the martyrdom of the population.'

No action or inaction of the British administration escaped criticism. If British troops suppressed terrorism they were guilty of 'provoking bloodshed'; if they failed to suppress it, they were neglecting their responsibilities. Moran in *Izvestia* called them 'experienced trustees of the Swastika'. Though Russia had no ideological love for Zionism, she could not resist the temptation to aggravate the problem on the spot by assisting the influx of illegal immigrants, if not of terrorists. In 1947 several ships loaded to capacity left the Black Sea ports of Russia's satellites in an attempt to run the British blockade.

At UNO, British policy was Russia's chosen target. Previously, Britain had been charged with holding on to Palestine at all costs in her own selfish interests. Her decision to quit, said Zaslavsky in October 1947, was an 'admission of bankruptcy'. British politicians should be 'put on trial for their failure and branded publicly in the sight of all nations'. It was shameful that the British should not be willing to put their troops at the disposal of the United Nations. In any case, said Zaslavsky, they were going to be withdrawn only because Britain 'had not the money' to continue governing Palestine in a spirit of terror. That was why the British were willing to 'exchange their role of independent masters in Palestine for that of police and hangmen controlled by the USA'.

If the propaganda sometimes made little sense, at least it never lacked virulence.

*   *   *   *   *

In Syria and Lebanon, the Russians aimed first of all to bring about the withdrawal of British forces and secondly to reduce British influence. When, in February 1946, the Levant Governments asked the Security Council to recommend 'the total and simultaneous evacuation' of British and French troops, Mr Vishinsky rushed in to defend their violated sovereignty. He was actually kicking very noisily at an open door, for Britain and France had no sinister intentions. They were quite willing to withdraw, though a little anxious about the security of the area in the absence of any effective UNO provision for safeguarding peace. They readily accepted a Security Council resolution which expressed confidence that withdrawal would take place as soon as practicable and that negotiations would be started with the Levant Governments for that purpose. Mr Vishinsky, however, vetoed the resolution—he wanted Britain and France to be reprimanded. His vigorous championship of the rights of small nations served its propaganda purpose.'It has become quite clear to us,' said a Lebanese deputy, 'that when our question was being discussed in the Security Council the States divided into two camps. One of them was on our side while the other took the opposite stand. The first camp was headed by the Soviet Union. We ourselves could not have defended our interests better than the Soviet Union did.'

Russia continued to keep a watchful and suspicious eye on British activities in the Levant States, encouraging and reporting all anti-British attitudes. In June 1946 *Tass* described the anxiety of certain Lebanese newspapers because, though it had been agreed that British evacuation should be completed by June 30th, a total of 137 British officers and men would remain a little longer 'to wind up affairs'. In a talk in Arabic in September, Moscow blamed the disturbed state of the two countries on British policy in the Middle East and British economic penetration. The most trifling incidents were given a hostile twist—nothing was too petty. In September, for instance, *Tass* reported from Beirut, 'Enjoying a monopoly of sugar imports into the Levant, Britain has lately imported sugar very dark in colour and of bad quality. This is causing discontent among the local population'. Without a flicker of a smile, *Tass* quoted a local newspaper as saying, 'We cannot agree with the Prime Minister that this "dark blessing" is heavenly food. It is rather the fruit of our submission and silent subjugation to British domination which goes beyond the sphere of political life and grows into the economic enslavement of the Lebanon'. The fact that British and American industrial advisers were being employed by the Syrian Government was noted. In January 1947, Moscow home service quoted an attack made by a Beirut newspaper on an agreement reached between the Lebanese Government and a British firm for developing and prospecting. 'There is no doubt that we need experts,' the paper had said, 'but why should we not get them from neutral countries which have no imperialist ambitions against us?'

* * * * *

Iraq was one of the Middle East countries where the maintenance of British power was most desirable on grounds of imperial interest and most difficult to justify on any other grounds. It was not merely that there was a valuable British oil industry to be protected; the territory of Iraq was so situated that it provided a fine strategic base, accessible through the Persian Gulf, for supporting Turkey and Persia. Its importance had been made clear during World War II when the Axis Powers had organized a dangerous *coup* and the allies had subsequently turned it into a vital military centre. But once hostilities were over evacuation of British troops began and by October 1947 GHQ Middle East was able to announce that the withdrawal had been completed.

Meanwhile, Moscow was fomenting anti-British feeling and encouraging Iraq nationalism. A Moscow broadcast in Arabic declared that the Anglo-Iraq Treaty of 1930—which gave Britain the right to maintain air bases and troops in the country— did not harmonize with Iraq's sovereignty. It 'gilded the chains which shackled Iraq'. But, said the broadcast, the people of Iraq had begun to awaken and a strong liberation movement was being built up. Certain parliamentary and political circles realized that the maintenance of the existing position was a clear violation of the country's interests. Had not the slogan 'Evacuation of the British from Iraq' been prominently displayed during demonstrations in Baghdad? Such a national movement, concluded Moscow, would of course be opposed by Britain, for Iraq was the most important link in the chain of British military bases in the Near and Middle East, and it was rich in oil.

In November 1946, *Tass* was reporting denunciations in Baghdad of the presence of British troops 'supporting with their bayonets a group of persons who monopolized power'. The trampling down of liberty, it said, had reached unprecedented proportions. In January 1947 Moscow home service quoted an accusation by a Baghdad newspaper that British imperialists were oppressing the Near East peoples, stealing their grain, usurping their freedom and menacing their security. In February, *Tass* was reporting mass arrests in Iraq and the cruel treatment of imprisoned 'democrats'. Ignatyev in Persian said that behind the anti-democratic methods used in the Iraq elections was 'the hand of a clever stage manager putting his machinery into motion'—the hand of the British imperialists.

Subsequent events raised doubts whether the 'stage manager' would be clever enough to maintain British positions in Iraq in the face of nationalist and communist opposition. Britain's hope was that she would be able to continue her special relationship with Iraq, while giving up the extra-territorial rights which were the chief target of the nationalists. At the end of 1947, therefore, a new Anglo-Iraq Treaty was negotiated which set up a Joint Defence Board, gave Britain considerable rights in wartime, but made no provision for British bases or the maintenance of British troops on Iraq soil in time of peace. While the Prime Minister of Iraq was signing the new Treaty in London, Iraq communists were joining with right-wing nationalists in staging anti-treaty riots and demonstrations in Baghdad, backed up by the denunciations of Moscow radio. As a result of the agitation, ratification of the treaty was refused by Iraq. Once again, Moscow had helped to make it difficult for imperialism to withdraw in good order.

*   *   *   *   *

Nowhere was Russia's desire to erode British positions in the Middle East made more clear than in her attitude over Egypt. Russian propaganda ranged itself uncompromisingly behind Egyptian nationalism. *Tass,* grubbing in the political refuse-heaps of Cairo, took care that every Egyptian criticism of the British, every unpleasant incident, every anti-British rumour, was sent home for transmission by Moscow radio to the Russian people and the world.

For orthodox communists, the dispute between Britain and Egypt was a textbook case. British capitalists were exploiting the country and were determined to go on doing so. That was the basic factor. British troops were in Egypt ostensibly to defend imperial communications, said Ignatyev in June 1946, but their real job was to protect British commercial interests. In the Sudan, Britain's sole concern was to maintain her domination and preserve her raw materials. For the time being, Moscow was a firm believer in the 'unity of the Nile Valley'. In December 1946 Fedorov in *Red Star* wrote of Britain's 'evil intentions towards the Sudan'. British attempts to hinder a settlement of the Sudanese question, said Hassanov in Arabic, were being concealed behind an assumed solicitude for the 'immature' Sudanese people.

No credit was given to the British for their earnest if fumbling efforts to reach agreement with the Egyptians on a new treaty which would safeguard the Suez Canal and permit a total British evacuation. Russia made no effort to tell the world that the British had already begun to withdraw from key positions on Egyptian soil; that there was no longer a British garrison in Cairo; that the magnificent naval base of Alexandria had been voluntarily abandoned, an event perhaps without precedent in the history of Empires; that the British had made so many concessions in the treaty talks that virtually everything was agreed except the future of the Sudan; that Egypt, in fact, had full sovereignty within her grasp as a result of purposeful British abdication.

What the Russians said was quite different. In the first place, according to the Moscow home service in September 1946, the British had been 'forced to agree to negotiate' because the movement for independence had become so acute after the war. This was not true, for the British could have stayed indefinitely in the unpopulated Canal Zone with little risk of incident. Secondly, said Moscow, the talks were not intended to have a satisfactory outcome. Their slow progress was due to the fact that Britain wanted to maintain her position and influence in Egypt and had no intention of withdrawing her troops. Serezhin, writing in *Izvestia* in September, said not only that the evacuation of British troops had not started but that the strength of British garrisons continued to grow. The number of troops, he declared, was not less than 200,000 and the building of new strategic bases was in full progress. Fedulov wrote in *Red Star* in October, 'Irrefutable facts demonstrate that these negotiations serve as a new manoeuvre on Britain's part to enable her not merely to delay her withdrawal but on the contrary to strengthen her position in Egypt'. According to Yermashov in November, the new draft treaty was actually an attempt to introduce 'worsened conditions'. Possibly what the Russians most disliked about the new draft was the provision for an Anglo-Egyptian military alliance and joint defence undertakings. 'In these proposals,' said a Moscow broadcast, 'the Egyptians see only a new skin for the same bitter wine.'

A broadcast in Persian in January 1947 quoted approvingly an Egyptian statement that neither in British history nor in present policy was there a precedent to show that Britain had ever given independence to any country. Nevertheless, the Russians did not cease to work and hope for what they regarded as the impossible. When Egypt took her case—her almost non-existent case—to the Security Council in August 1947, the Russians naturally gave it full backing. They would continue to support the Egyptians against the British until the final evacuation.

* * * * *

Burma's progress towards the status of an independent sovereign republic was punctuated by sceptical Russian jeers, constant imputations of British insincerity and untiring efforts to roll boulders in the path.

In December 1946, Mr Attlee announced that Britain intended to give Burma dominion status, but that if the Burmese people so desired they were free to leave the Commonwealth altogether. This statement, said Moscow radio, 'despite its outward radicalism', was not received by the Burmese with any enthusiasm. Although leaders of the liberation movement had agreed to go to London, a number of Burmese public figures— said Dyakov from Moscow—had pointed out that the British Government's statement was very far from concrete and gave no grounds for confidence that it would be realized.

In February 1947, after negotiations between Burmese and British had been successfully concluded in London, Izakov wrote in *Pravda* that the agreement was a typical document of British colonial policy, and that that was precisely how it was regarded by Burmese public opinion. *Red Star* told its readers that the essential demands of the Burmese had not been met and that British forces were to remain in Burma. The communists in Rangoon, following the Russian lead, said that no agreement should have been concluded and that unilateral action should have been taken by the Burmese to declare themselves independent. The acceptance of independence as a free gift, and without bloodshed, did not square with the dogma and simply could not be allowed. The communists, wrote *The Times* correspondent, 'seem bent on creating those conditions of anarchy from which their Marxist manuals have taught them the ideal state can in due course be built up'.

A Moscow broadcast in English openly sided with the Burmese extremist U Saw, a man after the Russians' own heart, who was later hanged by the Burmese for his part in organizing the murder of Prime Minister Aung San and his colleagues. U Saw, said Moscow, had pointed out that British diplomacy had gained a victory over the Burmese and that Aung San had signed the agreement 'with a trembling hand'. In July 1947, British efforts to safeguard the rights of Burmese frontier tribes before leaving were described by Klimov in *Trud* as reminiscent of the British policy of protecting small principalities in India. The agreement over the tribes had 'extended the key part played by the British administration'. In August 1947 after the assassination of Aung San *New Times* said that 'the British authorities clearly intend to use the present situation to the utmost in order to make Burma's colonial status permanent'.

Nothing could have been further from the truth. To the intense chagrin of the Burmese communists, the British made strenuous and successful efforts to re-form the Burmese government after the shattering blow it had received. In October, sovereign power was transferred to Burma and in the New Year the Republic of Burma was proclaimed in an atmosphere of the greatest goodwill. The lights of Marxism were going out one by one.

* * * * *

A good deal of anti-British mischief was made by the Russians over the Indonesian question. This dispute was primarily one between the Indonesians and the Dutch and the complex details need not trouble us here. But as soon as it became apparent that the British were deeply involved, the Moscow barrage opened.

Britain, it will be remembered, had been allotted the invidious task of rounding up the Japanese in the Netherlands Indies, restoring order, and handing over authority to the Dutch as soon as possible. In the process, British troops were fired upon by Indonesian nationalists and were obliged to defend themselves. But the British withdrew from the scene at the earliest possible moment and their greatest efforts were devoted to bringing about an enlightened settlement. Counsels of moderation were repeatedly pressed upon the Dutch; Lord Killearn and Lord Inverchapel were sent out to act as conciliators, and Britain welcomed the endeavours of UNO, ultimately fruitful, to produce agreement. In imperial history there is no chapter of which Britain has less reason to be ashamed.

To the Russians, anyone in conflict with the British anywhere was automatically to be regarded as an ally. Russia reported events in Indonesia with a partisanship which could not have been keener if her own troops had been involved. As usual, everything was black or white. The Indonesians were fighting for their freedom against Anglo-Dutch imperialism and the fact that they were led by a cruel, irresponsible and totally unreliable extremist minority whose claims to represent Indonesia were rejected by the mass of Indonesians themselves was, of course, ignored. Moscow agents were sent into Java to exhort the Indonesian Republic to press on with the struggle. Moscow radio represented the incompetent and arbitrary regime as a model of democratic government. In Moscow, an exhibition was organized in support of the Republic. A delegation was sent out by the communist-controlled World Federation of Democratic Youth, under a Soviet woman chairman, to make contacts with the Indonesians and leave behind an embryo Democratic Youth organization in Java. At a critical moment in the negotiations, when a settlement seemed at hand, the moderate Prime Minister Dr Sjahrir was kidnapped and held for some days by Indonesian communists. In the United Nations, Mr Gromyko invariably supported the Indonesian case and was rewarded by much-publicized letters of thanks from unrepresentative Indonesian bodies. Remote though the Netherlands Indies were from the Soviet Union, Moscow was taking a hand in a game where the stakes were high. For their size, these Indies were probably the richest territory in the world.

Every British action was twisted and maligned. One moment the British were being accused of whole-hearted co-operation with the Dutch in the brutal repression of a freedom-loving people. The next moment, it was being explained that the British were trying to mediate simply because they feared the bad effect that the conflict would have in India and Burma. Every effort was made to set the Dutch and the British against each other.

Nobody would believe, said a Moscow broadcast to Holland in August 1946, that Britain was defending Netherlands interests at the cost of her own gold and the blood of Indian and British soldiers. Obviously Britain had ulterior motives.

As usual, the Russians pressed day in and day out for the withdrawal of British troops. A broadcast by Baratov in June 1946 said that though almost all the Japanese were now under allied control, the date of the evacuation of British troops was being continually postponed. False allegations were made that the British were employing Japanese troops 'everywhere' against the Indonesians. The most reckless statements were made about the numbers of British troops involved. At the hands of Moscow radio, the British army achieved a mobility never before known in the science of logistics. On August 15th, 1946, a Moscow broadcast said there were 60,000 British in Indonesia—and that their campaign had already cost more than the whole Burma war! *New Times,* appearing about the same time, said there were 'two divisions'—say 25,000 men. These, it alleged, were engaged in beating up and torturing the Indonesians. One month later, Kopilov in a broadcast in Dutch said there were 'seven divisions' of British troops, equipped with 'poisonous chemical substances'. The Anglo-Dutch army knew no limit, said Kopilov, in applying this means of warfare against the peaceful population of Indonesia. It was perhaps odd, in the circumstances, that when British troops left Java the Indonesian Prime Minister should have said in a farewell message to British officers, 'Never before have we seen such qualities exercised by Europeans in this country—your endeavours will always be remembered here'. Or was it to be supposed that this apparent tribute was really an ironical reference to the use of phosgene?

When, in 1947, the Dutch lost patience with the leaders of the Indonesian Republic and resorted to military action on a considerable scale, the British Government did not attempt to hide its disapproval. The British press was almost uniformly critical and Australia, lodging a complaint against the Dutch with the United Nations, demanded measures to deal with this act of aggression. Britain and America were both anxious to end the fighting and get negotiations started again. Moscow sneered. It was difficult to imagine, said Cherniavski, that the mediation proposed by Britain would have any other aim than that of helping the Dutch imperialists to stifle the Indonesian people. Byelskaya said in a broadcast in English, 'It is obvious that before launching their latest operations against the Indonesians, Dutch ruling circles made sure of the support of certain Anglo-Saxon quarters'. In July the British and Americans were openly accused of 'instigating' the new colonial war.

After a brisk twelve-day campaign which if continued would have reduced all Java, the Dutch were persuaded, against their better judgment and as a result of strong Anglo-American advice, to end the fighting and resume efforts for a peaceful settlement. Zhukov in *Pravda* said that Anglo-American offers of good services in settling the conflict had come only when it became clear that the blitzkrieg on Java had failed.

*   *   *   *   *

It was over the Indian question that Russia displayed the greatest animosity towards the British Empire. In the post-war period, her propaganda on this subject showed a variety, an ingenuity and a lack of scruple which put it in a class by itself.

First, of course, there was the old theme of British colonial misrule—a topic which had long lent itself to communist exploitation. According to Moscow, everything about British rule in India was uniformly bad, and Britain was made wholly responsible for every evil in the sub-continent. *Tass* busily reported the Indian scene in terms of strikes, shootings, famine and disease. British rule was repressive, Indians were being kept in jail, Indian troops were being used in British wars, child labour was being employed in industry and agriculture, Indian labourers were being confined in fenced camps, and illiteracy was widespread. It was a classic example of capitalist and imperialist enslavement. Occasionally Moscow looked ahead to the time when this propaganda might have to be switched against Indian capitalism. In June 1947, for instance, Zhukov in a Moscow lecture dealt critically with the existing Indian parties and leaders who were 'mainly reactionary capitalists and industrialists'. A month later *Tass* from Delhi was giving publicity to a revolutionary appeal by Sarat Chandra Bose against the existing Indian parties. It was clear that the eventual departure of the British would be the signal for a new phase of the struggle, a fight to win India for world revolution.

In the meantime, however, the British were the main target and Russian propaganda developed several interesting themes as the various constitutional plans moved towards maturity. One form of attack—used, as has been seen, in the case of Egypt—was that the British were moving towards greater freedom for India because they had no alternative. Proposals made in May 1946, said Ignatiev in Persian, were in the nature of a compulsory gesture in view of the political and economic conditions in India and the general situation in the East. Zhukov in the Moscow home service mentioned three reasons for the British proposals—the increase of the mass anti-imperialist movement, the pressure of American imperialism which was pushing Britain out of her lodgments, and the strength of the Indian workers' movement which was frightening the Indian *bourgeoisie* and therefore making them more amenable to British suggestions.

Usually, however, the propaganda of the period assumed that the whole project of giving greater freedom to India was just window-dressing; that the British had no intention of giving up anything, that all the negotiations were imperialist manoeuvres, and that the British would in no circumstances leave India.

Great play was made with the charge that the communal problem was being used as an excuse for the perpetuation of British rule and was being consciously aggravated by British statesmen for their own purposes. Volodin in the home service said, 'There can be no doubt that the old principle of "divide and rule" lies at the root of the new plan'. The view that Indian peace was a British responsibility and that the British could not leave the country until the communal problem had been settled was described as 'hypocritical'. In September 1946 a broadcast in Rumanian noted the Hindu-Moslem clashes and observed that whereas all British and many Indian papers blamed both sides, clear-sighted Indian politicians placed the blame on a third party 'interested in kindling fratricidal struggle in India'. Dyakov wrote in *Izvestia* of British manoeuvres aimed at 'setting the Moslem League against Congress'. In December 1946 *New Times* declared, 'Only the granting of real independence to India can guarantee the settlement of her internal antagonisms; only this can knock the ground from under the feet of those elements who, at the instigation of reactionary circles from without, are struggling for their own private interests, plunging the country into the maelstrom of fratricidal war'. Dyakov, in an English broadcast, put the charge more succinctly. 'With India a scene of seething passions and massacres,' he said, 'the British would have an excuse for perpetual interference in India's internal affairs and would thus be able to retain their hold on the country.' In January 1947, *Tass* was reporting from Delhi that British agents were deliberately stirring up discontent on the North-West Frontier. A Moscow home broadcast in June 1947 said the idea of disunity and dismemberment ran like a thread through the British plans.

Even after independence had become a fact, the Russians continued to insinuate that Britain was doing its best to set the communities at each other's throats. When trouble broke out between India and Pakistan over Kashmir, Moscow radio accused the British of giving encouragement to the 'Free Kashmir' army and alleged that Afghans were being recruited for this army 'not without the knowledge of British officials'. The assassination of Gandhi, according to reports quoted by Moscow, was planned by the British Secret Service.

Throughout the period, the Russians purported to believe that Britain intended to encourage the princely States to stand outside any constitutional arrangements and so retain her own control over India from new bases. The official British attitude on this matter had been explained so positively and lucidly in the middle of 1947 that there could be no excuse for misunderstanding. Statements re-emphasized what the Cabinet Mission's Memorandum of May 1946 had said—that Britain would not be able to carry out the obligations of paramountcy after the transfer of power and that British troops would not be retained in India for such a purpose. The Viceroy, in blunt talks with the Princes and their Ministers, made it equally plain that individual states would not be granted dominion status and that Britain expected them to accede either to India or Pakistan. The British Government had already turned down an application from the Nizam of Hyderabad asking that his State should become a Dominion. The British were leaving no shadow of doubt that this time they were really getting out of India.

The Russians, however, ignored the evidence. In a home broadcast in June 1947, Volodin coolly told his listeners that the Indian States were to remain under the British Crown and that from their territory the British might be able to maintain control over the whole of India. A broadcast in Persian in September said, 'The Indian army will remain under the British. Large British forces will remain in India'.

Zhukov, after a visit to India, wrote in *Pravda* in May 1947, 'It would be crude self-deceit if one relied on first impressions and drew the conclusion that there is only a small number of British troops left in India. It is not a small number at all. It is not difficult to find this out after visiting Hyderabad, the largest of the Indian principalities. . . . The British themselves obviously make no secret of the fact that they are converting this great place into a military base. The Hyderabad impressions left no place for illusions that the British seriously intend leaving India. Even the inexperienced eye of a civilian could see that the work conducted here aims at the expansion and not the liquidation of British military objects. All of us who were surprised at the small number of British officers in Delhi and Calcutta were well-rewarded by the picture of the accumulation of British military forces in the centre of Hyderabad'. That phrase 'well-rewarded' suggests that the Russians felt some uneasiness at the prospect of their best Indian propaganda story melting away. It did melt away, of course—together with the whole of the British forces. When the first batch of British troops left Bombay in August, Prime Minister Nehru sent them a message. 'It is rare in history,' he said, 'that such a parting takes place not only peacefully but with goodwill. We are fortunate that this should have happened in India. It is a good augury for the future.' Nobody had told him, apparently, about Mr Zhukov's well-manned British arsenal in the fastnesses of Hyderabad State. Early in 1948 the British evacuation of India was completed.

Throughout, the negotiations which culminated in Indian independence were annotated by sceptical and abusive Russian comment. Talking on the Cabinet Mission's proposals in May 1946, Dyakov said, 'It is symptomatic that though the British Government has declared itself ready to make India independent, the proposals do not proclaim even dominion status for India, let alone independence. At the same time the police in India have been reinforced, the prisons are being enlarged, the enormous British army maintained'. He declared that most Indian leaders had cherished hopes of a change in Britain's policy towards India as a result of the advent of a Labour Government to power, but 'these hopes had soon been destroyed'. In *Izvestia* he wrote, 'While making certain concessions to the demands of the national movement, this plan, as was the case with previous constitutional reforms, envisages such measures as would give Britain new possibilities of weakening the national liberation movement'.

The home service said that the British Government's object in asking Nehru to become head of the new Indian Government was to make Congress responsible for the difficult economic position of the country. In October 1946 Britain was 'aiming at reinforcing by new conditions and by new means the rotting foundations of British colonial domination in India'. In June 1947, Zhukov said in a Moscow lecture that the British attitude to India had not changed and that the Labour Government had promised independence 'knowing they could turn it into a fiction'.

The partition of India, accepted by Britain with the greatest reluctance as the only practical solution of the problem, gave a last stimulus to Russian propaganda. The dismemberment of India, wrote Dyakov in *Izvestia,* had nothing whatever in common with the self-determination of her peoples and would hinder their unification in the struggle for actual independence. *Red Star* said that by artificially separating the industrial districts from the agricultural, the British intended to upset the country's economic life and to convert most of it into Britain's appendage for the supply of agricultural products. The historic aspirations of the Indian masses were being disregarded and the sole aim was to protect the interests of British imperialism. The Indian Communist party, which had favoured the idea of Pakistan as long as the British were against it, now condemned it as a British plot.

In the later months of 1947, Russian propaganda battled in vain against the flowing tide of great events. In August, Zhukov referred to the 'fictitious independence' that the half-hearted British reforms had brought to India, but there was little conviction left in the attack. From the communist point of view, the solution of the Indian problem had been an ideological disaster. Every Russian charge had been disproved; the dogma had been made to look ridiculous. It was satisfactory, of course, that the

British had departed, but regrettable that they had not been driven into the sea by howling mobs.

This was the moment when honesty required a modification of the dogma—when the facts, solidly ranged against the Russians, should have been acknowledged. But nothing of the sort happened. One simple incident throws into stark relief the conscious immorality of the whole Russian attitude.

In October 1946, Moscow had noted with some satisfaction that the new Indian Government, for all its supposed authority, had not dared to change its representative at the Paris Peace Conference. Its delegate, said the Russians, still behaved as a 'true vassal' of Britain. But by 1947 the Indians had appointed their own trusted nominees to represent them on international councils and the spokesman of India at UNO was the Ambassador to Moscow, Mrs Pandit, who was friendly to Russia and frankly opposed to many aspects of British policy.

When the Assembly of the United Nations opened in September 1947, Mrs Pandit was still to be found taking a highly independent line befitting India's new sovereignty. Nevertheless, in her speech she made a moving reference to Britain. 'In the past,' she said, 'we have not hesitated to criticize British policy but I wish to put on record the warm appreciation of the Indian people of the spirit which moved British statesmen to make a voluntary surrender of authority.' It could not be easy, she added, for a people to divest themselves of an Empire.

The Russians, throughout their press, reported Mrs Pandit's speech at considerable length. They deleted the passage in which she expressed her gratitude to Britain.

CHAPTER IX

RUSSIA AND BRITAIN

No attempt will be made here to describe or document the feelings of friendship towards Russia and the Russians which moved Britain during the early post-war period. The British people know what they felt; they know what their political leaders said, and what they did. They must be the judges.

The Russian attitude towards Britain, so far as it was vocal, was the attitude of an enemy. In time of war it is not customary to praise the enemy; the approved technique is to disregard such virtues as he may have and to concentrate on his shortcomings. That is precisely what Russia did. She poked and prodded at the social and economic structure of Britain like a marine surveyor looking for soft spots in a ship. The method and spirit were those of the late Dr Goebbels in his assaults on 'pluto-democracy'. There was the same indifference to facts, the same inflation of the petty, the same hyperbole of expression, the same repetitiveness of phrase, the same warped hatred. In Russia the press and radio, the theatre and cinema, the school and club and lecture-hall reflected in every ugly detail the morbid psychology of the communist rulers. It was a stereotyped, undiscriminating, uninspired hatred—the flat and automatic hatred of a desiccated dogma. There was nothing left of the Revolution's vibrant challenge. This was not the voice of the Russian people, who are generous and friendly and vital—it was the voice of the party gramophone, raucously reproduced by a worn needle in a deep doctrinal groove. But the party was in power, and what the gramophone said was Russian State policy, with the strength of a sixth of the world behind it.

There was no period of transition before the Russian attacks began, no pause to see what the wartime ally would do in peace. As the fighting ended, the 'shoulder-to-shoulder' record was taken off and the 'capitalist enemy' record put on. The offensive was mounted on a broad front. Britain was attacked as the home of unchecked privilege and ruthless exploitation, as a bastion

208

of entrenched reaction, as a country in the last stage of capitalist decay. All her activities were dissected and the remains contemptuously displayed before the world. Her post-war difficulties were reported with gusto and without sympathy. Her divisions—such as they were—were emphasized. No opportunity was missed to expose and exploit her inevitable discontents. *Tass* in London, well aware of its master's tastes and appetite, served up its news items well-dressed with the sauce of malice.

Unemployment in Britain was a popular theme—as long as it was rising. Strikes were conscientiously reported from London, and Moscow radio gave them world publicity. 'The unofficial strike of the London lorry drivers proves that not everything is as it should be on the labour front of post-war Britain,' said Moscow in a broadcast to Austria. The 'squatters' movement', in Russian hands, assumed the proportions of a small rebellion and appropriate lessons were drawn. 'Squatting' could not possibly happen in the USSR, Moscow radio told the Greek people, as there were 'no empty mansions or rich landlords to exploit the people's misery'. Russian comments on Britain's post-war housing problem read like an unusually ill-tempered Tory election leaflet. *Trud* wrote in October 1946, 'The present plan of building 110,000 houses—fulfilled only to the extent of 65 per cent—appears extremely meagre'. Britain's food shortage, her rationing problems and her black market, all received close and critical attention. In November 1946 Moscow radio was reporting wide discontent in Britain over demobilization delays. Russia, the self-appointed legatee of Britain's imperial estate, was as eager to speed 'demob' as any Serviceman hankering for Civvy Street. 'Many progressive leaders point out,' wrote Viktorov in *Pravda,* 'that the demobilization of the Army would make it possible to reduce the Budget and return hundreds of thousands of Britons to peaceful labour.' When Britain was gripped by a fuel crisis in the hard winter of 1946-7, Moscow gloated over the disaster. 'The Soviet Union,' said Mikhailov in a broadcast in English, 'knows nothing of such phenomena as are taking place these days in Britain, where shortage of coal has disrupted the whole economic life of the country.'

Britain's economic difficulties, it appeared, were due primarily to Mr Bevin's foreign policy, which the country could not afford, and secondarily to British reliance on America. The American

loan, wrote Viktorov in *Pravda*, had not only not eased the difficult economic position of Britain, but had proved to be a noose
around the neck of the British national economy, 'to be pulled
tighter and tighter as the enslaving conditions of the loan
materialize'. British prospects, said Yermashov, were 'dismal',
for Britain had 'placed herself in such a position that she had to
pay through the nose for the illusory help of her rich creditor'.
The only way of escape, said Shatilov, was for Britain to find a
new political orientation—towards Russia. Meanwhile, of
course, it was the workers who were bearing the brunt. In post-
war Britain, wrote Marinin in *Pravda,* there had been a tremendous increase in the wealth of monopolies, side by side with a
drastic lowering of the workers' standard of life. All the hard-
ships which Britain was now experiencing, he said, had been
thrust upon the working-class. The 1947 Budget, *Izvestia* recorded, had 'evoked discontent among the broad masses of the
people' because of its increase in indirect taxation.

A favourite Moscow theme was the growth of Fascism in
Britain and the reluctance of the authorities to suppress it. In
June 1947 Moscow radio was saying, 'The British Home Secretary has given the House of Commons to understand that open
Fascist meetings in the East End of London will not be forbidden even though held near German military camps'. Arkadyev
in *Red Star* said the British police were not hampering the Fascists but were deliberately persecuting all honest democrats, thus
creating the impression that certain British circles were deliberately cultivating the microbes of the Fascist plague. Regrettable
but minor anti-semitic incidents which occurred in several towns
after the hanging by Irgun of two British sergeants in Palestine
were characterized by *Tass* as 'real pogroms'. The grain of truth
had soon become a sandstorm. Moscow radio talked of 'a wave
of anti-semitic demonstrations'. A broadcast in Yiddish deplored the way in which Britain was 'trying to cover up the open
pogroms of Jews with a fig-leaf of diplomatic phraseology'. The
Fascists in Britain had reared their heads and adopted the
bloody Hitlerite pogrom tactics 'openly and unhindered'. Anyone asking how it could happen that a wave of pogroms could
take place under a Labour Government, said Moscow, would
get the answer that the police, unfortunately, had arrived too
late. How could the British police arrive too late not only at the

first pogrom but at the tenth and the fiftieth, when one remembered the efficiency of the intelligence service? 'The black and brown hordes' were mobilizing their forces. Another talk in English said it was difficult to conceive that all this was happening today in Britain. The difficulty was apparently overcome, however, for the talk went on to say that Mosley's pre-war raids on the East End were being repeated 'on a larger scale'. The people of Britain who had fought for their liberty now saw Fascist pogrom-makers at work unpunished.

Combined ill-will and ignorance occasionally produced propaganda items which one day may enrich an anthology of humour. In June 1946, the disintegration of Britain was foreshadowed when the Soviet provincial press was solemnly informed that the Scottish Nationalist Party would present a petition to the United Nations demanding self-government for Scotland. In December 1946, Moscow radio gave Hungarian listeners a sketch on the subject of caning in British schools. The Soviet paper *Ogonyok* published a photograph of a Londoner holding up his small child with reins and captioned it 'A loving father with his child. Children in London are often led on a leash like dogs'. During the Soviet elections in January 1947, six young communists wrote to the newspaper *Moskovski Komsomoletz* asking how candidates were selected in *bourgeois* countries. The newspaper referred them to the Eatanswill election in *Pickwick Papers* and said, 'Eatanswill is an imaginary place but what Dickens wrote correctly describes English reality'. Even British sport was not sacrosanct. After the visit to Britain of the Dynamo football team, Yakovlev wrote in *Sovietski Sport,* 'The profit motive with which British football is permeated presents one of the substantial reasons for the recent international defeats of British teams. The pound sterling will never replace the spirit of self-sacrifice demanded by modern football'.

Other attacks had a sharper edge. Special efforts were made to defame and ridicule the British army, past and present. No 'shoulder-to-shoulder' spirit could be detected in the film *Admiral Nakhimov* which had a remarkable sequence showing the headlong flight of a British Guards battalion during the Crimean War and another scene, most diverting to Russian audiences, showing the humiliation of a British officer caught in a lobster basket. In October 1947 two successive numbers of the

211

periodical *Literaturnaya Gazeta* presented British officers as cads and bounders. One story purported to describe how British naval officers in a Russian northern port during the war had scandalized the Russians by asking that British personnel should be provided with a brothel. In November, a contributor to *Red Star* told how he had advised a young man in Bucharest who wanted to see the world to join the British army, 'for then he would have a chance of misbehaving with the wealthy, trading in opium in Hongkong, getting drunk in Singapore or chasing young women in the wilds of India'.

So one could go on. These quotations are merely a few pebbles casually picked up on a vast and stony beach of conscious malice.

*   *   *   *   *

The most vituperative Russian comment on the post-war British scene was reserved for the Labour party and the Labour Government. This was fully in accordance with the dogma, which rated social democrats—except when it was hoped to use them for temporary tactical purposes—as the lowest form of political life. All communists know that the toughest road-block in their march to power is democratic socialism.

It took the Labour party a long while to get its true ideological bearings after the war. Its rank-and-file was soggy with emotion about Russia. Its local branches were permeated by apologists. 'Cryptos' and fellow-travellers spread their cloak, treacherous as green moss on a bog, across the gulf between tyranny and freedom and shouted that the bridge would hold. The ears of Labour stalwarts were sealed against harsh facts by a sense of loyalty and gratitude to Russia. In the General Election of 1945, one of the stoutest planks in Labour's platform was the claim that no one else could ensure good relations with Russia. 'Left can speak to Left,' said Mr Bevin, 'in comradeship and confidence.' So strong was the regard for the Soviet Union, so massive the ignorance and so stubborn the prejudice, that it is safe to say no power on earth could have turned the Labour party against Soviet policy by the end of 1947 except the Russians themselves.

Labour's point of view was well expressed in 1946 by Mr Morgan Phillips, the secretary of the party, who later was to have a high place in the hierarchy of the 'fascist beasts'. Shortly before a Labour party 'goodwill mission' was due to leave for Russia, he wrote, 'The Labour Party realizes that this is the moment for its personal approach to Russia. The memory of our wartime comradeship is a powerful incentive towards a deeper and more enduring understanding between the people themselves, and at this decisive time, when the adjustments and settlements between the victorious allies are by their very nature bound to become occasionally contentious, we feel that it is essential to world peace that the very real sympathy which developed between Britain and Russia during the war should be preserved and consolidated by every means. It seems to me to be the most natural thing in the world that the peoples of Britain and Russia, now both governed by socialist administrations, should wish to understand each other more thoroughly. Our approach to the final objective may be different, but we hope and believe that we are both striving towards the realization of the world of the common man.'

But while Labour spokesmen talked of comradeship, the Russians were already loading their guns. Communism, they knew, could not be expected to make much progress in Britain without Labour's close co-operation. The Labour party must therefore be split wide open, and the 'social fascist lackeys' of the party's right-wing utterly defeated, leaving the field to the Left. Club-footed, the Russians trampled their way on to the British political stage. Melnikov in July 1946 was attacking the 'Labour reactionaries' in harsh terms. It was much easier, he said, to recognize that Churchill, Amery and the like were the enemies of peace than to discover the real views and aims of those who mouthed lying phrases about co-operation, peace and even socialism. Moscow radio encouraged every dissension, applauded every 'rebellion'. It quoted the sayings and doings of Labour's 'fellow-travellers' with an enthusiasm which was tantamount to sabotage of their work. No Labour MP speaking his mind about the Government on any topic could feel secure from Russian support. Great publicity was given to the anti-conscription 're-volt' of Labour Members. 'The retention of conscription in peacetime is opposed to British traditions,' said Sergeeva hopefully. The foreign policy 'rebels' were awarded shadow-Cabinet status in the Russian press. Mr Zilliacus, though not yet qualifying for the Order of Lenin, was given many an 'honourable mention' as well as much advice about the tactics he ought to pursue. Of the document 'Keep Left', Moscow radio said, 'This manifesto is taken very seriously in responsible British political quarters'. *Pravda,* writing on the Margate conference of 1947, declared, 'Formal approval of Bevin's policy by the majority cannot conceal the deep divergencies existing between the broad masses of the British workers and the Labour leadership'.

The vigour and resource of Russian attacks on specific aspects of Labour policy made Mr Churchill's official opposition seem positively paralytic. The Government, said Hofman, was 'trying to keep up the armaments race in which steel, chemical, and other industrial aces of Britain have an interest'. Matveev, in the Russian home service, described the Government as 'the inspirer of the struggle against the Soviet Union' and showed how its 'alluring promises remained only on paper'. 'If the Labour Government has anything to do with socialism,' said *Izvestia,* 'it is this—it discredits the very idea of socialism by its activities.' Osipov said it was the policy of the Labour Government to shift all the economic difficulties on to the shoulders of the working-class without encroaching in the least on the interests of monopolists. To exert further pressure on the wages of the workers, declared Hofman, while simultaneously protecting the profits of the capitalists was the programme of the Government and typical of its entire policy. The nationalization of the railways was a 'measure for the benefit of shareholders'. The Labour leaders had shown 'a marked disinclination to nationalize the banks and basic industries'. Cuts in capital expenditure were 'a ruse to secure cheap labour later on'. Kuusinen in *New Times* wrote of Labour's policy as 'an ersatz socialism which does no good to the working-class and no harm to the capitalists'. Stolyarov in *Trud* said the leaders of the Labour party were not worried by the fantastic figures of capitalist profits but only by the publicity they might attract. They had 'denied social rights to the toiling masses' said another commentator. Mr Bevin had 'always betrayed workers in their hour of need'. Mr Attlee had 'always adopted a subservient attitude before monopolists'.

Once again, it should be noted that it was Russia and the communists who started the fight. Their aggression was not provoked by the Labour party and for as long as possible it was ignored. For two years, the Labour leaders exercised a monumental patience and restraint. One can search in vain for any trace of real animosity in their public speeches of the time. They were grieved, they were critical, but they were never hostile. Like Christiana, they stood wrapped in dignity and a white robe while the Moscow mud spattered around them. Not until the establishment of the Cominform in 1947—Russia's open declaration of war on social democracy—did Labour decide to fight. And no party ever went into battle with a heavier heart.

*   *   *   *   *

One of the most intriguing episodes in post-war Anglo-Soviet relations occurred in January 1947 when *Pravda* appeared one day with a prominently-displayed article under the heading 'Bevin Disavows Anglo-Soviet Mutual Aid Treaty'. The evidence for the startling allegation had been laboriously distilled from a speech which Mr Bevin had made the preceding December, in the course of which he had said that Britain was not tied to anyone except within the framework of her UNO obligations. In its context, the sentence could not reasonably be made to carry the meaning which the Russians attributed to it, but since there seemed to be a misunderstanding the Foreign Office and Mr Bevin issued clarifications. In the course of exchanges with Stalin, the Foreign Secretary underlined Britain's continued goodwill by offering, not for the first time, an extension of the treaty.

Stalin accepted the explanations which were pressed upon him. 'Your message and the statement of the British Government,' he wrote to Mr Bevin, 'completely explain the affair and do not leave any room for misunderstandings. It is now clear that you and I share the same viewpoint with regard to the Anglo-Soviet treaty.' But he went on to say, 'If one is to speak seriously of an extension, then before extending this treaty it is necessary to change it, freeing it from the reservations which weaken this treaty'.

Britain naturally tried to find out at once what 'changes' Stalin had in mind and in due course discussions were held in Moscow on the Russian proposals. The development was widely hailed in Britain as a hopeful sign. *The Times* diplomatic correspondent wrote of the possibility of 'a new and more friendly phase' in Anglo-Soviet relations and the happy turn of events provided a congenial theme for leader-writers. A Labour MP wrote to *The Times* suggesting that the moment had now arrived for Britain and Russia to become 'working partners'.

What was in the Russian mind? A Moscow home broadcast, pointing out that Anglo-American relations had 'acquired the nature of a military alliance' while British policy towards Russia was 'not consonant with the principles and demands of a treaty of alliance', seemed to suggest that Russia would be content if, in her military relations with Britain, she were put on the same basis as America. But the British Government had already proposed an exchange of British and Russian staff officers and a standardization of arms similar to that which existed between the United States and Britain, and Stalin had turned the proposal down. Such a plan assumed an eternally peaceful triangle, and Russia was thinking in terms of struggle. She wanted an ally against America, not a safe place in a *troika*. According to *Tass,* Stalin had said that an exchange of officers would be desirable but that at the moment it was not quite appropriate. People might interpret such a measure as preparation for war. Different organs of the press, he said, had blamed Britain and the United States for preparing for war by exchanging officers and standardizing training and armaments and the Soviet Union did not wish to be blamed in this way. A lamer excuse can rarely have been put forward at so high a level, for such a three-cornered development would rightly have been hailed throughout the world as a symptom of trust and an augury of peace.

Russia's real aims were made clear when *Pravda* published an article on the negotiations for a new treaty. 'One must strive to secure . . . ,' it said, 'that both parties should be under an obligation not to participate in any sort of agreements or actions which even indirectly would be aimed against one of the parties.' In black type, *Pravda* declared, 'The Soviet people rightly considers that treaties or agreements between Powers which have the object of establishing genuinely friendly relations between them must exclude the participation of each of the contracting parties in all *blocs* or action aimed at the other party, no matter how such participation may be disguised'.

In any but a Russian context, this would have made sense.

But, coming from the Kremlin, it meant that Moscow was trying to obtain by an international legal bond what she had conspicuously failed to achieve by other means—the unquestioning allegiance of Britain to Russian policies. Had Britain signed, she would, in the Russian view, have been morally bound to repudiate the defensive Truman Doctrine, to accept the Russian position over Greece, Turkey and Persia, and later to reject the Marshall offer since this would certainly be held to come under the heading of 'action directed at the other party'.

Why Russia thought it worth while to undertake so unpromising a manoeuvre must always be puzzling. The original allegation against Mr Bevin was printed in an article the theme of which was the opposition to Mr Bevin's foreign policy within the Labour party, and it is therefore conceivable that the whole purpose of the incident was to discredit the Foreign Secretary. To many, the most significant thing about the whole episode was that once again it was Britain who had to defend herself against a baseless Soviet charge, once again it fell to Britain to make a friendly overture, and once again it was the British who did the travelling in the interests of peace.

* * * * *

Trade between Britain and Russia had always, from the British point of view, been disappointing. To a great extent the two countries were economically complementary and large-scale exchanges would be mutually advantageous. But Russian trade policy reflected communist hostility to the West. The Soviet Government longed for the time when the area under its political control would be wholly self-sufficient. Exports were regarded as a necessary but temporary evil; imports as a reflection, unavoidable but humiliating, on Russian productive power. Foreign trade flourished only in periods of extreme Russian need. On the basis of existing evidence, it is pure illusion to imagine that a communist Russia will ever become a large and reliable customer for British goods, particularly manufactured goods, or that Britain can find economic salvation in developing an eastward at the expense of a westward trade.

Nevertheless, after World War II both countries had strong reasons for wanting to re-open trade relations. Russia needed capital goods to help repair her war-shattered fortunes. Britain badly wanted Russian timber and grain. The Labour Government was all the more anxious to get trade talks started because a trade agreement with Russia would be the most effective answer to critics who ceaselessly deplored Britain's economic dependence on America. Many Labour men also believed that a trade agreement would help to improve political relations.

As usual, the initiative came from the British. In February 1947 the Secretary for Overseas Trade, Mr Marquand, sent a message to Moscow saying he was willing to travel there at any time for discussions. His successor, Mr Harold Wilson, sent a similar message in March. Mr Bevin raised the question with Stalin at the March conference of Foreign Ministers in Moscow and in April Mr Wilson was flying to the Russian capital for a general exchange of views. In May, he paid a second visit for actual negotiations. In the field of trade, agreement was finally reached on all points after hard bargaining, but the discussions broke down on a financial question—the revision of the 1941 credit agreement between Britain and Russia.

Briefly, Russia wanted to revise in her favour the terms of interest and repayment of the large credit which Britain had advanced for the purchase of civil supplies. 'The concessions we were prepared to make,' said Sir Stafford Cripps afterwards, 'would have involved us in a heavy loss in the next three or four years.' Mr Glenvil Hall, Financial Secretary to the Treasury, subsequently indicated the extent of the contemplated concession. The maximum British offer would have meant a loss on capital repayment, in hard currency, of £26 millions in the first six years, to be recouped over the following ten years. Britain, in short, had been willing to defer her claim for £26 millions worth of dollars at a time when at home she was scraping the barrel for means to pay for dollar imports. But the Russians had asked still more. Their best offer would have involved a temporary British sacrifice of £34 millions worth of dollars. 'In view of our serious overseas financial position,' said Sir Stafford, 'we could not meet what the Soviet Government stated were their minimum terms.'

The breaking-off of negotiations was received with deep gloom by the British Left. It was suggested that the failure was due to American pressure, an allegation which was eagerly taken up by the Russians and flatly denied by Mr Wilson. He was, it seemed, taking the initiative for the resumption of the talks.

In August, Russia defaulted on a payment under her 1941 agreement. Having failed to get the modifications she asked for, she apparently felt entitled to alter the terms of her contract unilaterally and without apology. The British Government naturally asked for an explanation, but pointed out that of course any revision of the credit terms subsequently agreed upon would have retro-active effect.

While Britain continued to press for the resumption of the talks, Moscow radio was slighting, abusive and—as usual—contradictory. Britain, being down-and-out, naturally needed Russian help. That was the theme. 'It is well-known,' wrote Marinin in *Pravda*, 'that many British politicians, not to mention the British public, had certain hopes that these talks would lead to an easement of Britain's present and growing economic crisis.' Then came the contradiction. 'The British attitude proved that they not only showed no interest in a positive solution of the question of activizing Soviet-British trade but they actually showed a tendency to complicate the talks.' Finally came the abuse. Moscow radio told its English, Hungarian and Czech listeners that 'an activization of Anglo-Soviet trade clashes with the dollar diplomacy which has for some time dictated Britain's foreign policy'. *Pravda* accused Mr Wilson of 'misleading British public opinion' about the reasons for the breakdown and of trying to 'conceal from it the one-sided United States orientation of the Labour Government'.

Disregarding these verbal rebuffs, the ardent Mr Wilson made a third trip to Moscow in December 1947 to renew his suit, and an 'agreement in principle' was reached.

Whether or not it was right to conclude such an agreement was a question which only the negotiators, with all the relevant information at their disposal, could decide. Britain's need for animal feeding stuffs was pressing, and the 750,000 tons of coarse grains promised by Moscow would be invaluable. But the only basis on which the deal should have been judged was that of good business. Was it, all things considered, a profitable deal?

Yet when Mr Wilson announced his 'agreement in principle' to the House of Commons, Labour Members—without even knowing its terms—applauded as though the Minister had brought back 'peace in our time'. This was a political judgment. One Labour MP even suggested an 'official greeting' at the docks for the first shipment of Soviet grain. An 'independent' British policy, it seemed, meant to some Labour Members the sullen and barely acknowledged acceptance of £1,000 millions from the United States, and the decoration of the ports for a few hundred thousand tons of Russian oats and barley paid for by capital goods which would sell in any market and by a large bonus in the shape of postponed debt.

As far as the fundamental Russian attitude was concerned, the trade agreement would make no difference whatever. But the agreement might help, the Russians thought, to swing Britain the Russian way. The comment of Academician Tarle was revealing. 'In the British Parliament,' he said, 'when Minister Wilson spoke, expressions of enthusiasm took place which were quite unprecedented. The might of the USSR is the main support of those who do not wish to don the United States yoke.'

It may be that the agreement was commercially advantageous to Britain and that the larger talks envisaged would be still more fruitful. It may be that Britain was right to take all the initiative, to make all the effort. But to imagine that Russia's plans for world communism could be checked by a deal in machinery and grain was to set foot once more on the hard and painful road to disillusionment.

CHAPTER X

RUSSIA AND UNO

Like many other joint post-war enterprises, the United Nations Organization was built on an illusion, and was therefore bound to crack and crumble after a short life. Its underlying assumption was that all the Great Powers, including Russia, would work together after the war in good faith and a spirit of genuine co-operation for the same broad ends. There were no grounds whatever for this belief, and the reverse proved to be true.

From the very beginning, Russia regarded UNO as a theatre of war. Far from seeking to heal the wounds of the world, she devoted her main efforts to creating, aggravating and prolonging international divisions. She lived and worked for strife. Her manner was always quarrelsome and spiteful; in the later stages of the period, when Mr Vishinsky was accusing 'the Fulton heroes, American monopolists, psychopathic arch-ruffians, paranoiacs and gangsters of the pen' of 'warmongering', it became hysterical.

The Russian attitude to UNO was shown unmistakably in Soviet press and radio accounts of its proceedings. Debates were reported like battles. 'The first stage of the session has resulted in a victory for Soviet diplomacy,' said Izakov in November 1946. In the Moscow home service Yermashov talked of 'a series of major moral and political victories which have raised higher and further consolidated the authority of the USSR'. Leontyev wrote, 'The United Nations Assembly just ending was the arena for a major struggle between the supporters and opponents of democratic co-operation between nations. . . . It showed that the rallying of all the democratic forces and their firmness and determination in the struggle for peace are capable of defeating all the plans of the enemies of peace and democracy'. 'A triumph for the Soviet delegation and a defeat of the Anglo-Saxons', was a popular reporting phrase. Attacks by the Anglo-Saxons were usually 'repelled all along the line'. Russia's champions were cheered with uninhibited partisanship. Mr Molotov and Mr

Vishinsky were always making 'slashing attacks', speeches 'filled with irrefutable arguments', 'brilliant and annihilating replies', 'strong, straightforward and convincing statements'. By contrast, the western spokesmen 'mumbled inarticulately', made 'vulgar attacks' and invariably used 'hackneyed worn-out arguments'. Their speeches were reported in the form of garbled summaries interspersed with abusive comment. What President Roosevelt had planned as a Temple of Peace was to the Russians a pill-box in the international front line, and they blazed away from all its embrasures. No wonder the French delegate, M. Parodi, declared 'The general spirit of our work causes a certain disappointment'!

The General Assembly and the Security Council obviously provided an incomparable platform for Soviet propaganda. Simply because the world set such store by UNO, whatever was said there would attract attention. Here the Russian delegates could pour forth their diatribes, here Russia could pose self-righteously in the limelight as the champion of peace, the protector of small nations, the arch-enemy of fascism and imperialism. Here, too, the West could be put on the slab. Its reactionary aims could be exposed, its weaknesses probed, its selfish and sinister motives dissected. All the charges preferred by Moscow radio could be iterated and reiterated. Russia should come well out of the exchanges, for the West seemed indisposed to fight. Britain and America came to the council chamber armed ridiculously with an olive branch; they seemed to have no stomach for the long debates, no stamina. Full advantage would be taken of their weakness. In the end, UNO would probably break under the strain, but it would have served its purpose. To the Russians, UNO was expendable.

As long as it lasted, however, it was invaluable not merely as a propaganda instrument but as a shield for Russian actions. While UNO was in being, the West would be morally debarred from taking direct steps to curb the Kremlin's plans. The British and American peoples would naturally expect their Governments to be loyal to the new organization. Such was the Russian calculation, and such the fact. For nearly two years, neither Britain nor America felt free to make any move which could be represented as going outside UNO or undermining its authority. They were the prisoners of their own ideals.

The determination of the western Powers to make UNO the foundation of their policy would have been of little use to Russia had UNO in fact been equipped to take decisive action against clear breaches of law and justice. But Russia was comprehensively insured by the famous Principle of Unanimity. By means of the Veto, she could block any action of which she did not approve and defy the judgment of the world. She could turn an organization which was intended to be the guardian of peace and order into an impotent spectator of subversion and aggression. The Russians, of course, put it a different way. Unanimity, said commentator Lemin in July 1946, was 'a safeguard against the danger that certain reactionary imperialist groups would use the organization as a means of isolating socialist or new democratic regimes'.

UNO was not wrecked, however, because there was a veto provision in the Charter. In a world where Great Powers were still not prepared to abandon the inner defences of sovereignty, the veto as a last and exceptional resort was realistic. Had there been a will to agree among the Powers, it is doubtful whether the veto would ever have been exercised. What brought UNO to futility was the manner in which Russia employed the veto. At San Francisco the sponsoring Powers had said that it was 'not to be assumed that the permanent members of the Security Council would use their veto power wilfully to obstruct the operation of the Council'. But this was precisely what Russia did, precisely what she had intended to do. She used it to ensure that the Council should not work at all unless it worked in her interest. The veto was the saboteur's dream.

It was not surprising, in view of its great value, that Russia refused to countenance any tampering with the veto right. 'This principle of unanimity,' said Mr Vishinsky in October 1946, 'constitutes the basic foundation of the entire activity of the organization. . . . Even the slightest infringement of this principle is impermissible. The Soviet delegation believes discussion of any modification in this principle is impermissible.' Stalin denied that the veto had been used to excess. Mr Molotov said Russia had used it only in 'exceptional circumstances'. All attempts to weaken the veto power were denounced as efforts by the West to use its voting majority as a means of domination. 'For the principles of co-operation they would substitute rivalry and power politics,' said Moscow radio. 'The way would be completely clear,' said Mr Molotov, 'for the purpose of those groups and persons who want to accept nothing less than the docility of all peoples to their dictates and their sack of gold.' It was exactly the technique which had worked so satisfactorily during the writing of the treaties with Germany's satellites. The good-natured and trusting West had voluntarily extended its powerful wrists to receive the handcuffs, and when it complained that the metal chafed it was accused of violent designs.

In the light of the Soviet attitude, the efforts made by many delegates on many occasions to modify the veto right were bound to fail. There were always two courses and two only. One was to preserve UNO intact, with Russia and the Veto, for whatever these three were worth together in the scales of peace and justice. The other was to admit that the whole concept of UNO was built on error and to re-form the organization without Russia. No half-measures, no modifications would suffice. Mr Molotov was frank and realistic when he said, 'It is perfectly clear that rejection of the principle of unanimity among the Great Powers . . would in fact mean the liquidation of UNO'. For if Russia's blanket veto went, the organization would be worse than valueless to the Soviet Union; it would be a potential menace.

*   *   *   *   *

The whole history of UNO documents the charge that Russia used the organization for the dual purpose of attacking her ideological enemies and warding off the consequences of her own or her satellites' misdeeds and for no other purpose whatever. In the two post-war years, every single major subject on UNO's agenda was utilized by the Soviet Union for one or other of these two ends.

Offensively, she made propaganda charges over Syria and Lebanon and subsequently vetoed a Security Council decision designed to end the dispute; she made propaganda charges over Indonesia and refused to collaborate in the Council's efforts to achieve an agreed solution; she made propaganda charges over Egypt, over Spain, over trusteeship, over disarmament, and over the presence of allied troops in foreign countries.

Defensively, she used UNO to protect her own position in the

Greek, Persian, Albanian and Korean disputes. Over Greece, she used the veto like a flail and openly flouted the Security Council's will; over Persia she first 'walked out' of the Council and subsequently boycotted it; over Albania she defended a crime and vetoed its redress; over Korea she obstructed a UNO commission.

Some of these topics have already been touched on; others will be dealt with in later chapters. Here it will suffice to illustrate the Russian attitude, offensive or defensive, on four subjects which at various times occupied a great deal of the Security Council's attention.

* * * * *

Russia's desire to use the United Nations as a propaganda instrument was first revealed over Spain. Franco was fascist, he had co-operated with Hitler and Mussolini, his regime was hated throughout the democratic world. Russia would, therefore, represent herself as the protagonist in the anti-Franco cause. Moreover, by urging impractical and ineffective means of dealing with him, she would put the western Powers in the position of seeming to protect him. If by any chance she succeeded in overcoming western caution and bringing about fresh trouble in Spain, so much the better. Another civil war would keep western Europe in turmoil and communism would benefit.

The Russian thesis was that the Security Council should take action against Franco on the ground that his fascist regime constituted 'a serious menace to the maintenance of international peace and security'. This would have meant locking the stable door after the horse had been gone about two years. Massive though the iniquities of the regime were, it was fantastic to suggest that this isolated, discredited and destitute peninsula of fascism was a threat to peace in the post-war era within the meaning of the Charter. The time to deal with Franco extra-legally had been immediately after Germany's collapse. Not to have done so was conceivably a grave error of omission, but the error could not properly be made good through UNO machinery. The most painstaking research by a special sub-committee of the Security Council failed to a find a single ground for the charge that Spain was preparing an act of aggression. This being

H

so, it was equally certain that under its Charter UNO had no juridical right to intervene in Spanish affairs at all.

The western view of Franco had not been concealed. Both the British and American governments had repeatedly made it plain that they detested the regime and would welcome its overthrow. But they tried to be realistic. America declared that she was ready to take any necessary action under the Charter when the Franco regime became a menace to peace, but at present this was not the case. UNO pressure, she said, could not displace the regime; sanctions, even if legal, would only have the effect of isolating the Spanish people, plunging the country into political and economic chaos, and perhaps renewing civil strife in which different members of UNO might well take different sides. Britain also declared that she would do nothing to precipitate the shedding of blood over Spain's form of government, and the decision was right.

But every time the subject came up for discussion in UNO, Russia and her satellites repeated that Franco was a menace to peace and implied that western reluctance to take action arose from the fact that the West was not genuinely anti-fascist and was even in secret sympathy with the regime. Moscow radio said, 'One cannot overlook recent press reports that Franco is trying hard to obtain a loan in Britain and the USA'. *Pravda* wrote of western 'chicanery'. Borisova said in an English broadcast, 'By increasing her exports to Spain and recommending non-intervention, Britain is encouraging aggressors'. When the western Powers urged delay while the charge of being a 'menace to peace' was being investigated, Mr Gromyko played to the world gallery. 'International public opinion,' he said, 'will not be able to understand this course and still less to approve.'

For a long time, Russia pressed for a general severance of diplomatic relations with Franco—an instrument of policy which history had conclusively shown to be worse than futile, since it inevitably united an outcast people behind its Government. But the more the West hung back, the greater was the propaganda value of the proposal. In the end, Russia succeeded in persuading the Assembly of UNO to call on all its members to withdraw their Ambassadors and Ministers from Madrid, a step which in the main was loyally carried out. It had no practical effect whatever on the Franco regime.

Apart from using force, the only likely means of achieving Franco's removal was to encourage an alternative which might be acceptable to Spain. With this possibility in view, the British and Americans had talks in 1947 with the monarchist Gil Robles and the socialist Prieto. That the move was not to the liking of Franco was shown by a reference in the controlled Spanish press to 'the futile machinations of Mr Bevin's unpatriotic Spanish lackeys, a murderous revolutionary and a misguided renegade'. It was also not to the liking of the Russians, who had no desire to see Spain reconstructed on western democratic lines. *Tass* reported with approval a Uruguay newspaper's reference to Prieto as 'a defeatist and traitor now being groomed in the United States as Franco's successor'. It was not the first time that the attitude of Moscow had coincided with that of a fascist dictator.

* * * *

Another example of the way in which Russia contrived to use the United Nations as a vehicle for her propaganda was provided in 1946 when the Russians raised the question of the presence of foreign troops in non-enemy territories.

The propaganda value of the attack was high. A year after the end of the war, the territories where Britain and America still had troops read like a gazetteer. America had overseas expeditions in China, Egypt, Iceland, Greenland, many Atlantic and Pacific islands, and several of the Latin American republics. British forces were no less widely scattered. The presence of these troops abroad was, of course, largely due to the fact that America and Britain had borne the brunt of the overseas struggle with the Axis and had not yet had time to complete their withdrawals. But that was not the only explanation. Britain had a widely-dispersed Empire to protect, and unless she was prepared to abandon it—as Russia would have liked—the maintenance of some overseas bases was essential. America was torn between her hatred of imperialism and the need for global security in the face of an increasing Russian challenge. Whatever the justifications, the fact was that the Anglo-American position was vulnerable. The occupied non-enemy countries could be relied upon to fall in behind Russia on this issue.

The Soviet Union had made a skilful choice of ground. Her

227

own Empire, though vast in extent, was consolidated in one land mass. It could be protected by home-based troops at all points. Armies on the periphery could, and did, dominate surrounding areas without occupation. Moreover, Russia had perfected the political weapon. Where Britain and America needed troops to safeguard their interests, Russia could rely on the indigenous communist parties.

The Soviet attack was launched in the autumn of 1946, when Mr Gromyko proposed in the Security Council that UNO members should submit information within two weeks giving the strength and location of their forces in non-enemy countries, with details of air and naval bases and the strength of garrisons.

Moscow radio joined in. 'For British troops to be in all these non-enemy countries,' said Belskaya, 'is a gross violation of the sovereignty of these countries. Unrest, disturbances, clashes and bloodshed are the result. The withdrawal of British troops from foreign territory is today a positive necessity.'

Having failed in a second attempt to interest the Security Council in their propaganda campaign, the Russians switched their offensive to the Assembly in October 1946. The presence of foreign troops in non-enemy countries, said Mr Molotov, gave rise to 'serious uneasiness'. To camouflage the political nature of the attack, he had now thought up an additional reason for the census he required. It would, he said, be useful to the Military Staff Committee of UNO, whose task it was to study the question of the armed forces which UNO members would be asked to place at the disposal of the Council for world security purposes. 'The Soviet Union for its part,' he said, 'is prepared to submit such information to the Security Council.' And he added, innocently, 'Why should any one of us conceal from UNO the actual situation in this respect?' He prodded and goaded. 'It is clear to all,' he said, 'that no one will dare to refuse outright to present this information to UNO. Such a refusal would place any country in a position which would be difficult to explain to the peoples. . . . Let those who oppose the presentation of information say so frankly and explain their motives.'

Russia, with a fanfare of publicity, had already given the 'information' as far as she was concerned. She had announced that she had troops in Poland and Korea, without giving any details. Moreover, under the compelling gaze of *maestro* Molotov,

France had declared the insignificant total of her own forces in non-enemy territories and the Chinese delegate had been hypnotized into the rostrum to declare that all Chinese troops were back home. There, said Mr Molotov, was an example for Britain and America. Now let them follow suit. It was like a father encouraging his small child to swallow a glass of nauseating medicine by bravely sinking a small whisky-and-soda.

America and Britain were in a difficult position. They had no objection whatever to giving details of their troops abroad provided the information would help UNO to establish an effective security system—indeed, they had struggled hard to bring this about in the face of constant Russian obstruction. They did object to what was in effect a unilateral disclosure for Mr Molotov's political ends. The United States delegate said that America had nothing to hide, but why should the census not include all troops, both at home and abroad? Britain was interested in Mr Molotov's motives. What, asked Mr Bevin, was to be done with the information? If it was intended to help the Military Staff Committee, then it was obvious that the Committee would want to know much more than the details of the 10 per cent or so of troops stationed abroad. Mr Molotov wriggled. Allied forces in friendly States, he said, were an instrument of interference. Vaguely he felt that the information would be of great political importance to the Security Council which would then have a complete picture of what countries had forces abroad and where and how many, and be able to judge whether their presence had serious political significance. The Yugoslav delegate did not attempt to conceal the purely political motive. The purpose of the Soviet move, he said, was to enable the Security Council to decide whether British and American forces should be withdrawn from foreign bases.

The debate now became very complex. Britain wanted the problem to be considered in the context of general disarmament, where it seemed to belong. Russia brought herself to accept the American proposal of a census of troops everywhere, but declared that 'men do not fight barehanded' and that armaments should also come under the census. The British were prepared to accept this provided there was an 'international supervisory commission'. An attempt by Mr Vishinsky to get information about the atomic bomb through the back door had to be frustrated. The original Russian proposal had become lost in a jungle of debate about disarmament in general, and its propaganda value had therefore disappeared. Late in November, the Assembly approved a resolution requiring an almost immediate census of troops at home and abroad, but not of armament. Russia voted against it, on the ground that the proposal was now 'nebulous, involved and to a great extent meaningless'. A couple of weeks later the Assembly adopted a wider resolution on disarmament and the former decision about a census was revoked.

Throughout the discussions, Mr Molotov and Mr Vishinsky had held the initiative. They had lined up many of the small countries, including a very vocal Egypt, on their side. They had managed to give the impression that the West had something to conceal; that Britain and America were anxious to bury a clear and simple project under a mass of amendments. The *New York Times* commented, 'One thing is clear, and that is that the Soviet Union is definitely attracting sympathizers and potential sympathizers in the General Assembly'. Mr Molotov had been in splendid debating form. When the Philippines delegate had objected to a Russian proposal on the ground that it contradicted parliamentary procedure, Mr Molotov had retorted, 'I am grateful to the delegate of the Philippines for the useful lecture he has offered us about parliamentary procedure. I believe it will be particularly useful in the Philippines in the future when a Parliament exists there'.

Russia naturally exploited her advantage to the limit outside the Assembly. *Izvestia* wrote, 'The desire to hide in the shadow from international public opinion, from the control of publicity, stands out more and more as the line of British policy. . . . The Soviet Union was the first to state, openly and loudly, where and why its troops were and how and when they were withdrawn. . . . The attempts of the British and United States delegations to avoid a decision on the concrete proposal leads one to the conclusion that the British and Americans evidently have some serious grounds for concealing from the United Nations Organization the actual situation with regard to their armed forces abroad'. A broadcast in Persian in January 1947 said that the heated discussions had shown that Great Britain and the United States had been unwilling to furnish information about their armed forces in other countries, but that the Soviet proposal had been warmly welcomed in countries like Egypt, Abyssinia and Iraq, which were anxious for foreign troops to leave their soil.

* * * * *

The Charter of the United Nations had made enlightened provision for the future administration of dependent territories. As far as 'non-self-governing' territories or 'colonies' were concerned, the colonial Powers had declared that they recognized 'the principle that the interests of the inhabitants of these territories are paramount'. They had publicly and formally repudiated the old colonial system. They had undertaken to transmit regularly to the Secretary-General of UNO 'for information purposes' statistical data relating to economic, social and educational conditions in the territories. They had *not* given to UNO under the Charter any rights of interference in the administration of the colonies. This had been made clear in debate at San Francisco.

A separate section of the Charter had provided for the establishment of a trusteeship system under which the former mandated territories would be administered. There was nothing in the Charter to compel the mandatory Powers to place their mandates under trusteeship, but it was assumed that they would do so. By accepting the trusteeship system, the mandatory Powers gave a moral undertaking that they would govern the territories in accordance with an agreed code of principles, and rendered themselves liable to censure by UNO should they default on their undertaking.

These various commitments were shouldered by the colonial Powers voluntarily and gladly. Indeed, they themselves created the commitments. The trusteeship principle was the product and interpretation of British colonial policy, and it was the British Commonwealth and the United States who took the lead in establishing it.

Russia's part in the whole enterprise was about as constructive as that of a boy who sees a busy ant-heap and gives it a passing kick. Her self-appointed task was to represent trusteeship as a hypocritical cover under which the western Powers were consolidating their grip on exploited peoples; to smudge the clear line which the Charter had drawn between colonies and trustee territories, and to try to encroach by means of UNO upon the sovereign rights of the colonial Powers. In short, to make mischief.

At the 1946 Assembly, Mr Molotov complained of delay. 'One might think,' he said, 'that someone was intentionally hindering the formation of the Trusteeship Council. . . . Is not the prestige of our organization being undermined by the fact that for more than a year it has been unable to set up the Trusteeship Council, which should concern itself with improving the living conditions of peoples inhabiting the mandated territories of Great Britain, France, Belgium, Australia, New Zealand and South Africa? . . . Not a single step has been taken yet along this path by the countries which are tenaciously clinging to their mandates for Palestine and Tanganyika, Togoland and New Guinea and so forth, confining themselves so far to writing unsatisfactory projects and insubstantial declarations.' This was the characteristic opening growl. What Mr Molotov did not say was that the texts of three British trustee agreements had lain unacknowledged in a Moscow pigeon-hole for nearly ten months.

The actual terms of the trusteeship agreements provided the Russians with splendid opportunities for interference, insinuation and abuse. By the terms of the Charter, the agreements were to be framed by the 'States directly concerned'. Russia, who considered herself entitled to a finger in everyone's pie, declared herself 'directly concerned'. In her view when the Charter had said 'States directly concerned' it had meant the Big Five. She also objected to the trustee territories being made an 'integral part' of the territory of the trustee Power, though this provision had been considered administratively necessary under the old mandate system. It amounted, she said, to 'annexation'. The drafts reflected 'a tendency to transform the territories into components of the trustee State on a basis of inequality, of colonial possession', and were a retrograde step even in relation to the former mandate system. When in December 1946 the Assembly approved eight trusteeship agreements submitted by four Powers, Russia voted against them and refused to have anything to do with the Trusteeship Council which was set up. It was much more profitable to remain outside and make propaganda. 'The Soviet delegation,' said Orlov in an English broadcast, 'upholds the rights of nations to self-determination and the achievement of complete independence. It opposes retreat to the League system of mandates. It champions advance towards the great principle of equality and self-determination, the realization of which is awaited by the colonial and dependent nations.'

Mr Molotov had a number of most enjoyable field days over South Africa's request for permission to annex South-west Africa to the Union and her refusal to place it under trusteeship. There was nothing to compel South Africa to raise the matter at all, except a moral obligation, but once she had done so the Russians were merciless. The Ukrainian delegate declared that the natives in South-west Africa were deprived of the opportunity to get education, that 90 per cent were ill with tuberculosis, scurvy, venereal disease and other diseases, that they lived in reservations which were fenced with barbed wire and guarded by police and which in their conditions of desolation, filth and poverty recalled fascist concentration camps. Britain got the backwash of opprobrium. *Pravda* wrote, 'A shameful picture of disfranchisement, poverty, oppression and the extinction of the population of the British colonies is revealed every time the iron curtain over the colonial world is drawn aside'.

When the United States first submitted draft agreements for its trusteeship over the Pacific islands formerly under Japanese mandate, the Russians attacked them as 'a poorly-veiled tool of an expansionist policy and an integral part of an imperialist policy which seeks to establish a global system of bases and rule the world with American revolvers'. But when the drafts were presented for final approval, Russia surprised everyone by agreeing that they were 'entirely fair' and sent a nice Note to Mr Marshall saying that the Americans had made 'incomparably greater sacrifices' in the Pacific. In the words of the *Manchester Guardian's* gifted correspondent, Alistair Cooke, 'The Americans had expected to grovel before Mr Gromyko. But crouching before his inevitable whip, they looked up to see it was a sword he had in his hand and that they had been knighted'. But satisfaction was premature. The Pacific islands had been declared by America a 'strategic area' and as such would come under the ultimate supervision of the Security Council—where Russia had a veto.

Russia's disruptive propaganda was not confined to the subject of trusteeship. The most determined efforts were made to re-write the Charter at the expense of the colonial Powers. The Russians were not content with the Charter provision which required the submission to UNO of information about the social, economic and educational development of the colonies; they wanted political information as well, though in fact there was no shortage of published data. 'Their demand,' said *The Times,* 'proceeds not from a disinterested thirst for knowledge but from the calculation that its formal submission to the Secretary-General will give a pretext for international interference with the control of colonies which the Charter does not authorize.' That view of Russian motives was borne out by other projects in which the Soviet delegation took a leading part. With the help of India and several smaller states, Russia succeeded on one occasion in having a proposal adopted providing for periodical conferences of the colonial peoples in order that they might have the opportunity to express their wishes. Another resolution which she sponsored provided that the Secretary-General should convene an *ad hoc* committee to make recommendations on the basis of the information supplied by the colonial Powers. She even urged that UNO representatives should make annual visits to the colonies. All these attempts to undermine the sovereignty of the colonial Powers were completely outside the scope of the Charter, but Russia would not hear of a suggestion that UNO's jurisdiction should be clarified by the International Court. She always preferred agitation to clarification.

Russia was in a good tactical position to harry the colonial Powers, for once again they were vulnerable and she was not. She, of course, had no 'colonies'. It was true that she had annexed large alien territories around her borders as a result of successful war, but that was different. She had deported a large percentage of the populations to the interior of Russia, replaced them with loyal Soviet citizens, and incorporated the territories into the Soviet Union. Nobody had the right to interfere in matters concerning an integral part of Russia. When the representatives of a harassed colonial Power dared to refer to the subject of Russia's annexations, the Soviet delegate declared, 'It is well known that this has happened as a result of the free expression of the people's will'.

*　　*　　*　　*　　*

Three examples have been given of the way in which Russia used the United Nations to assist her aggressive propaganda campaign against the western Powers. The manner in which she used the organization to prevent effective action being taken against her interests in Persia and in Greece has already been noted and will be studied again later in connection with Korea. Undoubtedly, however, the most flagrant 'defensive' use of UNO arose out of the Corfu Channel incident.

On October 22nd, 1946, a British naval squadron was moving north between the island of Corfu and the Russian satellite state of Albania. It was keeping close to the Albanian shore, as was the normal custom of shipping, to avoid an uncleared German minefield on the left. The destroyer *Saumarez* struck a mine in the channel and the destroyer *Volage* took her in tow. An Albanian launch came alongside, asked what the ships were doing there, and returned to port without offering assistance. Shortly afterwards *Volage* struck a mine. Altogether forty men were killed and forty-three wounded.

A report was made to the Mediterranean zone board of the International Mine Clearance Organization on which Britain, France, Greece, USA and Russia were represented, and on its recommendation the British Navy swept the channel on November 12th and 13th, finding twenty-two very powerful German moored mines. Nine were identified on the spot and two were preserved. Examination showed conclusively that the mines had been newly-laid—within six months or less—and subsequent technical evidence on this point was not seriously disputed.

Britain accused Albania of a 'deliberately hostile act' in laying the mines and said she would bring the matter before the Security Council if reparation were not made. Yermashov in Hungarian said, 'Is it not quite plain and flagrantly proved that political pressure is being brought to bear on a small country which refuses to allow its sovereignty to be violated in any manner?'

After protracted and unsuccessful attempts to deal directly with Albania in the matter, Britain brought the dispute before the Security Council on February 18th, 1947, in the teeth of Russian objection. Sir Alexander Cadogan presented the charge— that a minefield had been deliberately, recently and secretly laid for three miles along a channel open to and frequently used by shipping of all nations, and that it had been laid either by, or with the connivance of, the Albanian Government since it came within 300 yards of the Albanian coast. This, said Sir Alexander, was a serious international crime and a crime against humanity.

The Albanian delegate, Kapo, denied that Albania had laid the mines or knew about them and said his government felt 'insulted'. The presence of British warships in the channel without permission was an infringement of Albanian national sovereignty—a 'provocation'. Mr Kapo then made a violent attack on the British attitude to the Albanian 'liberation' movement during the war, thus providing the only missing link in the chain of evidence—the motive.

Mr Gromyko supported Russia's protégé. Foreign ships which might have been responsible often appeared in Albanian waters, he said; ships had often been mined in places considered cleared and in any case British warships were 'bossing' in Albanian waters under the pretext of mine clearance. In short, Albania might not have known about the mines; if she had it was excusable; the British claim was unjust and ought to be dismissed.

Whether or not British warships were entitled to be in these waters was irrelevant to the main issue. It was pure chance that warships had been the first victims of the minefield—merchant ships might equally have been destroyed. Universally accepted international law, quite apart from the normal dictates of humanity, forbade the unnotified scattering of high explosive in any waters, even in wartime, and most of all in a recognized shipping lane. Only a short time before, UNRRA barges had been towed through this channel. There had rarely been a more callous or criminal act in peacetime than the laying of these mines. There had never been a clearer case.

When the Security Council met again in March, the Albanians—who had earlier hinted that the Greeks must have laid the mines off the Albanian shore without being noticed—now accused the British Navy of having laid on November 12th and 13th the mines which had blown up the destroyers three weeks earlier. The members of the Council spoke up strongly. One after another, they put the blame squarely on Albania. By a vote of seven to two, with one abstention (Syria), they declared that the mines could not have been laid without Albania's knowledge. Mr Gromyko, defender of the faithful, then applied his veto. Contemptuous of evidence, flouting the collective will and hating Britain, he made Russia's function in UNO plain by that one act.

The Security Council was now 'obstructed, sterile and impotent'. When in April Sir Alexander Cadogan moved that the dispute should be transferred to the International Court, the Soviet delegate took the opportunity to repeat that the British charge arose from political hostility to Albania and Mr Kapo ascribed the accusation to British 'greed'.

The Russian attitude, in all its studied malice, was perhaps made most clear in an article which appeared in *New Times* early in 1947. 'The history of these incidents,' it said, 'can serve as an example of how conflicts are engineered. . . . The true cause of Britain's reluctance to maintain normal relations with Albania is in the British Government's hostile attitude to the Albanian regime. . . . When the Corfu channel incident occurred, it was naturally regarded as an attempt on Britain's part to find some justification for the refusal to establish normal diplomatic relations and to blame the Albanian Government for the tension between the two countries. . . . The British attempt to represent the peaceful Albanian State as a dangerous aggressor originates in plans which have nothing in common with the interests of peace and security. The Anglo-Albanian dispute was fabricated for a definite purpose.'

And this was an ally!

CHAPTER XI

THE ATOM AND DISARMAMENT

If Russia had been willing to co-operate with her allies after the war, it is probable that the world would by now be able to look forward with confidence to the maintenance of global peace. An international authority could have been established to take full charge of atomic development, an international force could have been created to impose the will of UNO on any malefactor, and in a novel atmosphere of universal safety States might well have been glad to throw off the burden of their national armaments, as the peaceful citizen in an ordered community is glad that he need not carry a gun.

All these bright hopes were dashed by Russia. At a time when the majority of countries had realized that the clash of unrestricted sovereignties in an atomic age might destroy all, Russia raised hostility between groups of nations to the status of a principle. As has been seen, in the existing conditions she did not believe in international accord. For her, the struggle for world power was still to be resolved and international co-operation could come only under the aegis of communism, after victory. To accept a genuine world authority prematurely would be to abandon the ideological struggle, to betray the dogma. In such circumstances, there was never the least possibility that the long discussions in UNO about the atom, disarmament and the creation of a world force could have any fruitful outcome. The talks interested Russia only in so far as she thought she could extract material or propaganda advantage from them. They are worth studying mainly for the further light they throw on the consistent intransigence of the Russian attitude.

In the post-war world, control of atomic energy was rightly considered the key to the whole security problem. Attention was properly focused on the atom bomb not because it was the only weapon of mass destruction—there were many others—but because it was a unique and isolated weapon which could provide a simple test case. If the nations could agree on the major surrender of sovereignty and the vast measure of international control which would be required to tame the atom, all else would follow. The atomic bomb was the fortress of the disarmament and security problem; once the fortress was stormed, the support points would collapse.

History—if there is any unscorched bark to write it on—will have difficulty in criticizing the attitude of the United States towards atomic energy in the immediate post-war period. It was never true that the American monopoly of the bomb contributed to the division of the world. Russian policy towards the West had set hard in its mould before the existence of the bomb was known, and the bomb itself was no more than an additional excuse for an enmity already decided on. Had America followed the advice of the lunatic fringe and shared out its atom bombs among the nations like nuts at a party, Russia would have been much more dangerous but no less hostile. No propaganda can alter the fact that for the first time in history a nation possessing a dominant weapon made no attempt to force its will upon its neighbours. The charge of 'atomic diplomacy' was inevitable but baseless. The first eighteen months of America's monopoly coincided with a period of unbroken diplomatic conciliation by United States representatives. Far from desiring to exploit the hideous new weapon, America was quick to realize that international atomic control was urgent. Whatever the Russians might say, there was no precedent for such enlightenment. New ground was being broken. In the UNO Assembly Mr Hector McNeil said, 'Let Mr Vishinsky . . . tell us of some Soviet monopoly in armaments which the Soviet Government is anxious to place under international control and ownership'. There was no answer.

From the beginning, it was the West which took the initiative in seeking a workable and watertight atomic agreement, and Russia which displayed little interest in the project. It was the western Powers who were most acutely aware of the menace, who were most concerned about the possibility of an atomic armaments race. In November 1945 the British and Canadian Prime Ministers went to Washington to discuss atomic energy policy with President Truman and agreement was subsequently announced on the need for international control with full safeguards under the auspices of UNO. The expressed intention, generous as well as wise, was not merely to provide protection against the misuse of the atom, but to make its power available for peaceful purposes to the whole world. When the Foreign Ministers met in Moscow in December, it was the Americans who put the subject of atomic control at the head of the agenda, and the Russians who suggested that it should be moved to the bottom. It was the western Powers who urged and obtained Russian approval of preliminary proposals for atomic control. No sooner was the Moscow conference over than the British Government was steering a resolution through the Assembly of UNO, and the Lilienthal Committee appointed by Mr Byrnes was hard at work on the problem in Washington.

Concrete American proposals for international control of atomic energy were advanced in June 1946 in a memorable speech by Mr Bernard Baruch. 'We are here,' he said, 'to make a choice between the quick and the dead.' The substance of the proposals was that a world Atomic Development Authority should be set up, that it should be given very wide powers of control and inspection in all countries, that once the proposals had been accepted no country should have any further right of veto, and that as soon as effective control machinery had been set up America should hand over her stockpile of atom bombs, surrender her monopoly of knowledge, and thereafter be on terms of equality with all other nations as regards atomic energy.

Several things need to be noted about the Baruch plan before we proceed any farther. In the first place, a provision by which the American monopoly would be reduced by stages and finally given up only when an efficient system of control had been established was not just a clever American device to keep the atom bomb as long as possible and meanwhile to establish an espionage network in other people's countries. That was how it was presented by Mr Henry Wallace, who declared that the stages by which control would be imposed required the Russians to put their deuces on the table while leaving the United States to play her aces at her discretion. But in fact the plan was not 'cut-and-dried'; the Americans were by no means inflexibly wedded to the details of their proposal; the 'stages' were subject to negotiation and suggestions would have been welcomed. The fact was that the Russians never at any time made any serious attempt to clarify or amend the proposed relationship between the establishment of control machinery and the surrender by America of her monopoly. It is conceivable that had there been a will to agree, a plan could have been devised whereby the surrender of monopoly and the coming into force of a complete system of international control and inspection could have been a virtually simultaneous operation. The possibility was never tested. But the suggestion that America hoped, while still keeping her bombs, to be able to make a preliminary aerial survey of all Russia's industrial potential, was a monstrous and wilful perversion of the Baruch plan.

In the second place, the American requirement that atomic control measures should not be subject to a veto was basic. If, once the international undertaking were launched, any Power were permitted to use a veto to check inspection or block the imposition of sanctions on a violator, the whole conception of an atomic authority with adequate legal powers would fall in ruins. It might mean, in an extreme case, that a country would sign all agreements and then obstruct inspection on its territory, manufacture atomic bombs secretly and deny to the international authority the right to take security action in the world's interests.

In the third place, it must be emphasized that whatever suspicions the Russians entertained, they were in a splendid position to test American sincerity. If they really believed that America's stage-by-stage plan was a piece of chicanery, or that in the last resort the American Senate would refuse to agree to the surrender of stockpiles by the United States, now was the chance to find out. By pressing the matter to a stark issue they had everything to gain—assuming their own good faith. Nothing would have given them a greater political advantage in their struggle with America than a public demonstration that the Baruch plan was a fraud or a façade. If the Russians were so sure America was bluffing, now was the time to call the bluff. They did not do so. That suggested a very different Russian fear —that the Americans were in fact in earnest.

One final aspect of the Baruch plan must be stressed. In this— as indeed in any plan for any kind of international action to deal with armaments—an efficient system of inspection was the crux. All experience had shown, between the wars and since, that it was idle to talk of disarmament except in the context of security machinery on which the world could place reliance. No nation would disarm unless there were infrangible international guarantees. Confidence must come before disarmament, and confidence meant inspection. Without, inspection the nations would not trust each other, nor was there any reason why they should. Only a few years before Japan had signed a Naval Treaty at Washington and had at once proceeded to break it in secret. Precisely the same thing could happen over atom bombs. Moreover, Russia—a vast and almost hermetically-sealed police state—was just the sort of country where infraction would be easy. There could be no doubt whatever that unrestricted inspection was a condition of effective atomic control.

* * * * *

The Russian reaction to the Baruch plan was swift and hostile. Never was a constructive international proposal more recklessly misrepresented and maligned. Though it was patent to the whole world that the plan started from the assumption that America had an atomic monopoly and was trying to shed it safely, Mr Molotov declared that the plan originated in 'a desire to secure for the United States monopolist possession of the bomb'. The Russians preferred to exploit, rather than to elucidate, the proposal for an advance in 'stages'. Izakov in June 1946 declared that the American plan amounted to fixing a monopolistic position for the United States in the manufacture of atomic weapons 'for an indefinite period'. Why, he asked, were all countries bound to display blind trust towards the intentions of the United States while the United States itself maintained an attitude of distrust not only towards its partners but towards the proposed international control body as well. The American press, he declared, was 'chattering' about the need for nations to 'abandon their sovereignty' but what it really had in view was that all nations should sacrifice their sovereignty to the United States. 'The United States Government,' he said, 'evidently intends to determine at its own discretion the period of time during which it would allow the international organization to look into the secrets of the "atomic kitchen" gradually.' 'In this very mixed-up plan,' declared Izakov, 'every point evokes bewilderment and is pregnant with every sort of complication.'

Each new Russian comment further distorted the plan. A broadcast from Moscow in July 1946 referred to 'Baruch's plan . . . which provides for preserving the atomic weapon, preserving the monopoly of one State in that weapon, and utilizing it for bringing political pressure to bear on other countries.' A more wanton distortion could hardly be imagined. *Izvestia* declared, 'The Atomic Commission can become transformed into an independent organ in which the tune would be called by the country possessing the greatest quantity of atomic weapons'.

A grotesque summary of the Baruch proposals was given by Marinin in *Pravda* in July. 'The United States,' he wrote, 'holds the atomic weapon in its hands and manufactures it without any restrictions; the international control centre intensively collects information on world uranium and thorium deposits and furnishes the USA with this information. Should the USA find it suitable and advantageous, it will from time to time present to the international centre certain portions of the secret of production of the atomic weapon. And should the USA for some reason find this disadvantageous, it will resort to its Constitution—which demands that important international acts be approved by two-thirds of the votes of the Senate. Under Baruch's plan, the control organ is virtually deprived of all rights, since it does not enjoy any serious possibilities in face of the United States. It is virtually transformed into an international office for serving the needs of the American atom concern.'

In the light of this fantasy, a statement in a broadcast in Rumanian that America was finding neither the time nor the money nor the scientists for the peaceful exploitation of atomic energy and was stopping every attempt of the kind can only be regarded as a very subsidiary misrepresentation.

By December 1946, the Russians were referring to the 'notorious' Baruch plan, as though it were something shameful, and were attacking Mr Baruch personally as little better than a warmonger. In a speech ruefully philosophizing about the difficulties of getting men to live at peace, Mr Baruch had said, 'Peace seems beautiful during the brutalities of war, but becomes almost hateful when war is over'. The Russians, almost incredibly, twisted this to mean that he himself found peace 'hateful'. 'Such is the real face,' said *Tass,* 'of some peacemakers.' The speech was 'characteristic of Baruch', whose plan—declared *Izvestia*—

was made to suit 'American monopolists, bankers and stock exchange operators'.

Meanwhile, the Russians had produced a counter-plan. Presented by Mr Gromyko immediately after the Baruch plan had been made public, it proposed an international convention to 'outlaw' atomic warfare. The nations would simply agree not to use atomic weapons in any circumstances. The production and stockpiling of atomic weapons would be forbidden. All stocks of bombs would be destroyed within three months of the coming into force of the convention. The nations would declare any violation to be 'a serious international crime' and would undertake to pass legislation within six months providing for the severe punishment of offenders. Two committees were to be set up, one for the exchange of scientific information and the other to devise means of preventing the harmful use of atomic energy. Mr Gromyko took the opportunity to warn the nations against any attempt to modify the veto in connection with atomic control. Izakov declared that the distinctive features of the Russian plan were 'humanity, clarity and efficacy'.

This plan meant, and was of course intended to mean, that America would unilaterally disarm herself to the immense advantage of the Soviet Union. It was a missile hurled at an enemy rather than the foundation-stone of a security system. It left the menace of the atom wholly uncontrolled. All experience had shown that 'outlawing' a weapon did not suffice to prevent its manufacture and use if some nation thought it advantageous. It is inconceivable that the realistic Russians—who had poured such scorn on the Kellogg pact which 'outlawed' war itself—took their own proposal seriously. The Russian plan was strictly propaganda. Mr Gromyko knew that the western allies would oppose it because of its unrealistic nature, and then he would be able to denounce them as upholders of the atomic weapon. Marinin declared, 'The Soviet plan guarantees effective control over the observance of the convention, and the appropriate sanctions in the event of its violation'. It did nothing of the sort. The vague guarantees which the Russians had in mind would come within the Security Council framework, would be subject to the veto, and as a world defence against atomic warfare would be derisory.

For many months, the Atomic Energy Commission of UNO

discussed the two plans and failed to find any basis of agreement. In December 1946, the Commission adopted a plan closely modelled on the Baruch proposals providing for an international atomic authority with wide powers of control and inspection untrammelled by the veto. The plan was approved by ten votes to none, Russia and Poland abstaining. There was clearly no possibility that it could be carried into effect in view of Russian opposition, but the majority members continued to work on it in the hope that one day it might be needed.

* * * * *

From the Russian point of view, the intense activity in the Atomic Energy Commission was most regrettable. The western Powers had not merely sponsored and gained very wide support for proposals which Russia could in no circumstances accept; they had shown a pertinacity and enthusiasm in the Commission which had gone far to destroy the Russian contention that they did not really want atomic disarmament at all. In spite of all Mr Gromyko's efforts, the whole world was beginning to think that Russia was the nigger in the atomic pile.

In October 1946, Mr Molotov decided to make a move which would, he hoped, restore the initiative to Russia and at the same time thrust the Atomic Energy Commission into the background. In a hard-hitting and effective speech to the General Assembly of UNO, he called for a general reduction in armaments. In the General Assembly everyone was always against Sin and in favour of Disarmament and the speech was therefore assured of a good reception. Of course, said Mr Molotov, the Assembly should not be content to call in general terms for a reduction of armaments, but should specify as a primary task the prohibition of the manufacture and use of atomic energy for military purposes. It would be wrong, he declared, to postpone a decision on this question. The Russian plan to 'outlaw' the atom, rejected by the Atomic Energy Commission on the ground of its ineffectiveness, was once more in the picture. Mr Molotov, the great confusionist, had worked the trick again.

Walter Lippmann described the speech as 'a mighty counterattack'. Once again the western Powers were on the defensive. In the Atomic Energy Commission they had managed to cut a deep channel of technical achievement; now the stream of their activity had to be diverted into the delta of disarmament platitudes which was Mr Molotov's favourite terrain. Reluctantly, Britain and America took up and examined the flamboyant Russian resolution. The Americans produced a counter-resolution. Mr Molotov began to talk about 'meeting the United States half-way' on the disarmament question, and he got big headlines for a statement made at a banquet that 'we may already now assume that the proposals of the Soviet and American delegations can be brought into accord'. The professional optimists scribbled busily. In November Mr Molotov brought forward supplementary proposals for the international control and inspection of disarmament 'within the framework of the Security Council'. There were to be two control commissions, one for conventional armaments and one for atomic weapons. Mr Molotov knew there was no better method of squandering UNO energy than by the proliferation of commissions.

In December the Russian delegate was persuaded further to define his attitude to the use of the veto in connection with inspection—ground so well-trodden that it defied cultivation. His view was that the veto could be used while a decision on arms reduction was being worked out in the Security Council and it could be used in regard to Security Council decisions on the institution of committees for control over arms reduction and for the observance of the ban on atomic weapons. But once the control committees had been set up, they would naturally work according to the regulations the Security Council had laid down. 'Accordingly,' said Mr Molotov, suddenly emerging from a thicket of obscurity into the sunlight of clarity, 'it is quite wrong to represent the matter as if any state commanding the veto power would be in a position to prevent control and inspection.' Like a boy using a mathematical crib, he had the answer right even if it was not quite plain how he had arrived at it. The atmosphere in the Assembly became emotional as the two sides seemed to be coming together and the Canadian delegate declared, 'The peoples of the whole world will be grateful to the outstanding leader of the Soviet delegation who has today given the world fresh hope that we shall now be able to make great strides towards the realization of the dream of millions in all countries'.

However, the roseate dream was soon dissipated. As the discussions proceeded, it became apparent that Russia still had no intention of accepting any workable scheme of control and inspection, and that her main interest was to have the functions of the Atomic Energy Commission duplicated or perhaps superseded by an entirely new committee working on entirely different lines—Russian lines. Tempers began to fray. Mr Molotov blamed Britain for trying to treat atomic energy as though it were a separate problem. *Izvestia* accurately described Russia's constructive role when it wrote, 'The Soviet delegation with its consistent policy knocks the cards from the hands of its opponents'. Nevertheless, in the middle of December the Assembly was able to reach unanimous agreement on a disarmament resolution which was so broad that it was impossible to see what ends it served. It was left to the Security Council to give concrete form to the Assembly's wishes.

Reviewing the session, Viktorov wrote in *Pravda*, 'The course of the discussion showed that the enthusiasm of certain delegates was fully exhausted by their welcoming speeches'. Attempts had been made to 'drown the Russian proposal in a flood of casuistical resolutions'. Once again, a moral dichotomy was presented to the world. 'One tendency—characteristic of the Soviet delegation and of those supporting it—aims at going beyond formally raising the question of armaments reduction and endeavouring to secure a speedy and practical realization of measures for it. The other expresses a desire to avoid a practical realization.' Mr Molotov was represented as a great peacemaker. He had gone to the Assembly with bold proposals, he had forced them through in substance, and a unanimous resolution had resulted. That just showed what could be done when a country was sincerely devoted to the cause of peace and was not to be put off by a niggling pre-occupation with detail. There was no doubt that from the propaganda point of view, Mr Molotov had achieved his purpose and rescued the game.

When the discussions were resumed in the Security Council in the New Year, the United States and Britain were insistent that whatever was done under the Assembly's resolution should not undermine the work already carried out by the Atomic Energy Commission, whose authority must not be infringed in its field. The Council should refuse, said the United States delegate, to drop the report of the one commission that had completed the first phase of its work in order to set up another which would have to start all over again. In February the Americans proposed that the new commission should be called 'the Commission for Conventional Armaments', and that matters within the competence of the Atomic Energy Commission should be expressly excluded from its jurisdiction. This was opposed by the Russians, who were not in the least interested in what they knew was the futile task of pressing ahead with conventional disarmament, but were very interested in sabotaging the Atomic Energy Commission. When the American proposal was put to the vote, Mr Gromyko and his Polish colleague abstained from voting. They abstained again when the Council adopted a programme of work in accordance with the Assembly's resolution. Gradually, all the disarmament talks petered out. No progress was made at all in the discussions on conventional armaments and the gulf was seen to be unbridgeable when the Russian delegate declared, 'The system of control can come into force only when disarmament has been accomplished'.

* * * * *

It is now time to take a closer look at the root cause of failure in the whole field of discussion on atomic energy, disarmament and security. Deadlock invariably arose over the question of inspection and control. The record shows that from time to time the Russians appeared to be making minor concessions; to be moving, however slightly, away from flat negation. But there was no clarity or consistency about the movement. It was in March 1947 that Mr Gromyko gave the quietus to baseless hopes. He declared with calculated emphasis that Russia would accept no system of control which involved any international interference with the industrial life of Russia. Governments which supported such plans, he said, 'must have lost their sense of reality'. He objected to an international atomic control organ having the functions of ownership, management, licensing and supervision of mining operations and fission plants, or unlimited access to atomic plants for inspection. He objected to aerial surveys by agents of the international authority or to broad privileges of travel for its agents. He took his stand on the principle of national sovereignty. UNO's Atomic Energy Commission, he said, with its detailed plans of inspection, was just an international trust designed to perpetuate the United States atomic monopoly, and all that was missing in the Commission's report was provision for dividing the profits of the trust's operations! He disagreed that international action against any violator of any agreement should be exempt from the operation of the veto. He saw no danger that plants would be worked clandestinely for 'each nation would report faithfully a complete list of its factories'. In September 1947 the Soviet Government, asked by Britain to clarify its position, confirmed in a Note that in its view the functions of an inspectorate must be restricted and that all sanctions must be subject to the veto. Later, Mr Vishinsky underlined the Soviet attitude. In no circumstances, he said, could Russia accept foreign interference in atomic production plants.

Though it took the West nearly two years to get Russia's objections to any effective control and inspection publicly and finally clarified, her attitude could always have been deduced from first principles. From the Russian point of view, acceptance of the necessary minimum of international interference would have meant letting down the drawbridge to the enemy. Soviet Russia could never open her frontiers. She had too much to hide. Effective inspection would mean, among other things, that her scores of forced-labour camps and her millions of political internees would be uncovered, for the places she most wished to keep secret were naturally those which any conscientious inspectorate would want to visit. The grim foundations of the Soviet State—its police terror, its conditioned population, its tyranny—would be exposed. The insulated Soviet masses would make new contacts; the inward flow of dangerous knowledge would sap the whole political structure. The idea was quite fantastic. Of course Soviet Russia would never accept inspection.

*　*　*　*　*

The indifferent and finally the obstructive attitude of the Soviet Union to the establishment of an international force under UNO was equally predictable. It was true that the veto protected her against the operations of any such force; that she could prevent its legal use in any circumstances whatever where she felt it would be harmful to her interests. But there were dangers in the very existence of an international force. The time might come when the United Nations, veto or no veto, would decide to use an embodied force to assert their collective will even outside the framework of the Charter. The whole conception of a UNO with teeth was anathema to the Russians, whose hopes lay in creating trouble, not in maintaining order; whose interest was a divided, not a united world. Consequently, in the post-war period Russia did her best to obstruct the work of the Military Staff Committee, whose task it was to advise and assist the Security Council in establishing a police arm. Only after being repeatedly prodded by the Assembly and the Security Council did this Committee produce, in May 1947, a report which bristled with major disagreements. Russia's motives stood out plainly from her proposals. She demanded that each Power should contribute an identical contingent of force, which meant, for instance, that if one Power had no battleships the force would have no battleships either. She refused to agree that world bases should be put at the disposal of the force, insisting that between tasks it should be maintained in divided form on the home soil of its various contingents. This was tantamount to having no World Force at all, which was evidently what Russia wanted. When the subject was dropped, she was well content.

* * * * *

Surprise has often been expressed that, from the point of view of her own self-interest, Russia should have been so disinclined to bring under international control an atomic weapon which she herself did not possess and which for that reason was obviously a potential menace to her.

It can be assumed that the Soviet leaders weighed their decision carefully on this specific issue. The official Russian propaganda tended to make light of the bomb. Russian correspondents, after visiting the ruins of Hiroshima and Nagasaki, were allowed to say that the effect would be incomparably less in western cities and that the destruction could have been achieved more cheaply with ordinary bombs. No doubt such reports were intended primarily to reassure the Russian people.

What the Russian leaders did believe was that the bomb
would be of little use against large armies or widely-dispersed
industry. In September 1946 Stalin said the bomb was intended
to intimidate the weak-nerved but that it could not decide the
outcome of a war. He knew, of course, that on the outbreak of
atomic war his Red Army could march to the Atlantic without
serious opposition and that the atom bomb could hardly be used
against occupied western cities. He knew, too, that it was still
difficult to manufacture large numbers of bombs.

Moreover, the Russians confidently believed that with the
help of German scientists and the fruits of espionage they would
soon be able to manufacture the bomb themselves. Meanwhile
they had naturally no intention of provoking a war, and it is unlikely that they believed America would do so. They felt that
they had time.

Above all, the temporary risk arising out of the American
monopoly had to be weighed against the danger to the regime
if Russia's gates were once opened to the outside world. It is understandable that on a cool calculation the bomb seemed to
Stalin the lesser evil.

CHAPTER XII

RELIEF AND THE MARSHALL PLAN

One of the most bitter disputes between the Soviet Union and the western allies after World War II concerned the fate of Displaced Persons in the western zones of Germany and Austria. Of the pitiful human wreckage found there when the Nazis collapsed, by far the greater part had been returned home in a little over a year. The trouble arose over the 'hard core' of DPs—numbering some hundreds of thousands—who did not want to be repatriated. The bulk of these consisted of Poles who before the war had lived in the eastern part of Poland which had since been incorporated into the Soviet Union; Balts from Estonia, Latvia and Lithuania which had been annexed by Russia in 1940; and smaller numbers of people from many eastern nations which had come under Soviet domination. In other parts of Europe, there was a considerable Polish army which did not want to return to a communist Poland. The 'hard core', in fact, consisted largely of political opponents of the eastern regimes and was the direct result of Russian expansion and domination.

The Russian view was that all people who had been living before the war in the lands the Soviet Union had subsequently taken over were now Soviet citizens, and that it was their duty to return to Russia. Mr Vishinsky argued before UNO that if they failed to return they should be denied relief. The other eastern Governments likewise required the return of their own nationals. The western view was that people against whom no crime was charged ought not to be repatriated against their will.

The second problem concerned DPs who, in the eastern view, were 'war criminals'. There was no doubt at all that the post-war DP camps contained many criminal elements—men who had been guilty of 'war crimes' as well as many who for various reasons and in varying degrees had collaborated with the Germans. The difficulty was to decide what constituted 'war guilt'. There were Russian 'Whites', Yugoslav Chetniks and Ustachis, Hungarian 'Arrow Cross' men, Poles of General Anders' army,

Ukrainian nationalists—indeed, every European hatred, every minority cause seemed to be represented. Some, like the Poles, deserved gratitude rather than punishment; the Royal Yugoslav Army remnants were naturally hated by Tito but it was not clear that they had done anything to warrant summary vengeance at allied hands. Most of them were honest patriots. The western Powers had no desire to shield 'criminals' and made it clear that they were prepared to hand over to established Governments all those men against whom a good *prima facie* case of 'war guilt' could be made. They rightly refused to extradite large numbers of people on vague political charges, particularly as experience had shown that no fair trials could be expected in the eastern countries and that extradition was virtually equivalent to sentence.

In general, the West was as anxious as the Russians that the DPs should be persuaded to return home as quickly as possible and in the greatest possible numbers. Soviet propaganda often seemed to assume that Britain and America derived some sort of advantage from clinging to DPs. The opposite was true. These people were a huge administrative and financial liability. They consumed without producing; some of them got into serious mischief; all were wretched; and because they were almost all hostile to Russia and to communism they were a source of constant embarrassment and political tension. From every point of view except that of common decency and humanity, it would have paid the western Powers forcibly to repatriate them.

In their efforts to stimulate voluntary repatriation, the western allies and UNRRA used every means of persuasion they could think of short of force—and not far short. Russian and communist propaganda material and repatriation literature were freely admitted to the camps, while western literature was largely forbidden. Repatriation officers from the eastern countries were allowed to attend the camps in an effort to recruit volunteers. UNRRA officials pleaded, exhorted and sometimes came very near to threatening. The miserable inmates were subjected to organized and high-pressure agitation. 'The propitious time for the use of emotional devices will be left to the judgment of the district officers and area teams,' said one UNRRA order relating to Polish camps. Some UNRRA officials had to be reprimanded for putting DPs through a kind of political 'third degree'. To encourage repatriation, DPs were sometimes harried from camp to camp. Educational and cultural facilities were withdrawn. The inmates were constantly reminded that they had no prospects except in their own countries. The whole campaign was designed to make life so distasteful that only the most adamant would prefer exile under such conditions to returning home. The path of those who decided to go was sweetened, in some cases, by a gift of 60 days' food.

Though it was quite impossible to prevent anti-Russian feeling in the camps, every effort was made by the western Military Governments to stop organized propaganda. Agitation against any of the United Nations was strictly forbidden in DP assembly points. Specific Russian complaints were always checked, and if they proved to be well-founded action was always taken. The West tried to be loyal. It is possible to argue that loyalty went beyond what was reasonable. On the known facts, it is not possible to argue that repatriation efforts were half-hearted.

* * * * *

The Russians, as usual, impugned the motives of the West. They said that the British and Americans were deliberately protecting criminals and quislings, encouraging fascists, and keeping armed anti-Soviet formations in being for sinister purposes —charges which were all untrue. *Tass* in June 1946 quoted the Czech communist newspaper *Rude Pravo* for the statement that the western zones had become a shelter for all sorts of quislings and bandits. There were, it said, some 300,000 people, mainly Hungarians, Bulgarians and Yugoslavs, who though officially DPs were allowed free movement outside the camps and appeared to be carrying arms. 'The number of fascist gangs,' said the paper in a particularly wild allegation, 'exceeds that of the occupation forces of all four states together.' Writing in *Pravda* in July 1946, Viktorov declared, 'The American and British zones have become a refuge for notorious criminals, for Hitlerite hangers-on'. Arnoldov in a Moscow broadcast said that the notorious fascist Stepan Bandera was touring the United States zone inspecting White Guard military formations. In a number of fiery speeches to the United Nations, Mr Vishinsky produced long lists of 'war criminals' who were being given sanctuary in

254

the western zones. When the cases were investigated, it was usually impossible to find any trace of the persons mentioned.

The Russians pretended that the only thing preventing large-scale repatriation of the 'hard core' was the attitude of the western allies. In November 1946 *Tass* declared that systematic propaganda was being carried out in the western zones against the return of the DPs to their homes. A broadcast in English in November said that most of the DPs still in the western zones were anxious to go home. Another broadcast quoted the report of a repatriated native of Vilna to the effect that refugees who wanted to return were cruelly treated, and the statement of a Kharkov woman that the inmates of her camp had been frightened by 'White Guards' in British uniforms. When a group of Soviet citizens in one camp had issued two copies of a wall newspaper, 'The Motherland Calls', said this broadcaster, British officers had torn it down and had threatened the editor with detention and flogging. In May 1947, *Tass* quoted a Vienna report that the British were using force to prevent the repatriation of DPs in Italy, and were compelling the wives and children of repatriates to remain behind. At one camp 'Soviet citizens who expressed a wish to return home were escorted from the camp handcuffed'. Mikhailov, in an English broadcast on DPs, said 'Most of these people are victims of fascism. They were torn from their homes by the Nazis and are anxious to get back but they are kept from returning to their countries by the war criminals at work in refugee camps'.

It cannot be denied that pressure and force were sometimes used by inmates of the camps against those who wanted to go home. There were some bad incidents. But the charge that the administering authorities encouraged or tolerated such incidents was false. Refutation of Soviet propaganda allegations was hampered by the studied lack of detail in the stories.

What the Russians would have liked would have been a complete list of the names and addresses of the DPs in the camps, 'as then we would be able to arrange contact between the DPs and their relatives and friends' as the Ukrainian delegate told UNO in November 1946. But the western Powers knew that relatives would be used by the Russians as a means of coercion, and rightly withheld this information. They did, however, permit Russian and other liaison officers to attend the camps, with little effect. *The Times* correspondent reported from Vienna in March 1947, 'A Soviet repatriation mission, stationed permanently in the British zone, visits the Russian camp four times a week and waits for volunteers, but none comes'. The Russians alleged that obstacles were put in their way. In May 1947 Tsuriyupov wrote in *Red Star* that there were still 'hundreds of thousands of DPs' who had not had the opportunity of returning to their countries. He quoted a case of alleged obstruction. 'Searching for Soviet citizens in the British-occupied zone, Major Tikmazov accompanied by the chief of No. 626 Military Administration and an UNRRA representative visited two DP camps. In one of them the camp commandant, evidently forewarned, hastened to assure the Military Administration chief that there was not a single DP desirous of talking to the Soviet officer. Contrary to this assertion, on the appearance of the Soviet officer DPs in the camp began to gather in the courtyard with the obvious intention of engaging him in conversation. Tikmazov proposed approaching one of the groups but the Military Administration chief said that meetings were against regulations.' One can assume that the regulations were designed to safeguard the repatriation officers. DPs 'gathered in the courtyard' had a way of turning themselves into a lynching party. Only a few months before a Yugoslav official had been killed in a camp in Italy after he had defied the commandant's instructions and arrived without warning in a car flying Tito's flag to have a quiet talk with the inmates.

The British decision in 1947 to accept suitable DP immigrants to work in Britain provided the Russians with a propaganda theme exactly to their taste. Writing in *Pravda* in May 1947, Izakov said, 'This plan of mass recruitment of cheap labour from DPs is a plan to create in England a new reserve of serfs. The British working-class will be the chief sufferers from this. The creation of such a class will be a permanent factor in exerting pressure on the wages of the British working-class. Definite forces are attempting to use the DP problem for their mercenary aims, which have nothing in common with the interests of the people who are roaming in foreign countries far from their native lands'. A broadcast by Bilibin said that British and American reactionaries were building up artificial obstacles to repatriation in order to be able to form additional reserves of cheap labour for their colonies, dominions and other countries. A home service broadcast in May said that the British were recruiting DP labour by 'persuasion, deceit and threats'. Another talk for Russian listeners in June said that in Germany young DP girls had been forced to sign a contract obliging them to work for two years in Canada for a salary not even sufficient to give them a normal quantity of food. In July Korolkov wrote in *Pravda* that 'the recruitment of white slaves' could not be tolerated in the civilized world. 'Labour recruiters roam round the camps in search of cheap labour, persuading demoralized and frightened people.' But, as so often happened, Russian statements cancelled each other out. In an earlier broadcast these intimidated and exploited 'white slaves' had been denounced as 'followers of Nazism who prefer a life of ease in a foreign land to working for the restoration of the homeland'.

Russian propaganda about DPs in the British zone reached its climax late in 1947. Disturbed by the bad effect abroad of the decision not to release the Russian wives of British Servicemen, the Soviet Foreign Office complained in June in a formal Note that in spite of repeated inquiries in Germany no action had been taken by the British to repatriate Soviet children housed in orphanages, five of whom were mentioned by name. The Soviet press and radio developed the theme with gusto. These children, the Russians declared, were being kept in conditions of slavery; knowledge that the identity of their parents had been discovered was being withheld from them; they were being forced to become Roman Catholics and to 'forget the Russian language', their names had been deliberately changed, they were often whipped by the teachers and threatened with the 'police', and at one camp the favourite game taught to them was playing at war against the Russians.

Soviet public opinion was quickly mobilized in protest against such inhuman treatment. Shocked letters appeared in the newspapers and bereaved parents cried into the microphone. Women in the 'Red Rosa' textile mills in Moscow held lunch-hour indignation meetings. Letters were written to the British Red Cross. 'Surely,' cried Moscow radio, 'no British mother, no decent English man or woman, can hear about the forcible retention of Soviet children without crying "shame".' With its customary partiality, the British-Soviet Society hotly took up the Russian case. The charge was exploited on the Russian stage. A new play by Sergei Mikhalkov showed a Russian officer arguing desperately with a group of British officers in a DP camp in an effort to prevent the dispatch to Brazil of Russian children who were being deliberately represented as Poles or children of unknown nationality. Mikhalkov, when not writing plays, was a well-known author of fables.

Unhappily for the Russians, they had at last made an allegation sufficiently specific to be checked. Immediate investigation at the orphanages showed that the children in question—about 70 altogether—had been brought to Germany during the war from the Baltic States. In the absence of evidence to the contrary, they had been cared for by the British as orphans. They had not been ill-treated, or forced to become Catholics, or given different names. They had been educated in the language of the Baltic States from which they came. The members of the Soviet repatriation mission had been free to visit the orphanages at any time, and it was untrue that they had been obstructed in any way. The onus of providing *prima facie* evidence of the existence of parents was naturally upon the Russians, but none had been produced. Although repatriation of children to the Soviet Union had been going on for a long time under arrangements which were familiar to the Russians, no request for the return of any of these children had been made until the official Note of complaint. As soon as satisfactory evidence was forthcoming, the children were handed over to the Russians for repatriation.

One is tempted to describe this as the most dishonest campaign carried out by the Russians in the post-war period, but in such a field perhaps superlatives are out of place.

*   *   *   *   *

There are millions of people now alive in Europe who would be dead but for American aid in the post-war years. Many other nations contributed a quota to the vast total of relief—Britain herself spent £325 millions in non-recoverable assistance before May 1947—but the United States was the great, the universal provider.

American help for the war-shattered world took many forms —the transfer of accumulated lend-lease goods and war surplus stocks on generous terms, the granting of dollar loans, the voting of outright gifts, and the financing of the United Nations Relief and Rehabilitation Administration—UNRRA.

The total value of UNRRA aid was some £930 millions, of which the United States provided nearly three-quarters and Britain about 17 per cent. Of the countries which received assistance, several inside the Russian sphere of influence were high up on the list. The unconcealed hostility of many of these countries to America and Britain was not made an excuse for withholding supplies. Yugoslavia, for instance, which could apparently afford to maintain a large army, which was bitterly anti-American, and which on several occasions shot American aircraft out of the sky, received some 2,400,000 tons of supplies. Poland, whose communist-controlled government habitually broke its pledges to the West, received nearly 2,000,000 tons; Czechoslovakia received 1,500,000 tons; Russia herself received nearly 650,000 tons for distribution in the Ukraine and Byelorussia; Albania, which mined British ships and accused Britain of 'greed', received 180,000 tons. These are the impressive facts.

America resisted the temptation to use relief as a means of gaining either political concessions or economic privileges. In no case did she make internal political changes a condition of aid. She did not, for instance, demand that any country should drop its plans for socialization. She did not use her wealth to buy investments in the countries she assisted. In the main, she gave it away without expectation of return or reward. In so far as she exerted substantial pressure on the countries which she helped, it was pressure for reform—as in Greece and China.

In one or two cases, she reacted to specific breaches of faith by suspending or cancelling credits. In May 1946, for instance, she suspended a credit to Poland when an undertaking in connection with the loan appeared to have been violated, but the credit was restored in June after differences had been 'clarified'. A credit to Czechoslovakia was cancelled in October 1946, but only after a Czech spokesman at the Paris conference had charged the United States with using dollars to enslave Europe and it had been discovered that the Czechs intended to pass on a substantial quantity of American supplies to Rumania at a considerable profit.

To any unprejudiced observer, the most striking characteris-

tic of American aid was the way in which, year after year, it
continued to flow in spite of the insults and calumnies which
were heaped in its path. It surged over the rock of 'dollar diplomacy', it swept past the boulder of 'domination of small States',
it brushed aside the debris of 'capitalist monopoly' and it
flooded down into the plain, bringing life and hope to millions
of ordinary men and women. There were no conditions. Recipients were not even required to empty their mouths of American food before they shouted their abuse.

*   *   *   *   *

Soviet propaganda represented America as a rich mean country which was sending goods abroad only because it could not
use them itself or because it wanted to buy political influence.
In any case, said the Russians, much more could have been done.
Records covering a period of more than two years fail to reveal
a single lapse into gratitude. Not for the first time, Mr Vishinsky
was foremost in criticism. Forgetting the mountains of supplies
from America during the war—not just the aeroplanes and
tanks and trucks, but the petrol and the food and the materials
of every kind—he declared, 'For the United States, the war was
a source of enrichment'. Countries whose internal policies were
totally insulated from any outside influence except that of Russia screamed that America was using relief as a political instrument while they held out their hands for more. 'Progressive
circles abroad,' wrote Gorodetsky in *Izvestia,* 'regard the food
policy of the reactionary groups of the United States and Britain
as an instrument of political blackmail. . . . They are directing
their food policy either towards direct support for reactionary
groups which rule in various countries, or else utilizing food relief for the purpose of pressure on democratic governments in
the interests of reactionary circles.' Kudriavtsev, broadcasting
in English, said in October 1946, 'London and Washington are
trying to force their own conception of running the world down
the throats of all independent democratic countries, using the
ramrod of dollar diplomacy for the purpose'. In March 1947,
with more than half a million tons of American supplies in its
belly, Moscow told the Persians that the United States was assisting only those countries whose rulers were willing to consider

Wall Street interests above those of their own nation. In July 1947, *Pravda* published a cartoon showing 'Uncle Sam' with a large stomach labelled 'American loan' sitting on a prostrate Turkey while from the right-hand pocket of his jacket peeped a little man representing 'Turkish reaction'. To the left was an oil tower with the oil gushing straight into an American oil barrel. The cartoon was captioned 'Uncle Sam Helps'.

Another favourite charge was that the Americans were really doing themselves a favour by sending supplies abroad. They were protecting their profits by unloading their surpluses; it was ridiculous to suppose they were interested in relief for its own sake. 'American and Canadian statesmen,' wrote Professor Varga in *New Times,* 'consider it far more important to avert a possible fall in agricultural prices than to save the lives of millions of people, formerly allies in the war. . . .' He repeated the old charge that America was trying 'to exploit the need of other nations for the purposes of expansion and the extension of its influence'. Orlov, in a broadcast in November 1946, said, 'Very little American self-sacrifice would be required to ease the acute needs of the people of Europe and Asia. But there is not the slightest sign that the United States intends to make such an effort. . . . United States businessmen should stop playing with human lives for the sole sake of reaping profits. . . . Dollar democracy is supplemented with famine strategy'. Famine strategy! At just about this time, Alexander Werth was writing from Moscow, 'The urban populations of White Russia and the Ukraine . . . have been almost exclusively dependent for meat and fats on UNRRA's supplies, as I was able to observe during two visits there in the past year'.

In April 1947 Ilya Ehrenburg said in a direct broadcast to America, 'What you call generosity is in all other languages cupidity. You do not give; you buy and bribe'. What, after all, was common politeness but a step on the road to subserviency?

Even those immediately concerned in the receipt of supplies were churlish. Not content with looking a gift horse in the mouth, the Russians went over it tooth by tooth. In June 1947, Khomyak, director of administration of UNRRA deliveries attached to the Ukrainian Council of Ministers, said that though the minimum planned deliveries of food, industrial supplies and raw materials had been almost completely met, from the point of view of quality many of the goods were not up to the required standard owing to the 'unconscientious attitude' of certain American industrial firms. 'It is desirable,' said Khomyak, 'that before its departure the UNRRA mission in the Ukraine should adopt all measures for the full and punctual performance of the deliveries planned for the republic.'

Having consistently denigrated American actions and motives for two years, the Russians still saw no reason why they should not be granted a loan. In late 1947 Leontyev wrote in *New Times*, 'The surplus of dollars in the United States could easily be eliminated if American financial circles were willing to grant loans to other countries on equitable terms. . . . What could be more natural than a loan granted by a participant in the anti-Hitler coalition who did not suffer from enemy occupation or hostilities to another participant like the Soviet Union who had borne the main brunt in the struggle? But imperialist circles in the United States have so far fought a successful fight against the granting of credits to the USSR'.

Those 'circles' had certainly been given incalculable assistance by Russia herself!

*　　*　　*　　*　　*

The Marshall offer of June 1947 put the Russians in a worse quandary than any other post-war event. On the one hand, they badly needed large-scale economic help and so did their border satellites. To turn the offer down flat would create the worst impression in eastern Europe. A straight loan without any obligations whatever would be most acceptable and it seemed worth while to see if this could be obtained under the Marshall offer, however small the hope. At the same time, Russia could not possibly accept any offer which involved any measure of economic disclosure. It would never do to have the ex-enemy countries of eastern Europe sending delegates to the West to talk about their economic tie-up with Russia. Nor did Russia want any measure of European economic co-operation—that ran counter to the dogma. No breach must be made in eastern exclusiveness. There was a possibility, perhaps, that if Russia approved the plan Congress might reject it, but the gamble was dangerous. The best course seemed to be to investigate the possibility of unconditional aid; if that were not forthcoming, to make sure that eastern Europe stood out of the plan; and if western Europe accepted, to resort to sabotage. This policy, which was faithfully carried out, was fully consistent with the whole Russian approach to the post-war world. It may have been executed with a less sure touch than had marked other Russian actions in the post-war period, but there was never any question of a change of heart.

The reaction of the West to the Marshall offer was typical of the time. The Harvard speech of the Secretary of State was cautiously received in Britain and France until Mr Marshall made it clear that it applied to everything 'west of Asia'—in fact, that it included Russia. Then it was greeted with joy. There would be room in the lifeboat for everyone. It was a purely economic offer, not an ideological one. The wishful-thinkers had a brief but entrancing vision of a converted Russia throwing herself heart and soul into a joint European recovery programme. 'A bridge is offered to link East and West,' wrote *The Times*. Mr Bevin warmly welcomed this splendid new opportunity. M. Bidault, the French Foreign Minister, said, 'France will do her utmost to break the cycle of disagreement'.

Initial Soviet comment was cautiously unpleasant. Leontyev pointed out that dollar expansion was necessary to avert the economic crisis closing in on the United States, and drew attention to the 'stream of subservient comment' in the western press. Hofman declared that the plan was 'just another version of Truman's scheme for political pressure by means of dollars'. *Pravda's* tone was equally disagreeable but the dreamers were not unduly perturbed. 'We must not pay too much attention to the dialectical polemics of *Pravda*,' said the *New Statesman*.

Mr Bevin and M. Bidault made the most strenuous efforts to persuade Russia to join in a preliminary three-power conference. The French sent the Russians a formal invitation; the British Ambassador in Moscow gave it his country's eager backing. After some delay, and a characteristic grumble that the British and French had already concocted something behind Russia's back, Mr Molotov arrived in Paris with such a large staff that it looked as though he meant business.

Russia's decision to attend the Paris talks had a rapturous welcome in the press of western Europe. The bridge-builders were ecstatic. It was left to the communists to strike a jarring note. *Humanité* described Moscow's acceptance as 'a first check to the State Department which had wagered on a Russian refusal in order to throw Russia out of Europe'. This was the familiar communist attitude to America—one hand held out for dollars and the other drawn back to 'slug' the benefactor.

In Paris, Mr Molotov soon showed where he stood. He had no use at all for any suggestion that the European countries should try to integrate their needs and resources. There must be no hint of economic co-operation, which in Mr Molotov's language was always translated as 'interference in the sovereign rights of nations'. His idea was that the various countries should announce their individual wants and that America should satisfy them. He had come to Paris to jot down some items on the shopping list, and that was all. 'The Soviet proposal,' said Grishanin in a broadcast, 'has in view an Assistance Committee, the work of which must be limited to receiving appeals by European countries for American assistance, and the preparation from these appeals of a general programme of requirements.'

From all sides, Mr Molotov was assured that his anxieties about interference were groundless. Mr Marshall in a speech said there could be no more fantastic distortion than to suggest that American aid had been offered in order to fasten on the recipients some form of political and economic domination. Britain and France said over and over again that no one contemplated or would agree to any infringement of sovereignty; that any information would be 'supplied of their own free will by the countries desiring to take part in this action'. But Mr Molotov repeated all his allegations in a final statement which Mr Bevin described as 'a complete travesty of the facts'. It began to look as though the Soviet representative had received new and more emphatic instructions from Moscow. In threatening tones he declared that not merely would he have nothing to do with the plan but that if the West proceeded on its own it must 'face grave consequences'. The next day he returned to Moscow. M. Bidault, in particular, was shocked. No man had made greater efforts to co-operate with Russia, but this was the watershed of his endeavour. A few months later his exasperation was to spill over in UNO when, replying to Mr Vishinsky, he declared, 'The chief delegate of the Soviet Union has alleged that the French Government together with the British has only had in mind to connive with the American Government in order to alienate the political and economic independence of European countries. . . . As for endeavouring to enslave Europe, to divide it, to infringe upon the independence and sovereignty of states, I am sorry to say, for the tenth time at least, that this criticism goes against the truth'.

Following the precipitate withdrawal of Mr Molotov from Paris, Russia turned her attention to the dual task of blackguarding the West and making sure that the eastern nations kept aloof. Viktorov in a broadcast said 'The organizers of the conference consciously tried for its failure so as to free their hands for further activities'. A home service broadcast said 'It is precisely Bevin who, inspired by a Churchill-like hostility, has been making the greatest efforts to isolate the Soviet Union. It was with this aim that he came to Paris. . . . He did not need the three Ministers' conference in Paris except to prevent an agreement with the Soviet Union'. A later broadcast described Mr Bevin as the instrument of United States governing circles and said that in return for his services he hoped to obtain 'new US loans, primarily for his own country'.

Tass described the invitations to a wider conference sent out to twenty-two European nations by Britain and France as 'separatist action'. The eastern satellites of Russia, all of whom needed and longed for economic assistance, had no choice but to turn down the invitations. Finland refused 'on political and geographical grounds'. Hungary, which had gone so far as to appoint its delegation, said that 'to her greatest regret' she was 'not in a position to accept'. Czechoslovakia, having hurriedly accepted, was compelled by Russian threats to reverse her decision. 'Czech participation,' said an official statement, 'would be interpreted as an act directed against friendship with the Soviet Union.' Shamelessly, Moscow radio was to declare a few days later 'The refusal of Czechoslovakia in particular denotes the failure of the present conference'. The Czechs, snatched away from the lovely European party, were hastily consoled with an orange—a trade pact with Russia of dubious advantage.

Mr Molotov's chief argument against the Marshall plan had been that it sought to subordinate small countries to America. On his return home, he had immediately coerced half a dozen small neighbours, and had done it without even a decent covering of pretence. 'Rarely,' said the *Manchester Guardian*, 'has there been a more cynical exhibition of naked power. There is something at once tragic and horrible in the way in which Czechoslovakia, Finland, Hungary and Poland, against their saner judgment and the wish of the majority of their peoples, against their traditions of centuries, have been compelled by Soviet pressure to cut themselves off from the rest of Europe.'

When the Marshall countries gathered in Paris, the western Powers were still hopeful that the last word had not been said from the East. 'Everything that was in our power to do,' said M. Bidault, 'has been done to obtain a favourable answer from a unanimous Europe to the appeal made by the US Secretary of State. We shall be careful not to do or say anything that would alienate any nation, for we still hope that seats empty today will be occupied one day. . . .' But the Russian decision was absolute and the propaganda offensive was in full swing. *New Times* wrote of the 'dark adventurist aims' of the West. *Tass* reported the Paris talks as though the nations gathered there were racked with division and distrust, and as though the real business of the conference was the planning of an anti-Soviet conspiracy. 'No economic questions were discussed,' said *Tass* in one report. Everything at this 'so-called conference' was described in terms of 'struggle' and 'domination'. And this was to be the keynote for the future. By incessant propaganda in all fields and by the disruptive activities of her agents, Russia hoped to prevent the Marshall plan coming to fruition. She would do her best to fulfil the prophecy of Moscow radio—'The Marshall offer to aid Europe will fail'.

Russia's attitude to the Marshall offer revealed her plainly to all as the saboteur of European recovery, the opponent of co-operation, the autarchic tyrant of the East. It opened many eyes which before had been screwed up tight. Unfortunately, two valuable years had been wasted.

CHAPTER XIII

THE FAR EAST

Russia's post-war policy in the Far East was directed to the same broad ends and conducted in the same spirit as her policy in Europe and other parts of the world. Her aim was territorial expansion and a general increase of national and ideological influence without set limit. Some of her keenest ambitions had already been realized with the consent of her allies. By agreement, she had recovered the Kuriles and Southern Sakhalin from Japan and control of railways and ports in Manchuria from China. Having detached a considerable part of Outer Mongolia —Tannu Tuva—and quietly incorporated it into the Soviet Union, she had subsequently consolidated her position in the rest of the territory. She was beginning once again to penetrate Sinkiang. Inner Mongolia had long been a stronghold of the Chinese communists. As a result of their activities, Russia hoped soon to be in a position to control the whole of Manchuria, while China proper offered a most promising field for successful civil war. In Korea, the Russians had all the foothold they needed for their further plans. They would have liked a greater say in the affairs of defeated Japan, but since America was unwilling to grant it they would have to be patient and put their hopes in the disruptive power of communism. Farther afield, the Pacific positions of the old imperialist Powers could be steadily undermined by propaganda and agitation among the native populations. There is no indication whatever that the idea of honest co-operation for joint purposes in the Far East ever crossed the Russian mind.

*   *   *   *   *

Korea, a strategic peninsula jutting out from Manchuria towards Japan, had already been the subject of two Far Eastern conflicts before World War II. In 1894 Japan had 'liberated' it from the suzerainty of China and in 1904 had 'protected' it against Russian imperialist designs. Five years later, after briefly enjoying the status of an 'Empire', it was annexed by Japan. Many Koreans were driven into exile and those who remained were treated as a subject race. Only the emigrés kept alive the cause of national independence.

At the Cairo Conference in 1943, the United States, Britain and China agreed that after the defeat of Japan Korea should 'in due course' become free and independent. At Yalta, Roosevelt and Stalin reached informal agreement on the same lines. It was thought that a period of trusteeship would probably be needed to prepare the country for re-emergence as an independent state after the years of tutelage during which Koreans had been permitted only a minor part in administration.

As Japan went down in defeat, the Russians accepted the Japanese surrender in the northern half of the peninsula and the Americans in the southern half, in accordance with an earlier decision of the military commanders. Zones of operation were delimited by the imaginary 38th parallel of latitude which roughly bisects the country. The Americans had never supposed that this boundary would have anything but temporary military significance and their plans had been drawn up on the assumption of Korean unity. But the Russians, following their usual practice, sealed off their zone at the 38th parallel.

Developments in Korea now followed a familiar pattern. The Russians had always intended, if they could, to obtain exclusive control of the whole peninsula. The first step was to impose a subservient communist regime on the northern half. 'People's committees' sprang up under the guidance of Korean communists brought in from Russia and China, and in February 1946 a Provisional People's Committee of Northern Korea was established. In March a law was passed redistributing the land. Other 'reforms' were carried out with equal ostentation. Hostile elements were encouraged to go south into the American zone, thus relieving the northern food shortage. Late in 1946 elections were held. 'All democratic parties and public organizations,' wrote *Pravda* in November, 'numbering some five million members will appear as one *bloc* with a common programme widely approved by the popular masses.' Voting for or against the *bloc* consisted of dropping a pellet into one of two boxes in open town squares under the scrutiny of armed guards. The 'United

National Democratic Front' consequently won a famous victory. *Tass* reported that 99.6 per cent of the 4,356,000 voters went to the polls, and that 96.9 per cent of the ballots were in favour of the Front. A totalitarian regime under communist control was soon working smoothly along routine lines, backed by a newly created Korean army several hundred thousand strong. The considerable industries of Northern Korea were linked not with the agricultural south, but with eastern Russia.

By comparison with the tough and purposeful policy of the Russians, the administration of the Americans was weak and muddled. They had no desire to establish their own form of government in Korea; all they wanted to see was the setting up of a sovereign Korean Government for the whole country without unnecessary delay. In the meantime, they were content with a negative policy of maintaining order. For the sake of administrative convenience, they unwisely retained a number of Japanese officials in their posts in the early period. They rightly refused to recognize a 'Korean People's Republic' which had been hurriedly set up by the communists in Seoul in September 1945, and they disbanded the 'People's committees'. But they were reluctant to impose their own political and economic measures. The steps which they did take often had unhappy results. Their efforts to free the Korean economy from controls led to profiteering and inflation, and half-hearted attempts to plant the seeds of western democracy in such unfavourable soil resulted in a multiplicity of parties and a political bedlam. The Americans, in short, were well-meaning but largely ineffective. The plain fact was that they just did not want to be there.

The Russians, having disciplined their own zone, followed their usual practice of stirring up as much trouble as possible in the zone of an ally. Their propaganda, both locally and from Moscow, was strident and sustained. The Americans, they said, had failed to weed out collaborationists; had adopted a friendly attitude towards the Korean Democratic Party which harboured pro-Japanese elements; had tolerated anti-Soviet sentiments; had shown a repressive attitude towards 'people's organizations'; had encouraged 'landlords and industrialists', and had co-operated with Korean emigrés who wanted to preserve 'feudal and semi-fascist social relations in Korea'. There was no 'people's unity' in the South, where—Smolensky lamented in a

May 1946 broadcast—'political parties are fighting each other'. Communist agents were sent into Southern Korea to help foment strikes and disturbances and in October 1946 something like an armed insurrection was instigated. The Soviet radio subsequently accused the Americans of 'unprecedented terror'. An interim Southern Korean 'Parliament' with advisory functions, established in November 1946, was an easy target for Russian criticism as a paradise of 'landlords, officials and collaborators'.

The Americans were not interested in a war of zones. From the first, they had worked for unity. At the Moscow conference of Foreign Ministers in December 1945 they had proposed that a Joint Soviet-American Commission should be set up to unify such things as currency, transport and trade, and to make a move towards the restoration of Korean independence. An agreement had finally been reached on the basis of a Soviet draft which provided for such a Commission and also for the establishment of a Korean Provisional Government to operate under four-Power trusteeship for five years.

These plans came to nothing. The Russians no more desired a unified Korea than they desired a unified Germany, unless it could be under their sole control. American disillusionment came slowly in long and weary meetings of the Commission, where the Russians further exercised their talent for obstruction and delay. Plans to form a provisional Government broke down because the Russians would not agree that any political party should be consulted which did not accept the idea of trusteeship. Most Koreans strongly objected to trusteeship; indeed, all parties of any importance did so until the communists, by a dexterous overnight twist of policy, came out in support of the principle and thus qualified for consultation. To record the details of the protracted and involved dispute would be tedious; basically the Commission's efforts were fruitless because the Russians did not want them to succeed. After the first breakdown, the Americans tried several times to re-open the discussions at a higher level and in 1947 it seemed for a time that a basis of understanding had been reached. In August, however, the United States abandoned hope of bilateral agreement and suggested four-Power talks—a proposal which the Russians rejected.

The Russians were now ready to play their ace card, which had been protruding from a sleeve for some time. In September

1947 they suggested that all foreign troops should be withdrawn from Korea by January 1948 and that the Koreans should be left to settle their own affairs. Since the only armed force then left in Korea would be the strong puppet army of the North, Russia knew that she would have no difficulty in obtaining control of the whole peninsula. The Americans naturally rejected the plan.

In the 1947 Assembly of UNO, Mr Marshall asked for action on Korea. By a large majority, UNO decided to set up a Commission which would supervise the transfer of power to a national Korean Government, to be elected with proper safeguards against coercion and equipped with its own and exclusive armed force before the withdrawal of Russian and American troops. The Russians declared the proposal 'unjust and illegal,' announced that they would boycott the Commission, and subsequently refused to allow it to enter North Korean territory. Once more Russia had thwarted the will of UNO, once more she had refused reasonable co-operation with a former ally, once more she had dug in her heels in a territory which had come under her temporary control as a result of a common victory.

*   *   *   *   *

In the circumstances which prevailed, a clash of wills between the Soviet Union and the United States over post-war China was inescapable. America wanted a prosperous China with which the world could trade, a united China, a China which would be strong enough to withstand Soviet pressure and would therefore be able to contribute to stability in the Far East. Russia wanted to encroach on China's territory and interests, and in due course to bring the whole country under communist control. American policy, in practice, was inclined to be defensive and inhibited; Russian policy, as usual, was aggressive and crude.

The story begins at Yalta, where President Roosevelt and Mr Churchill made big concessions to Russia at China's expense, and without her knowledge, in return for a Soviet promise of eventual participation in the Japanese war. It was secretly agreed that the naval base of Port Arthur in the Liaotung peninsula of Manchuria should be restored to Russia; that the nearby commercial port of Dairen should be internationalized and Russia's 'pre-eminent interests' recognized there; and that Manchuria's strategic railways—formerly the Chinese Eastern and South Manchurian railways—should be placed under joint Soviet-Chinese control. China was otherwise to regain full sovereignty in Manchuria. As a result of this agreement, which the United States and Britain promised should be 'unquestionably fulfilled', Russia would recover in relation to China virtually the position which she had enjoyed in the days of Tsarist imperialism before 1904.

On August 14th 1945, the date of the Japanese surrender, China signed a treaty with Russia which covered these and other points. The Soviet press was naturally jubilant. Russia was to have the right to use Port Arthur and a large slice of neighbouring territory as a naval base, though civil administration would remain with the Chinese. Dairen was to become a free port with a Soviet citizen as harbour-master, but again civil administration was to be exercised by the Chinese. The Manchurian trunk railways were to come under joint management. Russia repeated that she recognized China's sovereignty over Manchuria. Moreover, the sovereignty she recognized was specifically stated to be that of the Nationalist Government of Chiang Kai-Shek, as the Central Government of China. This latter undertaking was re-affirmed by Mr Molotov at the Foreign Ministers' meeting in Moscow in December 1945.

One of the subsidiary points covered by the treaty was the future of Outer Mongolia, a territory where Soviet influence was very great but over which China had long claimed sovereignty. In an exchange of Notes, the Chinese Government undertook to recognize the independence of Outer Mongolia if a popular plebiscite confirmed a desire for independence. Russia had no doubts about the outcome of such a plebliscite, which in due course was held under her auspices. The vote, according to a Russian report in November 1945, was taken 'on the broadest democratic basis' and was exercised mainly with the thumb. Of the 487,409 citizens of the territory who took part in the plebiscite (98.4 per cent of the whole), 487,409 or 100 per cent voted for independence. There was not a single misplaced thumb. China subsequently implemented her undertaking by entering into diplomatic relations with Outer Mongolia.

As far as the other provisions of the treaty were concerned, Russia made no attempt to carry out her bargain in letter or in spirit. Her troops had occupied a large part of Manchuria in the closing hours of the war with Japan and far from respecting China's sovereign rights in the territory had proceeded to loot it as though it were the land of a conquered enemy. Russia's method of implementing a promise to help China with 'material resources' was to strip Manchuria's industry, which had been intensively built up by the Japanese and which China hoped to receive intact as some recompense for her immense losses at Japanese hands. The Red Army had soon removed almost all the machine tools and electrical equipment. In some coalmining areas, not enough power plant was left to keep the pumps working and many mines were flooded. Much equipment was removed from iron and steel plants and in two major centres of chemical production about 30 per cent of capital equipment was removed. Manchuria was reduced virtually to an agricultural economy and a generation would pass before its inhabitants regained the opportunities they had lost. At one time, the Russians were willing to hand back a part of their booty, but only on condition that the Chinese Government agreed to 'joint operation' of the industry that remained—a proposal which was outside the terms of the treaty and was naturally rejected.

The provisions giving China rights of civil administration in Port Arthur and Dairen were not fulfilled. Both ports were treated as Soviet property and every effort by China to obtain her rights was obstructed. A Soviet broadcast in May 1946 by Tripolsky, describing life in Port Arthur, said, 'The Soviet people in far-off Port Arthur do not feel divorced from their motherland'. There was, indeed, no reason why they should. The provision that Dairen should become a free port was also a dead letter, and both ships and personnel entering the port had to obtain clearance from Moscow.

Moreover, Manchuria was not handed back to Nationalist China. When the Chinese Government tried to re-establish its authority there, every obstacle was put in its way by the Russians and the Chinese communists, who had acquired large quantities of Japanese arms. When Central Government troops were transported to Dairen in American ships, the Russians refused to allow them to land. Other convenient ports had passed into Chinese communist hands with Russian connivance. When the Red Army evacuated Manchuria in May 1946, it was not the forces of the Central Government but Chinese communist troops who moved in to a concerted timetable. Far from implementing their agreement to recognize the authority of the Nationalist Government, the Russians always gave the fullest moral backing, if nothing more substantial, to their communist co-conspirators. By the end of 1947, the Nationalist forces had been driven out of most of Manchuria and there was every prospect that the whole territory would in due course become a Russian-controlled satellite state. The Soviet Union had stepped straight into the shoes of Japan.

As far as the Russians were concerned, the intentions behind the Soviet-Chinese treaty had been fraudulent. Rarely had an international agreement been so totally disregarded. This did not prevent a certain Vassiliev writing in *Red Star* that in Manchuria Russia had been 'faithful as ever to its international obligations'.

Meanwhile, America's feelings about the developing situation were very mixed. In the first place, she wanted the authority and strength of the Nationalist Government to be fully restored; to that end, she gave it great material and moral assistance. The help included military stores and installations, military advice and training, ships, trucks, machinery, railway equipment and much besides. In value it totalled hundreds of millions of pounds. In addition, America transported three Chinese armies by air and eleven by sea in order that the Nationalists might help to round up the Japanese and re-assert their control in the liberated Centre and North of the country. Inevitably, civil war flared up between the Central Government and the communists. The Americans became uneasy; the Russians increasingly abusive. Though Moscow had itself undertaken to support the Central Government, it castigated the Americans for actually doing so. They were 'fomenting civil war'. With naïve frankness *Pravda* wrote in July 1946, 'The reactionary forces of China would have been routed long ago if they had not been able to rely on American help'.

America was aware that without continued aid of all kinds, Nationalist China might fail to withstand communist pressure. On the other hand, Americans were far from favourably disposed to the corrupt and repressive regime of Chiang Kai-Shek and were embarrassed by the need to bolster him up. In a heroic attempt to bring about a peaceful solution of the Chinese struggle and create a united and independent China, General Marshall tried for many months to mediate on the basis of a military truce, the creation of an integrated Chinese army, and the liberalizing of the regime. While his efforts were at their height, a Moscow broadcast referred to America's 'cruel policy' of trying to spread civil war in China. When the attempt was finally abandoned as hopeless and General Marshall branded both sides as incorrigible, a broadcast by Perevertailo described the abandonment as 'dictated by the wish to give Chinese reaction a free hand'.

The withdrawal in 1947 of all but a token force of American combat troops and the withholding of further military aid to the Central Government in the absence of real reform eased America's conscience. It by no means solved the problem. A reactionary and unpopular Government had been unable to destroy Chinese communism even with American help; it might well succumb to it if help were denied.

The danger was never as self-evident in Britain as in the United States. Many people were inclined to accept the view—expressed by Stalin at Potsdam—that the Chinese communists were 'not real communists at all' but just agrarian democrats. Such an attitude was naturally fostered by the Chinese communists themselves. In April 1946 one of their leaders, Chou En-lai, dissociated his party from the Russians, saying that it was 'rather in favour of the American style of democracy'. But the Chinese Communist party was always firmly built on Marxist foundations and its chief, Mao Tse-tung, had been well-grounded in the Moscow school. Whatever the immediate domestic aims of the Chinese communists might be, one thing was certain. If they ever achieved power in China, their foreign policy would be as closely linked to that of Russia as was the policy of Bulgaria or Rumania. They had made that fact apparent in their attitude to the European war, which had exactly reflected Kremlin views. A communist China would be an immense reinforcement of the Russian *bloc* in the world struggle, and the civil war could not safely be regarded except in that context. To prevent China falling completely under Russian influence was, and is, as much a British as an American interest, for the world is one.

*   *   *   *   *

275

Russia was at war for five days with a Japan already on the verge of military collapse. Before the meeting of the Big Three at Potsdam in July 1945, the Japanese Ambassador in Moscow had asked whether the neutral Soviet Union would agree to act as mediator to bring about a settlement of the war. Though Japan was not yet quite prepared for unconditional surrender, her will to fight had vanished. On August 6th the first atomic bomb was dropped. At midnight on August 8th-9th a Russian declaration of war became operative. In the early hours of August 10th the Japanese made the approach which was to end in their unconditional surrender on August 14th.

Those are the bald facts. There will always be argument about the relative effects of the atomic bomb and the Russian declaration in speeding the Japanese surrender. There can be no argument about Russia's fighting contribution in the Far Eastern theatre. It was negligible.

Russian propaganda gave the impression that in addition to bearing the brunt of the war against Germany the Red Army had been largely instrumental in defeating Japan as well. Mr Byrnes has told us in *Speaking Frankly* how in Moscow in 1945 he was shown a Russian film which had a scene described as 'signing the surrender terms' with Japan on 'a battleship'. 'There was no statement that the battleship was the *Missouri* or even that it was a United States ship. The entire scene might well impress many Russians as the ending, on a Soviet battleship, of a private war between Russia and Japan.' That was no doubt the intention. A new myth was being created. By the time the first anniversary of the surrender was reached, *Izvestia* was writing, 'The day of reckoning came when the Soviet armed forces in the Far East, acting from various directions, dealt a shattering blow to imperialist Japan. Owing to this the Second World War, which threatened to be long-drawn-out . . . ended quickly'. Another newspaper declared, 'The decisive role was played by the Soviet Union, by its glorious armed forces. The smashing defeat inflicted by our troops on the Japanese armies in Manchuria, Northern Korea and Sakhalin forced the Japanese Government to accept unconditional surrender'. At about the same time, a broadcast in English on the Soviet contribution said that Japan did not agree to surrender until the Soviet Union had routed the cream of her ground troops 'in hard fighting which cost Japan

276

674,000 officers and men'. One does not need to be a military historian to know that those last ten words, as a description of a five-day war, are ludicrous.

Though Russia had received an enormous tonnage of American supplies to build up an army which largely did not fight, and had been paid in Japanese territory and Chinese concessions for a contribution which she did not make, she regarded herself as entitled to an equal voice with America in regard to defeated Japan. Mr Molotov even suggested that Marshal Vassilievsky should be joint Supreme Commander with General MacArthur, and subsequently the Russians continually complained of the subordinate role allotted to them in Japanese affairs.

In fact, American decisions concerning the control of Japan were not directed against Russia. The view of many Americans was that as their country had played so large a part in the war against Japan, they should decide occupation policy. Nominal roles were at first assigned not merely to Russia but to the British Commonwealth also. Indeed, when the Americans suggested on their own initiative as early as August 1945 that an advisory commission should be established to carry out the surrender terms, it was Russia who seemed satisfied and Britain who objected on the ground that the Commonwealth's part should be more decisive.

Whether, in general, it was proper and expedient for America to exercise what amounted to a near-monopoly of control will not be argued here. What is quite clear is that she was morally entitled to do so as far as Russia was concerned on far stronger grounds than that of relative contribution. The Russians had placed American and British representatives in subordinate positions in those enemy countries which the Red Army occupied —Rumania, Bulgaria and Hungary. The western members of the Control Councils in those countries were ciphers. Russia had already made it clear that in her view possession was the whole law. She had no claim to any different treatment in the case of Japan.

In post-war Japan, Russia showed the same tendencies and followed the same propaganda lines as she had done elsewhere. Her purpose was to discredit the Americans, obstruct administration and divide the country against itself in readiness for the final ideological struggle. Fault was found with every aspect

277

of the Supreme Commander's work. The Soviet press and radio criticized the agrarian reform plans, the trial of war criminals, labour legislation and the progress of demilitarization. All Japanese who were not communists were 'reactionary' and anyone engaging in industry was a 'monopolist'. Japanese discontents were exploited and strikes were sympathetically reported.

If Russia had been given a more decisive role in Japan, she would have induced the same paralysis of action there as she was able to do in so many other spheres. Whether or not such power was withheld from her for the right reasons is beside the point; what matters is that, happily, it was withheld. As a result, it was possible to avoid the deadlock and frustration which had been encountered in every other field of allied endeavour, and to give Japan a start on the road to enlightenment and freedom.

POSTSCRIPT

WHEN THE idea of this book was conceived, shortly after the end of World War II, British public opinion was confused and divided about Soviet intentions and the 'fellow-travellers' were vocal and persuasive. But the Soviet leaders, who won so many tactical battles in the post-war period, were compelled by the dogma to throw away their best hope of strategic victory—the support which they had banked in the West. Today, the apologists are as discredited as the Men of Munich. They have crawled under the stones, and the West has at last taken up the Soviet challenge. The evidence marshalled in the preceding chapters should help to confirm the necessity of that belated step.

It has fallen to our generation to fight yet again, and on a world scale, the age-old duel between tyranny and freedom. That is the heart of the struggle between the Soviet Union and the West. The question is whether the eventual World State is to be based on respect for individual rights of thought and belief, or whether it is to be a vast prison of the spirit. In this conflict, there are only two sides. Social democrats in western Europe may like to pitch their tents a little away from the encampment of American capitalism, but fundamentally there are no irreconcilable differences between these two. Britain under a Labour Government is no more an ideological half-way house between the United States and the Soviet Union than a man at the top of the Rockies is half-way between the Earth and the Moon.

Having accepted the challenge, we must not be deflected from our course by false hopes. There is no likelihood that the aims of the Soviet Union will change as long as the present regime lasts. They may seem to change, but we must not again mistake manoeuvre for conviction. When the real change comes, there will be no doubt about it. The impact of returning honesty and freedom will be as resounding as the shouts of revolution.

This Soviet regime has earned our automatic and permanent distrust. It has so debased the currency of language that its words are worthless. It has shown itself so unprincipled that we should no longer desire to co-operate with it on any terms whatever.

We should consciously desire its downfall, as we desired the downfall of the Nazis. There will be no hope of international understanding and secure peace while it persists.

Russia must be prevented from making any further physical encroachments by the knowledge that war would result. There is no other way. But we should recognize that the long-term world struggle will be fought out mainly in the minds of men. For us, many of the weapons of peace lie unexploited. Certainly we must deal forcefully with force, but we shall gain more in the long run by dealing truthfully with falsehood. The West has nothing to conceal and not very much to be ashamed of. Soviet communism is rotten through and through. Let us start with a total war of facts.

Any other sort of war is in the highest degree unlikely unless we bring it about by our own folly. The West will not start shooting. Physically as well as morally, the cost would be too high. Only morons talk lightly of war in an atomic age. Russia will do nothing to start a general war as long as the West is strong and united. Only by the narrowest of margins did she survive the German attack. There is no possibility that she will deliberately challenge the combined power of the United States and the British Commonwealth and the rest of the democracies. Nations do not provoke war when they know it will bring them no advantage.

The prospect would be very different if Russia could divide the American and British people against themselves. Then Russia might think a war worth while; then she and the communists might win. But Russia can sow dangerous divisions only if the West fails in its practical undertakings. If the complex and far-from-uniform way of life which Russia likes to label 'capitalism and imperialism' fails to evolve in a peaceful and orderly manner, then of course communism may triumph. Another economic disaster like that of 1931 would almost certainly be fatal to democracy. The prime task of the West is to disprove the validity of the dogma.

If we can show that the communist predictions are wrong and that capitalism can develop and change without breakdown, if we can build better than the communists and provide security and prosperity without destroying freedom, then the communist parties will retreat, their cause will decay, and the foundations of Soviet power will begin to crumble. In the end—far off though it may be—not merely the satellite victims of imperial communism but the long-suffering Russian people also will be liberated. Then, but not before, free men may be able to create a united world.

INDEX